101 Best Home-Business Success Secrets for Women

Proven Ideas and Strategies to Help
You Start, Manage, and Profit from
Whichever Business You Choose

Priscilla Y. Huff

Prima Publishing

Chapter 6: Financing Your Venture   136

Chapter 7: Marketing Plan   168

Chapter 8: Advertising   189

Chapter 12: Managing and Maintaining a Profitable Business   317

Chapter 13: Going Online   335

Acknowledgments

I wish to acknowledge and thank each of the women quoted and profiled in this book for taking time from their busy businesses and family schedules to share their experiences and success tips with my readers. The efforts and hard work of these and other women business owners have opened "entrepreneurial doors" for women all over the world to begin ventures that give them more control over their lives while doing what they enjoy.

Special thanks to Prima Publishing's editors and publicity department, and my copyeditor, for their encouragement and assistance with this project.

Introduction

This is my sixth book on the subject of home and small businesses for women. I have been writing for some sixteen years—profiling women entrepreneurs, offering business ideas, resources, and tips gathered from my research, interviews with women business owners, and my personal experiences as an owner of a home-based writing and publishing business.

When I started my writing services business, I had three small sons and worked at various part-time positions to help support my family. I started writing as a "stringer" for a local weekly newspaper for a few cents a word. This taught me the basics of interviewing, photography, and—more importantly—how to put together a feature story.

When a new editor was hired who wanted only staff writers to write the features, I no longer had a market for my stories. What I did have were published clips and valuable first-hand writing experience. With that background, I was able to land a freelance assignment with the magazine *Income Opportunities (IO)* for a story about my sister-in-law and her friend's unique home business, "Educational Clowning." Suddenly I was able to find women-owned home businesses starting and thriving all over my small suburban community—five on one small-town street alone, which were featured in IO and other small-business publications.

While writing regularly, I sent a proposal to a small publisher, Pilot Books, which published my first tiny book, *Home-Based Business Ideas for Women*, in 1993, and later, *Directory of Home-Based Business Resources*. These little books helped when I submitted a proposal to Prima Publishing for a much larger book: *101 Best Home-Based Businesses for Women*. This book has sold to date over 100,000 copies; is in its second, revised edition; and has been a featured selection of several national book clubs.

I now write full-time, publishing the newsletter *"101 Best & More Home-Based & Small Businesses for Women* and *UPDATES: The Latest Facts, News & Tips for Self-Employed Women,"* am currently marketing a syndicated column called "The Self-Employed Woman," and am beginning to expand my small publishing business: LITTLE HOUSE Writing & Publishing.

What is my purpose in telling my own story? To show you that being an entrepreneur is an ongoing process that grows as you learn (and make mistakes!) along the way. I belong to several business owners' organizations, regularly read business and trade publications, attend annual women's entrepreneur conferences, and continually strive to educate myself in areas of business management and writing—all with the goal of staying current with the news and gaining the knowledge I need to help my customers (readers) and my business prosper.

Many women ask me how to start a home business *today* that will generate the profits they need to support themselves *tomorrow*. In reality, your business may take two to fifteen years to provide enough money for you to work from your home full time (though there are exceptions). Business experts say that two-thirds of all home businesses are started on a part-time basis—a practical but hectic way to start when you put a business into your already overloaded schedule!

Many of the successful female entrepreneurs I have profiled in my articles and books over the years (including those mentioned in this book) have started their businesses modestly and in their spare time. Polly, an active grandmother, has started three different businesses while working part-time at other jobs. Regina uses one business (a home cleaning service) to support herself while she works at her passion—creating and selling her unique jewelry—on weekends. Starting a business on the side gives you the advantage of time to master that "learning curve"—to gain the necessary know-how and business management skills you need to eventually make that transition from part-time to a successful full-time business.

That's why an entrepreneur must be inquisitive, undaunted by mistakes, patient, and persistent enough to seek answers to all the questions she must ask to ensure survival of her home and/or small business! This quest takes time (and money), but the good news is that people and resources are available to help you every step on the road to entrepreneurship! As you hone your entrepreneurial skills, remember to network with other business owners and people related to your industry. Networking and exchanging information with other women business owners, writers, and small publishers have helped me obtain leads and practical advice I might never have discovered on my own—plus I've gained a number of good business friends along the way.

In my previous books, I presented over 300 home and small business ideas for a woman's business. In this book, I compile 101 of the best success secrets (and more) from women entrepreneurs and business experts for the purpose of giving you practical and useful information you can use to make your chosen home-business idea(s) a successful reality.

As the next century begins, my hope is that you will join the more than 3.5 million home-based, women-owned businesses in the U.S. today that provide full- or part-time employment for an estimated 14 million people (National Foundation for Women Business Owners). May you fulfill your own dreams as well as those of your loved ones and your communities.

I sincerely wish each of you "101 Best Wishes for Your Success in your Entrepreneurial Ventures!"

Priscilla Y. Huff

1

An Introduction to Home-Business Success

The future belongs to those who believe in the beauty of their dreams.
—Eleanor Roosevelt

• SUCCESS SECRET 1 •

Understand the growth and future of women-owned home-based and small businesses.

In the past ten to fifteen years, women's business ownership—much of it home-based—has been an unprecedented business phenomenon. Knowing that millions of women are succeeding in business just might provide the incentive you need to join them. Here are some revealing statistics about this entrepreneurial movement:

❖ According to the U.S. Census Bureau, the number of women-owned businesses in the United States reached 6.4 million in 1992 (increased to 7.7 million in 1994), representing one-third of all domestic firms and 40 percent of all retail and service firms.

❖ Businesses owned by 9.1 million women today generate $3.6 trillion in business revenues and employ 27.5 million people (National Foundation of Women Business Owners [NFWBO]).

❖ In the last 10 years, the number of self-employed women has increased at six times the rate of men (SCORE Association—Service Corps of Retired Executives), with the number of women-owned businesses increasing by 78 percent in the past decade (NFWBO).

❖ More than 3.5 million women business owners are home-based and provide full- or part-time employment for an estimated 14+ million people (NFWBO).

❖ The Small Business Administration (SBA) states: "In today's economy, home-based businesses are a growth industry to watch."

❖ Many wealthy women entrepreneurs started from their homes, creating successful companies such as Mrs. Fields Original Cookies and the Lillian Vernon Corporation. If you read *Working Woman (WW)* magazine's profiles of "America's Top 500 Women-Owned Businesses" (May 1998), you will find that many started from home offices and today own businesses with revenues in the millions. The top-ranked company in the *WW* May 1998 issue had annual revenues of $4.5 billion with the 500-ranked company having 13.2 million!

The bad news for those starting a business is that experts say it may take three attempts to get one business to thrive. The good news is that entrepreneurship offers the *potential* for women to earn far more than they can by working for someone else—especially when the job outlook predicts growth for women in the next several years. The Department of Labor says that six of the ten occupations that will provide the largest number of jobs for women from now until 2005—cashier, janitor or cleaner, sales clerk, waitress, food-server, and home health aide—pay annual wages that classify a family of four at the poverty threshold.

Entrepreneurship Benefits Women
Provides more earning potential.
The average wage-earning job offers less earning potential that is possible for entrepreneurs. According to the U.S. Department of

Labor, nearly seven out of ten women in 1995 earned less than $25,000. The NFWBO says that some 8 million women-owned businesses in the U.S. generated nearly $2.3 trillion in sales during 1996. Although owning a business often means you'll work more hours than you would if employed for someone else, it also provides you with unlimited possibilities for other income-earning options throughout life.

Provides better job security.
The days when people, perhaps your own mother and father, worked for one company for their entire work lives are gone. Companies are bought and sold, downsized, moved, absorbed into larger companies, or dissolved—often with little or no notice to workers. Those who lose their jobs are often forced to take lower-paying jobs with other companies because their present job skills are obsolete and they *lack* the skills new jobs require. Entrepreneurs "invest in themselves." They learn to depend on their own ingenuity to problem-solve and feel gratified knowing that the business decisions they make—even wrong ones—are due to their efforts.

As this book is being written, the U.S. economy is good, as is evidenced by the lowest unemployment rate in years. What many people do not realize is that supporting a family today requires an average of two incomes—sometimes $2\frac{1}{2}$ or 3! Average worker wages today have not risen in proportion to the cost of living, which has doubled over the last 20 to 30 years. Many people who are homeless or at the poverty level *are* employed, but they're often called the "working poor" because the minimum-wage jobs they hold cannot support a family. Many such families are headed by single mothers.

Helps in "balancing" a career and a family.
Though more of today's companies are "family-friendly" and are often highlighted in publications such as *Working Mother*, many working couples are still scrambling to find the best solutions for child care. Some take a "tag-team" approach in which the father stays home with the children while the mother works, then the mother goes to work when the father comes home. This can be not only exhausting for these couples, but hard on their relationship as well.

Having a home-based business gives a woman more flexibility to balance her schedule around her family—sometimes including

Home-Based Business Start-Up Tips

Before you start any home business, ask yourself these three crucial questions:

1. *Are you and a home business compatible?*
   Bert, who has owned a successful, home-based antiques business, had watched her mother sell antiques on the side while raising her family. This experience gave Bert the idea to try her hand at selling items at flea markets. She enjoyed the customer contact, liked being at home with her two small daughters, and realized her own home with its house and barn located on a busy intersection was ideal for her business idea. She has had a thriving business there for over fifteen years. Bert says: "I easily put in forty hours a week with my business, but I have been able to arrange my hours and vacations over the years to suit my family."
2. *Is your business idea(s) suitable to run successfully from a home office or base?*

aging parents. (This is especially true for baby boomers—the "sandwich" generation.) She also has more opportunity to participate in community and/or altruistic activities. This does not necessarily translate to more time—in fact, the home-based entrepreneur may have less time because of her venture's demands. It does mean, however, that she can better control *how* she uses her time.

Gives a sense of pride, purpose, and enjoyment.
Many people hate their jobs, but feel "trapped" due to financial obligations. A woman can start a business doing work she enjoys. If she cannot afford to leave her "day" job, she can begin on a part-time

Obviously, some businesses lend themselves better to working from home—computer-related businesses, such as desktop publishing and consulting services, for example. You must first consider all factors, such as customer traffic, signs, zoning restrictions, inventory, deliveries, and laws. For example, Jane bakes a variety of homemade cheesecakes and other desserts for her customers. She is permitted by the state of Pennsylvania to use her own kitchen for commercial purposes (it must pass state inspection); other states require cooks to use a licensed commercial kitchen outside of a home.

3. *Is the number of potential customers large enough to warrant the existence of this business—in other words, is there a market for your business to make the money you want and/ or need?*

Fifteen years ago, Deborah, a certified teacher who had taken a leave of absence to raise her children, received so many requests to tutor friends' children that she knew she could start an educational service in her community that parents would need and want.

basis and look forward to the time when she might turn it into a full-time venture.

Enables women to be role models.

Statistics show that entrepreneurs "beget" entrepreneurs. Children and other young persons will be encouraged to try independent ventures when they see their mothers, aunts, sisters, and even grandmothers become entrepreneurs. In addition, women business owners avail themselves of mentor-protégé programs to a much greater extent than do men who own businesses (NFWBO).

Self-employment is not for everyone, but many women say this about their businesses: "I love what I do so much that I don't consider it work!" For these women and many others, entrepreneurship provides the best way to combine all their "worlds"—family, work, community, and future!

For More Information
Books/Publications

America: Who Stole the Dream? by Donald L. Barlett and James B. Steele (Philadelphia, PA: Andrews & McMeel, 1996).

Chaos or Community? Seeking Solutions, Not Scapegoats for Bad Economics by Holly Sklar (Boston, MA: South End Press, 1995).

Entrepreneur Magazine: Starting a Home-Based Business by Entrepreneur Magazine Group (New York: John Wiley & Sons, Inc., 1996).

Homemade Money, 5th ed., by Barbara Brabec (Cincinnati, OH: Betterway Books, 1997).

The Millionairess Across the Street by Jennifer Basye Sander and Bettina Flores (Chicago: Dearborn Financial Publishing, 1999).

The Small Business Start-Up Guide, 2nd ed., by Robert A. Sullivan (Great Falls, VA: Information International, 1998).

Working Woman magazine (May 1998).

Internet Sites

< www.crafter.com/brabec > Barbara Brabec. Author of *Homemade Money* (listed above).

< www.toolkit.cch.com > Business Owner's Toolkit. Has a *SOHO Guidebook* that includes business start-up tips.

< www.workingwomanmag.com > *Working Woman* magazine's Web site.

Statistics Sources

< www.census.gov > Census Bureau.

< www.nfwbo.org > National Foundation for Women Business Owners, 1100 Wayne Ave., Suite 830, Silver Spring, MD 20910-5603.

< www.score.org > SCORE (Service Corps of Retired Executives).

Other Helpful Start-Up Tips

❖ Assess your strengths, whether natural or gained from your experience, that you can use in your venture idea.
❖ Determine how you can bolster your weaknesses. Perhaps you can enroll in accounting and other business courses, find experts who can advise you, or get on-the-job experience.
❖ Grow one step at a time and at a pace that allows you to learn as your business develops.
❖ Realize you *will* make mistakes. Learn from them and then move on.
❖ Find a mentor—another woman business owner, a spouse, a friend, an agency or association representative—with whom you can consult whenever you need support or business information.
❖ Make a bank your friend. Ask other business owners for referrals in your community for banks that are "friendly" to micro-businesses.

• Success Secret 2 •

Weigh the pros and cons of home-business ownership *before* you start a home-based venture.

The NFWBO says the greatest reward of business ownership for women is gaining control over their own fate. Here are some of the pros as well as the cons listed by women who earn money from home:

Pros:
❖ Being home with your children (though most mothers of pre-schoolers have some sort of child-care arrangement—spouse, grandparent, local baby-sitter—so they can set some regular hours to conduct business).

not reach her and she did not return their telephone calls. She was so overwhelmed with work and family matters that she didn't want to answer the phone for fear that it might mean more work than she could handle.

After a good business friend (who was frustrated with her lack of responsiveness) explained why he was not going to do business with her, the desktop publisher realized she would have to change her business operations. She has since reorganized her work schedule to focus on her target customers and has sped up her reply time to same-day responses.

A major reason customers use home-based businesses is they feel they can get special attention directly from the business owner —you. Treating all customers with respect and professionalism will help you develop the customer loyalty that will sustain you even in recession times. Word-of-mouth referral is one of the common ways home businesses get customers, but reputation can go both ways. Poor customer service will also be noted and passed along to others in your community.

Mistake: Not keeping family and business separate.
Before you ever open a home business, discuss the limits that signify your working and your not working—what is and what is not business. Having three telephone lines into your home may be a joy to any teenagers who live with you—but let them know if and when they can and cannot use those lines for personal calls. A closed office door, a sign posting your office hours, working at your desk, or some other method to signify when you are the business owner and when you are the mother or wife will help prevent interruptions while you are running your business.

Mistake: Inadequate technology for your business's needs.
To be competitive in your business, you will need the basic technology your industry requires. "Basic" does not mean the latest piece of equipment with the most "bells and whistles," but rather the equipment that will produce the best results at the best price. You can always upgrade your technology as your business begins to make money.

Lorain first used second-hand saws and sanders when she began making her popular wood toys; but when she saw the craftsmanship that some other exhibitors were displaying at craft shows, she realized the limitations of her equipment. She enrolled in an evening woodworking class at a local vocational-tech school and learned which were the best heavy-duty machines for her business as well as improved her skills in order to produce top-quality toys.

Mistake: Lack of a business plan.
Starting and running a venture without a business plan is like building a house without blueprints. You may get it built, but the foundation may not support it for long. Annette, who started a concierge business (assisting others with errands, shopping, and such) was disappointed when she got no response to her advertising. She realized that in her conservative community, people considered it frivolous to pay for such a personal service. However, when she advertised in a nearby community, she got more responses; the neighboring community included many professional working couples who needed Annette's service and were willing to pay for it. Annette says: "If I had written a business plan and researched who my potential customers were, I would have saved myself time and money."

_____

For More Information
Books
Every Business Is a Growth Business: How You Can Prosper Year After Year by Ram Charan and Charles Burck (New York: Times Books, 1998).
Secrets of Self-Employment: Surviving and the Ups and Downs of Being Your Own Boss by Paul and Sarah Edwards (New York: Putnam Publishing Group, 1996).

_____

• SUCCESS SECRET 3 •

Be aware of and know how to overcome common obstacles to women's entrepreneurship.

Many women want to start a business, but for a number of reasons never see their ideas become realities. Here are some of the major obstacles they face:

Financing

In recent years, many women have relied on credit cards for business start-ups or financing. However, the NFWBO says that more women-owned firms are relying on business earnings and that their sources of financing are now quite similar to men's. Here are some realistic funding sources for women business owners:

✤ **Specialty loans** are now being offered by local banks where a one-page application can land you an unsecured credit line or loan ranging from $2,500 to $50,000. Contact: Wells Fargo/ National Association of Women Business Owners (NAWBO) Program (800) 359-3557, ext. 120; Bank of Women/America, Inc. (213) 680-3375.

✤ **Micro-loans** offered through private and SBA-backed agencies. Contact: Local SBA office, Small Business Development Center, or Women's Business Development Center for a micro-loan lender in your area < www.onlinewbc.org > .

✤ **Cash awards** are often available. To get information about them, see the library reference guide *Awards, Honors, and Prizes* (Gale Research, Detroit, MI).

For More Information
Publications

Access to Credit: A Guide for Lenders & Women Business Owners of Small Businesses. Order from Federal Reserve Bank of Chicago, IL 60604.*

The Small Business Financial Guide, MasterCard International: (800) 821-6176.

Self-Confidence

Any person will have a few self-doubts when starting a new venture, and women are no exception. "What if my business fails?"

---

*Financing information supplied by Kimberly Stanséll, author of *Bootstrapper's Success Secrets: 151 Tactics for Building a Business on a Shoestring Budget.*

"How will I balance a business, family concerns, and my regular job?" are just some of the considerations that erode a woman's confidence.

A good way to get self-confidence is to discuss your fears and concerns with other women in business or with a mentor. Most women entrepreneurs are willing to share tips and help one another succeed in business by encouraging new entrepreneurs and assisting them in finding the right resources to get the business up and running.

Networking Opportunities

If you're used to working with others in an office setting, being the sole owner (and perhaps the only worker) in your business can make you feel isolated and miss the feedback from others. To help solve this problem, you might try these ways of networking with other women:

❖ Join a local **chamber of commerce** (many chapters have women's groups within their organization).

❖ Join a **trade association** related to your business.

❖ Find other woman entrepreneurs on an **Internet business group** with whom you can exchange e-mail about solving business problems or participate in a work-from-home chat group.

❖ Form a **local group** of women entrepreneurs in your own community.

❖ Join a **national women's business group** such as NAWBO or Women Incorporated.

Commitment

Many women have trouble saying *"No!"* to outside commitments such as parent/teacher school groups, community activities, or even some family events. One keynote speaker at a conference for women entrepreneurs stated that the biggest challenge for women in the next century will be to find *balance* in their lives.

To balance your life, you have to prioritize what has to be done—the needs of those who depend on you, the bills you need

Success Secrets for Entrepreneurs*

Here are some other success secrets offered by women entrepreneurs:

Know which ways to maximize sales opportunities. —Patricia C. Gallagher, successful self-publisher, child-care business owner, and parenting consultant

If you want to have a business working with your hands, do not buy all your tools at once. I suggest you start with a few basic tools and build a few projects to see whether this is what you really want to do. —Lorain, toy-maker

Keep organized.—Sandy and Charlene, former owners of a home-party craft business

My advice for any women who want to become entrepreneurs is to start a business in something that is familiar to you and that you truly believe in. Do not let anyone discourage you from accomplishing your dreams.—Chris Carroll, former owner of a home-cleaning service and publicity agent for her comedian husband, Jimmy Carroll

to pay, the requirements of your new business, and "free time" for yourself (don't forget to factor this one in!). After assessing your "must" commitments, then and only then should you venture to give time to "causes" about which you feel strongly and want to support. The NFWBO states that "Women business owners in the U.S. are more likely than men entrepreneurs to participate in volunteer activities and to encourage their employees to volunteer."

Often, you can promote your business while you help others by (for example) presenting a class for women's self-help groups or donating a product or coupon for your service at a charity auction. Just remember: It is better to say "No" more often and really help a few than to say "Yes" to many and end up helping no one!

Uncertainty—What Business?

Unsure of what business to start? The following tips can help you decide what business is best for you.

✤ **Brainstorm** what you like to do and what you *might* like to do and think how it might meld together with your "must" commitments, goals, and dreams.

✤ **Research** all the potential ventures that interest you. Visit your library, talk to women business owners, or work or volunteer in a business to gain experience and to see whether you really would like to do this work full time.

✤ **Plan** the steps you will need to take to make your dream a reality. Write a rough business plan and focus on the customers you will need to reach and evaluate whether the market out there is large enough to support your business!

Uncertainty—How to Start?

Don't know where to start? Finding information for your business is vital to your success. Helpful sources include:

✤ The U.S. Small Business Administration (800-8-ASK-SBA), Women Business Development Centers (< www.onlinewbc. org >).

✤ Your state senator or the representative of your state's department that assists small and women's/minorities' businesses.

✤ Your local chamber of commerce and home-based business associations.

✤ Other women entrepreneurs.

If you persist in seeking the answers you need (and they are out there!) as well as find the right people to help you, chances are you will succeed in your own business—no matter what obstacles you may face.

1. **Do not think that just because you know your business— cleaning, teaching, desktop publishing, or whatever— you will have a successful business.** Skills, knowledge, and experience are valuable assets to bring to a business idea, but it is just as important to know how to *manage* your business to success. Charlene and Sandy, partners in a home-party craft business say: "Our craft parties were bringing in money, but we did not know if we were really *making money* until our accountant showed us how to keep records so we could monitor our expenses."

2. **Develop a support network of business and legal professionals, other entrepreneurs in the same industry as you are, media contacts, and supportive family and friends.** These people will be crucial in helping you solve the problems your venture will experience, especially when you face what seems like insurmountable odds.

3. **Be persistent.** Polly had four different businesses before she found one that was successful—making handmade soaps. If you know it is a good service or product, others will discover that, too!

• SUCCESS SECRET 5 •

Have dreams but also have realistic expectations in achieving them.

You may dream of owning a multimillion-dollar business but realistically know it will take more than just wishing to make it happen. Here are some practical steps to help you become a successful home corporate giant:

1. **Put your goals on paper.**
   Instead of talking about your business dreams, turn them into goals by taking the first step: writing them down on paper. Dreamers talk, doers act. Writing them down will help make your goals believable to you. There are some women who have attended a local women's entrepreneur conference

each year, but are not one step closer to starting their business. Others have already started one or two sideline businesses while working at a full- or part-time job.

2. **Write the steps you will need to reach that *first* goal.**
   Do you need to establish a business name or do preliminary market research? Make each step manageable so you feel you're getting closer.

3. **Keep a vision for your long-range goals.**
   Do, however, make sure your short-term goals all work to help you toward that end result.

4. **Be flexible in your entrepreneurial journey.**
   Patricia C. Gallagher started an at-home child-care business so she could stay home with her children. She was so successful that she wrote and self-published the book *Start Your Own At-Home Child Care Business* and sold it to two major publishers, plus self-published several other books on writing, child care, and parenting. Because of her varied experiences as an entrepreneur raising four children, Gallagher is also earning money as a public speaker at conferences and organizational events.

5. **Enjoy the process.**
   After all, though earning money is important and does validate your business, a big part of starting a business is that it defines your life and who you are.

For More Information
Books
Bootstrapper's Success Secrets: 151 Tactics for Building Your Business on a Shoestring Budget by Kimberly Stanséll (Franklin Lakes, NJ: Career Press, 1997), < www.kimberlystansell.com >.

Working Solo: The Real Guide to Freedom & Financial Success with Your Own Business, 2nd rev. ed., by Terri Lonier (New York: Wiley, 1998), < www.workingsolo.com >.

Internet Sites with Start-Up Information
(See also Resources on page 398.)

Home-Business Survival Tactics

Here are some pointers to keep in mind as you start to make sure you *stay* in business!

❖ **Learn** all the pluses and minuses you can about the business you're starting.

❖ **Be legal.** Know the licensing and zoning requirements, certifications, inspections, and so forth that apply to your business. Ignorance will not suffice for defense should you fail to comply with regulations.

❖ **Monitor** your business's financial matters and track expenses and income on a regular basis.

❖ **Create** a work space that is functional and separate from your home life.

❖ **Review** your business plan regularly to analyze your progress and direction.

❖ **Reward yourself** (and your family) for both small and large accomplishments. It will help your motivation and express to your family you appreciate their support.

< www.ivillage.com/work/index.html > The Women's Network (iVillage). Priscilla Y. Huff and other home-business experts write weekly columns, host weekly chats and message boards, and offer profiles of successful women entrepreneurs in many types of businesses.

< www.toolkit.cch.com > The Business Owner's Toolkit.

———

• SUCCESS SECRET 6 •

Establish your business's ethics.

Seventy-six percent of women entrepreneurs surveyed by the NFWBO offered at least one policy or practice that was consciously different from what was followed at a former place of employment. Differences most frequently mentioned include offering flexible scheduling; being more understanding about time off; and treating, valuing, respecting, and acknowledging that employees are important.

One successful woman entrepreneur says: "I made up my mind a long time ago that I would never consciously make money with my business as the result of someone's mistakes or misfortunes." You may not realize it, but your business will reflect your standards, your philosophy, and your ethics. Americans do not really begrudge success—only when the successful person is stingy with her money. Today customers expect you to "give back" something to your community, especially when you have been blessed.

Here are some guidelines for establishing your business's ethics:

✤ **Be honest** in your dealings with your customers and business associates. If you make a mistake, acknowledge it, make reasonable amends, and then take steps to ensure that it will not happen again.

✤ **Be fair**—treat all customers and employees with equal respect. Check to see if your trade industry recommends a code of ethics to follow. It will help legitimize your business. For example, the Direct Selling Association has an ethics code for its members, which include Avon; Mary Kay, Inc.; and others.

✤ **Follow your instincts,** common sense, and the "Golden Rule." One woman entrepreneur says: "If something I am requested to do does not 'feel' right, even if it appears to be potentially lucrative, I do not do it."

✤ **Exchange information** freely with others in your industry. You never know what leads they may give back in return.

Having a vision of the business principles you plan to follow will help you react, should you ever face a moral dilemma in your business practices.

2

Starting-Out Steps

The secret of achievement is to hold a picture of a successful outcome in mind.

—Thoreau

• SUCCESS SECRET 7 •

See if you have what it takes to be an entrepreneur.

Do you have what it takes to be an entrepreneur? Here is a self-test:

1. Do you set goals for any projects you tackle?	Yes	No
2. Are you self-driven to achieve the goals you set for yourself?	Yes	No
3. Do you feel limited in your present job and wish you could run a business *your way?*	Yes	No
4. Do you generally complete a project to your satisfaction, no matter how many hours it takes?	Yes	No
5. Are there other entrepreneurs in your family?	Yes	No
6. Are you a creative problem-solver?	Yes	No
7. Are you afraid of failure?	Yes	No

8. Do you enjoy competition?   Yes   No
9. Are you good at working with people?   Yes   No
10. Do you have business management skills
     or experience?   Yes   No

If you answered "yes" to eight of the ten questions, you have a good idea of what it takes to be an entrepreneur. If you answered "yes" to six or seven out of the ten, you show promise. If you answered "yes" to five or fewer of the questions, you might want to get more experience or training in the industry in which you want to start a business—or contract with people who are strong in the areas you are weak.

Traits of an Entrepreneur

Entrepreneurs are a unique group of people. They have a self-confidence and charisma that distinguishes them from others. They are non-conformists and tend to ask many "whys?" and "why nots?" and love it when they are told "It will never work!" or even "You're crazy!" They enjoy the challenge entrepreneurship gives them and are driven to succeed. Here are some other common entrepreneurial characteristics:

Risk-Taker

Entrepreneurs are generally non-conformists with courage to try something that they (or others) have never tried before.

Self-Motivator

Entrepreneurs are self-driven to take the steps necessary to achieve their personal and business goals. They have that "fire-in-the-belly" determination and high energy to put in the hours they need to succeed.

Unafraid of Failure

Statistics show that it may take as many as three attempts to start a business before one succeeds. Entrepreneurs know that failure itself is not bad; they learn from their mistakes and persist until they succeed.

Military Service Positions
Relate any experience, training, and education you had in the military to civilian occupations.

Hobbies
What starts out as a hobby for some women often turns into a full-time business. In "following your passion," you can combine both a love of what you do and the knowledge gained into a winning, profit-making venture.

Interests
Write down what interests you and investigate what skills and training you might need to start a business in those areas. Brainstorm for several related ideas and research their possibilities.

Because each person and enterprise is unique, honestly evaluating what you can (or cannot) contribute to an entrepreneurial idea will help you determine what business will realistically work for you and your potential customers—and hopefully lead to a long-term, successful business.

For More Information
Books
The Joy of Working from Home: Making a Life While Making a Living by Jeff Berner (San Francisco: Berrett-Koehler Publishers, Inc., 1994).
Which Business? Help in Selecting Your New Venture by Nancy Drescher (Grants Pass, OR: Oasis Press, 1997).

Now that you have assessed your skills and strengths, here are four tips to help you find the best business idea(s) to suit you:

1. **Read books and publications.** Peruse the business sections of your local library and bookstore and you will find many books presenting home-business ideas. Such magazines as *Entrepreneur's Business Start-Ups, HomeOffice, Income Opportunities, Small Business Opportunities, Spare-Time,* and many others list business ideas and home-business success stories,

plus provide valuable how-to information and resources to help you start a home business of your liking. (See "Magazines & Publications" on page 405 under Resources.)

2. **Carry a tablet with you at all times.** Jot down ideas that come to you, or those you hear in conversations, on the radio, or see on television.

3. **Read your local papers.** See the trends and needs that exist in your community. What was not needed last year may be needed this year.

4. **Give a new twist to an old idea.** One woman in a small town was always rescuing sick and abandoned animals, so she started a "pet" taxi and ambulance service. She also developed sidelines to her businesses of building "cat yards" and selling pet foods, plus running a nonprofit animal adoption service.

Once you have a solid list of business ideas that interest you the most, you will want to narrow your list. Of course, three criteria that any business idea must meet are:

1. That a market exists for your business.
2. You can afford to start it (in terms of money and time).
3. You have the expertise to conduct this business.

Do not even list a business idea that does not meet these basic requirements, unless you plan to research it further to be certain whether it is or is not possible.

Choosing the best business idea for you is only the beginning in your quest to having a successful home business. For many, this is as far as it goes. Others go on to the next steps that turn their business ideas into a working reality. Do not be afraid of going forward to the next stages of your business start-up—millions of women are doing it every day, and so can you!

_____

For More Information
Books
Finding Your Perfect Work: The New Career Guide to Making a Living, Creating a Life by Paul and Sarah Edwards (Los Angeles: J. P. Tarcher, 1996).

Unique Business Ideas

How many times have you heard about a unique business and said, "Why didn't I think of that?" Here are some pointers to help *you* get that business idea that everyone else wishes they had thought of first! Pay attention if you hear people saying:

❖ They wish there were some device or business to help them do something easier.

❖ They wish they knew of a device that would save them time doing a certain task.

❖ They absolutely hate doing some chore or task.

❖ They wish something did not cost so much.

❖ They are interested in learning something but don't know where to start.

❖ They are tired of the "same old" way of doing things or operating something.

Working Solo: The Real Guide to Freedom & Financial Success with Your Own Business, 2nd rev. ed., by Terri Lonier (New York, NY: Wiley, 1998).

Internet Sites
< www.workingsolo.com > Site for above book *(Working Solo)*.

• SUCCESS SECRET 9 •

Understand fully how home-based, self-employment options operate.

For years, women have been earning money from home in ways other than owning a business—from being distributors or sales representatives for larger companies to running a franchise, having a vending route, or even operating hot dog carts. Options such as network marketing and franchising (see below) may also be money-making opportunities you'll want to investigate for yourself.

Network Marketing (MLM and Direct Selling)

Here are several frequently asked questions about MLM and direct selling opportunities:

Q: *Please explain the terms MLM, direct selling, and network marketing.*

A: Both direct selling and MLM (multi-level marketing) pertain to "network marketing," in which you, the "distributor," purchase the rights from a company to market its products to customers within a given territory (not always exclusive).

As a distributor, you are self-employed and set your own hours. Generally, you purchase a starter kit with order forms, samples, and supplies for direct sales to consumers. Popular items sold this way include toys, cosmetics, and many others. Distributors sell one-on-one with customers, through party plans or both.

In MLM, distributors not only sell a company's products but enlist others to sell these products/services under their supervision—called "downline." You, the "recruiter," would then receive a "compensation"—a percentage of your enlistees' sales.

Q: *What are pyramids?*

A: Pyramid business scams (which are illegal!) operate where a few people at the top make money from the many at the list's bottom who generally lose their initial (and often substantial!) investment. Many pyramids disguise and tout themselves as legitimate MLM opportunities.

Q: *How can you evaluate a network business opportunity?*

A: Michael Klimek, MLM consultant and author of the *MLM Truth Reports*, advises: "First look at how long the company has been in the network marketing business. History shows that most MLM companies never see their third year in business."

Other tips for determining a network opportunity's legitimacy include:

❖ Taking time to research the company. Do not be rushed or pressured!

❖ Contacting the Direct Marketing and Multi-Level International Association to see if the company is a member.

❖ Checking for any complaints with the Better Business Bureau and attorney general's office in the state of the company's headquarters.

❖ Finding out the initial investment. Legitimate network marketing companies usually offer affordable start-up materials.

Marla Berchard, a full-time network marketing professional and consultant advises: "To maximize financial success, it is critical to select a company that has four elements:

1. A compensation plan rewarding part-time distributors and full-time professionals, but not at each other's expense.

2. A stable company providing outstanding customer service. Products that are competitively priced and of excellent quality, get results and are *consumable* (very important!). With consumable products you generate repeat business instead of always having to find new customers.

3. Duplicable training, support systems, and mentorship. This is where the phrase, 'you're in business for yourself, but not by yourself,' comes into play. There should be a complete system that includes leadership, training, marketing tools and resources (both on and offline) that make financial success in network marketing attainable for anyone with the desire to enjoy it!"

4. Do your company research with calculator in hand and your common sense, as well as your intuition, highly activated. Learn how to sort through company and product 'hype' and apply proven business principles to make a sound and informed decision. Tap into resources to help you learn what pitfalls and 'red flags' to avoid. Above all else, find a good mentor. This is a great industry that presents tremendous opportunity for women entrepreneurs. If you truly possess the desire and motivation to succeed and are willing to work hard to achieve it, then there is absolutely no limit to what you can do!"

For More Information
Books/Publications

Home Businesses You Can Buy: The Definitive Guide to Exploring Franchises, Multi-Level Marketing and Business Opportunities Plus: How to Avoid Scams by Paul and Sarah Edwards and Walter Zovi (New York, NY: Putnam, 1997).

Inside Network Marketing by Leonard W. Clements (Rocklin, CA: Prima Publishing, 1996).

Opportunity World magazine, 28 Vesey St., #257, New York, NY 10007-2701; $11.97/year.

Start Your Own Network Marketing Company: Build Your Business with a Proven System by Angela L. Moore (Rocklin, CA: Prima, 1998).

Internet Sites/E-mail Addresses

"Evaluating Network Marketing Compensation Plans" by Marla Berchard. For a free copy of this report and others, e-mail: mbhb@home.com.

< www.fraud.org > The National Fraud Information Center. Scam updates.

< www.mlmcentral.com/mlmtruth/ > Online MLM newsletter by Graeme Clark and David Warren. Michael Klimek authors their *MLM Truth Reports*.

< www.netbusiness-secrets.com > NetBusiness Secrets. Articles on network marketing.

< www.noboss.com > The National Organization of Business Opportunity Seekers.

< www.pmignet.com/nmo/index.html > Doug Mayer's network evaluation tips.

Organizations

The Direct Sellers Association of Canada, #3-100 West Beaver Creek Rd., Richmond Hill, Ontario L4B 1H4 Canada.

The Direct Selling Association (DSA). 1666 K St., NW, Suite 1010, Washington, DC 20006; < www.dsa.org >. Has a "Code of Ethics" for members, which include Avon; Mary Kay, Inc.; and others.

order to understand their operations. Make a list of questions to ask about anything that is not clear.

❖ Visit several of the franchises in operation and talk to their franchisees to get some feedback about what they like and do not like about the company and doing business.

❖ If possible, visit the headquarters and ask permission to observe the training sessions.

❖ Ask if there is financing available.

❖ Ask about the company's expansion plans, and whether their franchises have exclusive territories or compete against one another.

❖ Ask if this franchise can be operated from a home-based office.

❖ Consult with a lawyer familiar with franchise agreements.

Tanya Wallace, co-author of *Moneymaking Moms,* and founder and franchisor of Toddlin' Time parent/toddler playgrounds, says the women franchisees who purchase a franchise, "usually find that purchasing a franchise is much easier than starting a business from scratch, simply because it is a turnkey operation. Procedural and marketing manuals are complete and tested, and the business itself has been established and proven in a given area." Wallace continues: "There is also a home office to rely on for assistance in structuring the business. It is often a more attractive option than starting a business on their own."

For More Information
Associations

American Association of Franchisees and Dealers, P.O. Box 81887, San Diego, CA 92138-1887, < www.aafd.org >. "A nonprofit trade association representing the rights and interests of franchisees and independent dealers throughout the United States." Also has publications on entering a franchise venture, financing, and other information concerning franchises.

International Franchise Association, 1350 New York Ave., N.W. Suite 900, Washington, DC 20005-4709, < www.franchise.org >. Internet site has the *Franchise Opportunities Guide Online*® as well as a listing of companies, code of principals and conduct, membership information, and listing of publications on franchise opportunity topics.

Books/Publications

Entrepreneur Magazine and *Entrepreneur's Business Start-Ups* magazine regularly feature the latest available franchise (as well as free small- home-business news and advice). For copies, visit your favorite bookstore or newsstand; write for subscription information to Entrepreneur Media Inc., 2392 Morse Ave., Irvine, CA 92614; or visit their online sites (listed below).

Franchised Business, edited by Ann Dugan (Dover, NH: Upstart Publishing Co., 1998).

Franchise Fraud by Robert L. Purvin (New York: John Wiley & Sons, 1994).

The Franchise Handbook, 1020 N. Broadway, Suite 111, Milwaukee, WI 53202. Write for subscription information.

The Franchise Opportunities Handbook: A Complete Guide for People Who Want to Start Their Own Franchise by Lavern Ludden (Ed.) and the U.S. Department of Commerce (Indianapolis, IN: Jist Works, 1995). Contains information on more than 1,500 franchisors.

Franchising 101: The Complete Guide to Evaluating, Buying, and Growing Your Successful Franchising Magazine, 16885 Dallas Parkway, Dallas, TX 75248. Write for subscription information.

A Woman's Guide to Her Own Franchise Business by Anne Small (New York: Pilot Books, 1986).

Government Sources

The Federal Trade Commission, Public Reference Branch, Washington, DC 20580, < www.ftc.gov >. The FTC provides a free information package about the FTC Franchise and Opportunity Rules.

Internet Sites

< www.betheboss.com > Be the Boss—franchising information and resources.

< www.BizStartUps.com > *Entrepreneur's Business Start-Ups* magazine.

< www.EntrepreneurMag.com > *Entrepreneur Magazine.*

Beware of Franchise Fraud

All franchises are *not* created equal, so you will want to protect yourself from franchise fraud. Here are some warning signals that the franchise is not what its owner wants you to believe:

* The franchisor's UFOC shows that some of the key people have been involved in a bankruptcy or a material litigation in the past 10 years.
* Did the franchisor ask about your background? Legitimate companies want good people as franchisees to help their company thrive.
* Other franchisees of the company are dissatisfied with the support given them (or voice other complaints when you interview them).
* The franchisor lacks a mission statement.
* Operations of the franchise are within one another's territory and competing for the same target customers.

If everything does seem okay, but your intuition is doubtful or you believe you are not really suited to the restrictions a franchise can impose, then look into other franchises, or "go it alone" and start your own company.

< www.franchise1.com > and < www.busop1.com >. *The Franchise Handbook* (see Books/Publications on previous page).

< www.HomeOfficeMag.com > Entrepreneur's HomeOffice Online: find information about home-based franchises.

< www.pilotbooks.com > Pilot Books has been a leading U.S. publisher of franchising information since 1959.

< www.sfmag.com > *Successful Franchising Magazine* (see Books/ Publications on previous page).

———

Other Business Opportunities Including Vending and Carts

Other self-employment ventures you may want to investigate are licensed business opportunities. These company-owned ventures are similar to franchises but are concerned more with the products' sales. Each company defines the terms of their agreement. Here are several types of business opportunities:

+ **Wholesaler.** You sell the company's products to retailers and other distributors who sell directly to the customer.
+ **Licensing.** In this agreement the *licenser* gives the *licensee* permission to sell products using the name and trademarks of the company. For example, if you are a crafter, you could not replicate a well-known cartoon character in your work and sell your product as that character without a specific license to do so.
+ **Distributorship.** In this agreement, the distributor sells the company's products but cannot use the company's trade name as part of its own trade name. Popular items sold this way are vitamins, cosmetics, and toys.
+ **Vending Machine Routes.** In this venture, the entrepreneur usually has to purchase the machines and pay the location owner a percentage of the sales. Below are some helpful resources to which you can write for additional information.

For More Information
Associations
The Independent Vendors Assn., P.O. Box 71023, Des Moines, IA 50325. Magazine; proposal kit.

Mobile Merchandizing Association, P.O. Box 54472, Los Angeles, CA 90054. Newsletter, resource directory, and book (*From Dogs to Riches*—see Books below).

Denise Clark, author of *From Dogs to Riches,* started selling hot dogs from a mobile cart in 1987 to help pay for her pre-law education. She has since expanded her operation to owning a number of carts that have annual earnings in the six figures. She continues to expand her business while pursuing her law degree on a part-time business.

The National Bulk Vendors Assn., 200 N. LaSalle St. #2100, Chicago, IL 60601. Has booklet, *Introduction to Bulk Vending.*

Internet Sites

< www.vendingconnection.com > Helpful information and links for vending businesses.

Publications

Vend-All's *Tips & Tricks* ($15 for booklet), 35136 Center Ridge Rd., North Ridgeville, OH 44039.

Vending—The Real Deal (1997) by D. Chester ($59.95 + $10.00 handling and priority shipping). Order via the Internet (enter "vending" in major search engines) or send check, cash, or money order to The Vending Service, 159 Stonebrook St., Simi Valley, CA 93065.

✤ **Carts & Kiosks.** These are technically not home businesses, but depending on the location, you may be able to have them in an area outside or near your home or just do them on a seasonal business. You can rent them at shopping malls or purchase a mobile cart and travel to different locations. The ideal location and a good product can be a winning, money-making combination.

Books

From Dogs to Riches: A Step-by-Step Guide to Start & Operate Your Own Mobile Cart Vending Business by Denise Clark (Los Angeles, CA: MCC Publishing Co., 1992).

If you decide to invest in any of these self-employment options, be very cautious and investigate each opportunity thoroughly. Consult with a lawyer if you have any doubts about contracts or other details.

For More Information
Internet Sites

< www.noboss.com > NOBOSS (The National Organization of Business Opportunity Seekers). "The Web's largest database of detailed information on 100 + home-based businesses that can be launched with capital investment ranging from $50 to $5,000."

Organizations

American Business Opportunity Institute, c/o Andrew A. Caffey, 3 Bethesda Metro Ctr., #700, Bethesda, MD 20814. A national information clearinghouse and seminar company specializing in business opportunity and franchise investment and regulations. Send a business-size, self-addressed stamped envelope for more information on publications and programs. Caffey is an attorney and an internationally recognized specialist in franchise and business opportunity law.

The National Organization of Business Opportunity Seekers, 8281 Northwind Way, Orangevale, CA 95662.

• SUCCESS SECRET 10 •

Do not limit yourself to just one product, service, or business.

Sometimes a home business can offer more opportunities than just one business.

Options for you to consider.

❖ **Spin-offs.** Polly made different brands of potpourri mixes to put in various sewn items and sell. She loved the fragrances so much that she decided to incorporate them into creating handmade soaps which she sells to various craft and gift shops.

❖ **One for profit, one for your passion.** Regina uses one home business to help her fund another. She cleans homes during the week and on the weekends sells her own specially designed jewelry at artisan shows and specialty shops, a business that fulfills her creative outlets.

❖ **Seasonal.** One woman featured in a business magazine has three businesses based in her area: She is a ski instructor in the winter months; grows fresh herbs to sell to restaurants in the spring; and makes flavored vinegars in the summer which she sells to gourmet cooking shops.

Six Ways to Find Spin-Offs in Your Current Business(es)

1. Self-publish your expertise in books, booklets, or publications. People love to read success tips by someone who has "made it." Offer these for sale especially in your industry. Patricia C. Gallagher ran a successful at-home day-care business and then put her practical experiences into a book that she sold to two different publishers.
2. Create software of templates, mini-programs, or training manuals for other entrepreneurs in your industry based on your experiences.
3. Offer yourself as a workshop leader, keynote speaker, or panel participant for industry conferences.
4. At the end of the talks, or for persons who are not able to attend conferences, offer audio or videotapes or transcripts of the tapes.
5. Write articles (online or through print media) and/or columns in industry or consumer publications that will reach your target audiences.
6. Check whether your local cable or radio show will allow you to have a regular show about your expertise.

Here are some tips for handling multiple ventures:

❖ Keep each business completely separate (even if they are related)—especially with your records, advertising, accounts, and so on. Consult regularly with your accountant to monitor your financial statements.

❖ Have a separate business plan for each venture including short- and long-range goals, market research, and planning, and review them regularly.

❖ Contract with a home-based, virtual assistant for a few hours a week to help you keep up to date with correspondence so you can concentrate on the business's services, production, and marketing.

✤ Use customer feedback and market research to improve and expand each business and possibly find lucrative spin-offs in these businesses.

As I tell women in my business workshops, one man in my community has eighteen businesses, so why shouldn't you someday?

• SUCCESS SECRET 11 •

Learn how to avoid home-business scams.*

You know the old adage: "If it sounds too good to be true . . . it usually is!" However, many people who are frustrated with their present jobs and would love to stay at home and work fall victim to the increasing number of work-at-home scams that appear on the Internet, in newspapers and magazines, and in other media. The National Consumer League estimates more than $200 billion is lost to home-business scams and fraud each year!

Be suspicious of all ads like the ones saying they pay people to "stuff envelopes or assemble crafts at home." And beware of those full-page ads that never tell you exactly what work the person in the picture is doing at their kitchen table (where else?) but *do* tell you that she has made millions doing this simple and easy job, and all you need to do is send them $49.95 and you can learn how to do it, too! Here are some tell-tale signs of a home-business opportunity scam:

✤ Promises huge profits running this business in your spare time.

✤ Asks you for money before they send you any business details.

---

*If you wish to find *legitimate* opportunities for companies that hire home workers, you first must determine if it is *permissible* in your state or in accordance with federal regulations. Check with your state legislator's or federal office of the Department of Labor for what is and is not permissible. Some states, too, require that you obtain a "homeworker's certificate."

❖ Refuses to give names (addresses, telephone numbers, etc.) of others who have invested in this business opportunity.

❖ Requests money for work-at-home sources.

❖ Very willing to negotiate the price of the home-business opportunity if you complain about the high prices—these scam artists want to get whatever money you are willing to spend!

❖ Refuses to send you a demo disk if they are selling business software.

❖ Wants to sell you the business opportunity but offers no advice on how you can market this business in your community.

❖ Pressures you to sign a contract without giving you time to check out the company.

❖ SENDS YOU E-MAIL SOLICITATIONS IN CAPITAL LETTERS!

One older couple in my community took a second mortgage on their home to invest $15,000 in a business opportunity that included a computer and software for three different business packages (all out of date). They were promised free support in their business start-up. This couple even flew out to the company and interviewed the owners and observed their headquarters.

Unfortunately, the couple had no experience or training in any of the business packages they purchased or knew nothing about business start-up and marketing. They also had not done any market research in their community to see if such business services were needed. They would have been much better off if they had taken that $15,000 and invested in their own business venture— one they knew and one that had a market existing for it! (Note: this company was finally charged with false advertising and ordered to pay back the money it took, but the victims only received a small percentage of their investments.)

You may be anxious—even desperate—to start a business, but take the time to thoroughly research your business ideas and *do not spend a single penny* until you are satisfied with the credentials of the company with whom you are dealing. Better yet—avoid them altogether! Better to "invest in yourself" and start a business based on your own expertise and strengths. Chambers of commerce, home-based business groups, U.S. Small Business Administration's small business development and women's business development centers, and other sources can all help you get information you need to start a successful (and legitimate) venture in your own community!

If you suspect a scam or you have been a victim of one, contact one or more of the following:

✤ The Consumer Protection Agency and Better Business Bureau in your area. They can tell you whether complaints have been lodged against the company you have been dealing with.

✤ Your state attorney general's office or the attorney general's office in the state where the company is located.

✤ Your local postmaster. The U.S. Postal Service investigates fraudulent mail practices.

✤ The advertising office of the publication, radio, or television station that ran the ad you answered. Report your experience to them.

✤ The Federal Trade Commission (FTC). This commission cannot help resolve individual disputes, but it can take action if there is evidence of a pattern of deceptive or unfair practices. To register a complaint or receive their free *Work-at-Home Schemes*, write to *FTC*, Washington, DC 20580; call (202) 326-2225; or visit their Web site: < www.ftc.gov >.

✤ The National Fraud Information Center. To get updates on the latest frauds, scams, or to report a fraud of which you have been a victim or one you suspect is a fraud, write to The National Fraud Information Center, P.O. Box 65868, Washington, DC 20035; call (800) 876-7060; or access < www.fraud.org >.

✤ Council of Better Business Bureaus has *Work-at-Home Schemes* (Publication 204) available free. Write to Publications Dept., 4200 Wilson Blvd., Arlington, VA 22203; or visit their Web site: < www.bbb.org >.

For More Information
Books
The Work-at-Home Sourcebook, 7th ed., by Lynie Arden (Metairie, LA: Live Oak Publications, Inc., 1999).

---

are trying to start new lives. There is nothing quite like the feeling of giving others some hope and encouragement.

✤ **Give yourself some time to relax and enjoy life**—whether you exercise, spend time with friends and family, or read that latest book by your favorite mystery writer!

Overcoming Work-at-Home Fears

Many women say they would love to start a home business, but they are not good at approaching people, or that they are afraid of failing. As was mentioned previously, entrepreneurs are characteristically risk-takers and not afraid of failing, but just because you do not like to take risks or feel too shy to promote yourself doesn't mean you cannot be a business owner. Here are some methods to help you overcome your fears:

✤ Attend small business expositions, or a women's entrepreneur conference sponsored by Women's Business Centers, Small Business Development Centers (SBDCs) and organizations such as the Junior League of Oakland—East Bay, Inc.'s annual Women's Business Conference held every spring. These conferences give you opportunities to take workshops in business areas that you need support, including how to market yourself and your business.

✤ If you have to make sales calls ("cold-calling"), write out a "script" and practice what you are going to say.

✤ Be prepared with promotional materials, business cards, and samples of products if you visit potential customers or exhibit at a trade show.

✤ Look and act confident, even if you do not feel it. Realize that everyone gets the jitters and the more you do something, the better you will get at doing it. Iris Kapustein, who owns Trade Show Xpress, a trade show consulting firm, reassured me before we went on a television show together: "You will do fine because you are talking about your business—*you* are the expert."

✤ Realize that failure is only bad when we fail to learn from it. Remember that some business studies show that many entrepreneurs required three attempts at starting a business before one succeeded.

Challenge yourself a little bit each day, and you are sure to surprise yourself with the results!

For More Information
Books
Inc. Your Dreams by Rebecca Maddox (New York, NY: Penguin, 1996).
Seven Secrets of Successful Women by Donna and Lynn Brooks (New York, NY: McGraw-Hill, 1999).

Internet Sites
< www.womensu.com > Women's U. A virtual university to help women achieve their goals, including a page of helpful motivational books.

• SUCCESS SECRET 13 •

Learn how to do market research to determine whether there are potential customers for your home-business idea.

Finding Your Customers—Your Niche
No matter what business idea you consider, if you do not have customers for your service or products, your business cannot succeed. To determine the potential, you have to identify your target market (the customers most likely to patronize your business) and whether there is a "niche" (some service or product that is not yet being provided to those target customers).

Sue Barrett, who has been involved in a variety of home businesses and also operates the Home Business Center Web site, says: "If you are just starting a business, establish parameters of your target market by asking the following:

1. What are their demographics?
2. What are their needs and requirements?
3. What benefits do they want?
4. What are their concerns about your type of product or service?
5. Who is your competition?

"Knowing your target audience will minimize the risks of doing business. It will uncover and identify potential problems. It will help you recognize opportunities in the marketplace that otherwise would be missed. It can save you time and money by focusing your energy on the potential BUYERS."

For More Information
Books
Finding Your Niche by Lawrence J. Pino (New York, NY: Berkley Publishing Group, 1997).

Internet Sites
< www.homebusinesscenter.com > FA Publications, 31 N. San Mateo Drive, Suite 144, San Mateo, CA 94401-2865.

How to Analyze Your Competitors
In your quest to find target customers, you need to analyze your competitors and study what they are and aren't providing to their customers. Here are some suggestions:

❖ **Study their advertisements** to see which services or products they are pushing. Get copies of their promotional materials. Then see if there is a service or product they do not provide.
❖ **Do informal surveys** of your target customers at business trade shows or events, or via the telephone, flyers, word of mouth, ads in the newspapers, or direct mailings with response cards.
❖ **Test a product and or service** similar to your competitor's by offering a free consultation or sample and then ask for feedback about its quality.

Be Smarter Than Your Competitors

No matter what business you start, you are likely to have competition from other businesses for some (or all) the same customers. Here are some tips to help you get an advantage.

✤ **Be available more hours or at times when your competitors are not.** For example, you might run a child-care business that has hours on weekends or some evenings for parents who are students or work evening shifts.

✤ **Surprise your customer with little extras.** Provide free estimates with no obligation. Send them thank-you notes or congratulatory cards on special occasions. Offer them special sales. Sue Marx, who has a home-based salon, offers refreshments and free handmade ornaments to all customers during holiday seasons.

✤ **Be honest with your customers.** If you make a mistake, take steps to rectify it. Tell them immediately when you cannot handle a certain request, and keep a list of others they can call. When we did the lawn care, we also had requests to rototill gardens or trim trees. We did not have the equipment to do that, but we did have a list of recommended business owners who performed those services.

✤ **Treat all customers with respect.** You do not have to like every customer, but you do have treat each as a person, with professionalism and common courtesy.

✤ **Communicate!** Be available for your customers and be sure to get back to them promptly if they have a question. Kathy Barndt, a lawyer with a home office, says: "I often answer my own business telephone even though I have a secretary. My clients are surprised and pleased that they can often talk directly to me."

Let them know if you are having a problem completing a project. Make sure you understand exactly what the customer wants (do not assume *anything!*). Send out "customer report cards."

✤ **Be bold and honest** and contact your competitors directly and ask them if there are customers' jobs that they cannot or prefer not to handle. My husband and I did lawn care on the side a couple of years ago, and discovered a niche of mowing the tiny lawns of townhouse owners. We received the tip from an owner of a large lawn- and tree-care business, who told us it was not worth his time to mow small lawns and preferred to mow business sites. We had more business than we could handle mowing these little lawns!

✤ **Call your competitors,** and tell them you will be grateful for any smaller referrals and that you are worthy of their recommendations.

• SUCCESS SECRET 14 •

Know the tasks you must do before you quit your day job.

Options to Consider Before You Quit Your Day Job
You may have dreamed of starting a home business for various reasons, but before you tell your boss off and quit your day job, consider these tips:

1. **Start While at Your Present Job**

    ✤ If there are company benefit plans, see when they will increase in value and if and when you might receive money from them.

    ✤ Schedule routine physical, dental, or eye examinations covered by your company's health insurance. Determine the cost of the health coverage if you had to pay for it.

    ✤ Update your references. If your boss commended you for doing a good job, ask if she would put in writing and place it into your file.

    ✤ Take courses, training sessions, etc., paid by your employer that you could use in a future business.

2. **Develop a Financial Plan**

   ❖ Make sure you have good credit. If not, take the time to establish it—preferably while you are still employed.
   ❖ Save money. Try living on the bare minimum to see if you can get by on less money when you start your business. Put the savings toward your venture. Moonlight at a part-time job. Experts recommend you save two years' living expenses—the average time for a business to become profitable—before quitting to start a full-time venture.
   ❖ See if you will be getting a severance or retirement package that could help finance a business or pay living expenses.

3. **Evaluate Yourself**

   ❖ Ask yourself and the honest opinion of others if you have what it takes to be a business owner. Setting goals, flexibility, self-discipline, confidence to take calculated risks, willingness to market yourself and your business, and other characteristics are all important for an entrepreneur.
   ❖ Evaluate your skills and/or education to decide whether you need additional training for your venture.

4. **Prepare for Your Business Start-Up**

   ❖ Write a business plan you could take to a banker.
   ❖ Do thorough market research for your business idea. Use both primary research (asking persons directly for feedback) and secondary research (collecting data and demographic information from business organizations, legislators, and government agencies) to develop a customer profile and to discover whether a market exists.
   ❖ Start your business part time—as two-thirds of new business owners do.
   ❖ Develop a business network of experts and contacts in your industry and in the community in which you will be doing business. These will be invaluable in getting referrals and clients.
   ❖ Set goals—long-range and short-term—to establish a plan of action.

Be Self-Confident

You will have "nay-sayers" who may try to discourage you, but if you believe in yourself, you will be more likely to succeed than someone who listens to the pessimists and is overwhelmed by self-doubts.

For More Information

Books

This Is Your Life, Not a Dress Rehearsal: Proven Principles for Creating The Life of Your Dreams by Jim Donovan. (Buckingham, PA: Bovan Publishing Group, Inc., 1999).

Internet Sites

< www.jimdonovan.com > Author of *This Is Your Life, Not a Dress Rehearsal*, listed above.

• SUCCESS SECRET 15 •

Fully consider your family's involvement and their concerns when you contemplate entrepreneurship.

As a new business may demand even more time than a job outside the home, it may cause conflicts and build resentment between you and your spouse and other family members. Here are some guidelines to help you prevent this from happening.

Working with a Spouse

Jim and Nikoo are a husband-wife team who write historical romance novels under one pseudonym, May McGoldrick. Jim, an English professor at a local college, and Nikoo, an engineer, share in raising their children and in developing their joint writing career. They say: "We want our life relationship with one another to be distinctly separate from our work relationship. This is sometimes tough, but this is how we go about it.

"We consider each novel that we write as a 'product.' As collaborative writers, each of us is contributing to the process of creating that product. However, we force ourselves to remember that 'we' are not the same as the 'product.' In separating ourselves (or at least distancing ourselves) from the product, we avoid investing all of our feelings of 'self-worth' in it. Sure, we produced it, but we also have other things more important in our lives. By thinking this way, we make ourselves less defensive about our contribution, and our relationship as a couple can continue to operate and develop (and maybe even flourish) on an entirely separate plane of existence." Nikoo and Jim McGoldrick, AKA May McGoldrick, authors of *Flame* (Penguin/Putnam, 1998) and *A Marriage of Minds: Collaborative Fiction Writing* (Heinemann, 2000).

Author Azriela Jaffe advises a woman to ask herself the following questions before entering into a business with her life partner:

❖ "Do you have the kind of relationship that thrives on plenty of time spent together?

❖ Does distance make the heart grow fonder, or do you prefer to spend as much time as possible with your mate?

❖ Do you each have unique skills and interests to contribute to the venture, and a shared passion for the product or type of business?

❖ Have you worked out a way to resolve conflict?

❖ Are you willing to share power and control with your spouse?

❖ Have you considered the financial risk of 'putting all of your eggs in one basket'?"

Jaffe continues: "Remember this: Rewards for entrepreneurial marriages are enormous—and so are the risks. Be sure that you are coupling for the right reasons, and that you communicate up front about your concerns and fears. And then, keep the communication open as you proceed!"

For More Information
Books
The Home Team: How Couples Can Make a Life and a Living by Working at Home by Scott and Shirley Gregory (Cambridge, MN: Panda Publishing, 1997).

What Successful Entrepreneurial Couples Do

❖ Assess their strengths and skills and match them accordingly to the business's tasks.
❖ Integrate the business with the family but don't allow it to interfere with the sheer enjoyment of family activities.
❖ Show appreciation for each person's contribution to the business with positive comments and support instead of criticism and ridicule.
❖ Regularly plan business goals together.
❖ Share household chores and child-rearing.

Honey, I Want to Start My Own Business: A Planning Guide for Couples by Azriela Jaffe. (New York, NY: HarperBusiness, 1996).
Let's Go into Business Together: Eight Secrets to Successful Business Partnering by Azriela Jaffe (New York, NY: Avon Books, 1998).

Internet Sites/E-mail Addresses
< www.isquare.com/crlink.htm > Visit this site for a free online newsletter for Entrepreneurial Couples, or e-mail Azriela Jaffe: < az@azriela.com > .

———

Working with Two Entrepreneurs under the Same Roof
With technology affordable and increasingly sophisticated, more couples are conducting two or more home businesses from their homes.

Here are some solutions to the unique problems that dual home businesses under one roof present:

Equipment and Supplies
It makes sense to share supplies, printers, and a fax machine, but couples are advised to have a separate telephone for each busi-

ness and possibly separate computers, depending on the specific requirements of each business.

Scheduling
One couple has what they call a "power meeting" at the beginning of each week to discuss and plan their schedules as well as the household and family's errands and activities.

Division of Work and Pleasure
Home-working couples respect one another's working time and limit the interruptions so work can be accomplished. One couple "meets" in the kitchen for lunch and for occasional walks in a nearby park when the weather is nice.

Office Space
Organization and separateness are the keys here. Let each set up the space most suitable to the business, and do not allow one business's papers, records, and so forth to "spill over" into the other's area.

For More Information
Books
He Works, She Works®: Successful Strategies for Working Couples© by Jaine Carter, Ph.D. and James D. Carter, Ph.D., (self-published, 1995).

Internet Sites
< www.cartercarter.com > Authors of *He Works, She Works*, listed above. For price and ordering information, write to (their) Family Renewal Institute®, 720 Turkey Oak Ln., Naples, FL 24108.

Integrating Home and Work Space
Of course, one of the reasons many women want to work from home is to stay home with their children—usually with pre-school children, but older children and teens may need even more

support these days. A few years ago in a home-business magazine, a woman gave this reason for deciding to bring her office
"home" even though her children were in school. "The principal
called to inform me that my son was cutting school and spending
the time with others at a home where the mother was away working. I told him he should call that mother and let her know what
was going on. He said to me, 'I am!' "

It can be especially hectic to work from home with children.
Here are some tips by women who do:

- ❖ **Involve your children when possible.** Patricia C. Gallagher,
  entrepreneur, marketing expert, self-publisher, and mother of
  four children, says to involve your children so they really feel
  they are contributing, and celebrate with them when something
  special happens in your business. (Gallagher at one time had
  their family van painted with the cover of her book and took off
  on a cross-country book tour with her three daughters—until
  she realized she was pregnant with her fourth child!)
- ❖ **Try to keep to a working schedule** so your children will know
  when you are and are not working. Have a sign posted or a signal that means you are busy at the moment.
- ❖ **"Spend some time planning** *how* you will use your time, and
  always allow for the unexpected by scheduling 'just in case'
  time," says Caroline Hull, co-author with Tanya Wallace (mothers of a total of eight children) of the book *Moneymaking Moms*.
  "I think so much of our stress occurs because things get out of
  balance and the roles of mom and moneymaker start to conflict.
  Time that is spent on time management and planning is always
  time well invested."
- ❖ **Realize family "emergencies" can happen any time** and disrupt
  your business schedule. Allow for this by having back-up plans
  and giving yourself extra time to complete a project.
- ❖ **Set some regular time** to spend specifically with them. One
  mother sets a timer and spends fifteen minutes every hour or so
  playing with her children.
- ❖ **"Do not forget why you are home in the first place,"** says Liz
  Folger, home-business author and mother of two daughters. "For

me it's to raise my daughters myself. Raising doesn't mean saying, 'I'll play with you in a few minutes' every time they come
to me for my attention. Take time for your kids. They grow up
so quickly, and you can never have yesterday back. Live today
to the fullest."

✤ **Take advantage of home and office technology**—portable
phones (with mute buttons), headsets, voice mail when you
cannot come to the phone, baby monitors or intercoms to keep
track of what is happening in your home, half-doors so you can
bar pets and little ones from your office but still communicate
with them.

✤ **Have at least one "strictly business" telephone line** that is
off-limits to your children or at least until "office hours" are over.

✤ **Stress "business hours" to your clients** so they know that your
having a home office doesn't mean they can call 24 hours a day;
politely give them the hours you are "open" for business.

✤ **Take advantage of "spouse" coverage** and concentrate on doing the most important jobs during those times.

✤ **Take advantage of time**—those many, small blocks of uninterrupted time to do some work—children's naps, an hour before
everyone gets up in the morning or in the evening when they go
to bed.

These are just a few of the many tips home-working Moms use
to run a business.

Work hard, but not to the point of being a workaholic. Make
time to relax and reap the benefits of working from home—earning
money at a business you enjoy while being with those you love!

_____

For More Information
Books
Home but Not Alone: The Work-at-Home Parents' Handbook by Kather-
ine Murray (Indianapolis, IN: Jist Works, 1997).
*How to Raise a Family and a Career Under One Roof: A Parent's Guide
to Home Business* by Lisa Roberts (Moontownship, PA: Brook-
haven Press, 1997).

Child-Care Options

Even though your primary reason for working from home is to be with your children, most women have some sort of child-care option so they can work for uninterrupted periods of time. Here are some of their strategies:

✤ "Share" a nanny with another home-working mom.
✤ Hire a baby-sitter or teenager after school to come into your home a few hours a day or week while you work.
✤ Enroll preschoolers in a nursery school one or two days a week.
✤ Join a community mother's group where you barter baby-sitting hours.

Mompreneurs: A Practical Step-By-Step Guide to Work-at-Home Success by Ellen H. Parlapiano and Patricia Cobe (New York, NY: Berkley, 1996).
Moneymaking Moms: How Work at Home Can Work for You by Caroline Hull and Tanya Wallace (New York, NY: Citadel Press, 1998).
The Stay-at-Home Mom's Guide to Making Money: How to Choose the Business That's Right for You Using the Skills and Interests You Already Have by Liz Folger (Rocklin, CA: Prima Publishing, 1997).
Work at Home Wisdom: A Collection of Quips, Tips, and Inspirations to Balance Work, Family, and Home by Andi Axman and David H. Bangs, Jr. (Dover, NH: Upstart Publishing Co., 1998).
Working at Home While Kids Are There, Too by Loriann Hoff Oberlin (Franklin Lakes, NJ: Career Press, 1997).

Internet Sites

< www.bizymoms.com > Liz Folger. Author of *The Stay-at-Home Mom's Guide to Making Money* (listed above).
< www.ivillage.com/work/index.html > Authors of *Mompreneurs* (listed above) host a weekly chat for The Women's Network.

• SUCCESS SECRET 16 •

Know the legal requirements of your home business.

It is well worth your time and money to consult with an accountant and lawyer specializing in small business matters when setting up your business!

Zoning Matters

Home Office Computing Magazine has published a listing of top cities in the United States that are home-business "friendly"; however, do not assume that your area is as receptive to home ventures. Your first step is to *know* the zoning restrictions where you live. Pick up a copy of your local government's laws and read it thoroughly. If you need a permit or license, find out the specifics and assess whether you can work within the parameters set down.

Most of the women I interviewed were told by their local government officials that as long as their business did not cause their neighbors to complain or caused undue traffic or noise into the neighborhood, they could do business and would not even need a zoning permit.

Illegal Home Businesses

It is very important that you're aware that some kinds of home businesses may be illegal, according to local, state, or federal regulations. For example, many home sewing businesses are in violation of the Fair Labor Standards Act. Check with your local authorities, your state's office that handles small businesses, and the U.S. Department of Labor for the current laws regarding home workers before you start up your business.

Here are some additional tips to avoid zoning conflicts:

✤ Be considerate and do not annoy the neighbors. As long as your business does not interfere with your neighbors' lives (through noise, excess traffic, fumes, etc.), they should leave you alone. (In my community, a row of houses on one street had six women with different home businesses!)

✤ Keep your business within bounds. If you begin to expand and need a building or more storage space, you may want to consider renting in another location.

✤ Meet with clients at their offices or rent office space by the day or as needed from a member of the Executive Suite Association.

✤ Move to a less restricted or more home business "friendly" neighborhood!

✤ Write the laws! Join with other home-business owners in helping to have some input in any of the ordinances to be made regarding home businesses.

How to Determine Your Legal Structure

To determine which form is best for your business, you will need to decide under which auspices you will operate. There are a number of legal structures, each with guidelines, but you are most likely to function under one of these three.

Sole Proprietor

This is the most common form of business structure for micro-businesses and those just starting up with hopes of expanding. With this form, you keep all the profits but are responsible, too, for all the losses.

General Partnership

This is a verbal—preferably written—business agreement between two persons defining the ownership interests of the partners and other important matters. Unfortunately, many partnerships eventually break up due to conflict of direction, division of business duties, or life changes.

Ellen Parlapiano and Patricia Cobe, co-authors of *Mompreneurs*, say: "The first step to a successful partnership is to have a shared vision. Both partners have to be working toward the same goal—even if they have very different approaches and work styles. Then, as you both progress toward that goal, it's essential to be flexible and accommodating of each other's differences."

Corporation
With this structure, the corporation becomes an entity unto itself and is separate from your personal life. It must have officers, and profits and losses are reported separately. The advantage is that if you incur debts, your personal assets cannot be taken.

Additional Legal Matters
+ Check also with your state and federal regulations regarding your specific business. Jane Mitchell, who creates specialty cheesecakes, was required to pass an inspection of her kitchen before the state gave her a license to bake from her home. Many other states do not permit commercial cooking from home.
+ Obtain a Federal Tax ID number. With sole proprietorships, this is your Social Security number; but many business forms require a federal Employer Identification Number (EIN). Contact your accountant, Small Business Development Center, or your local IRS for the form.
+ Learn what taxes you will be required to pay—such as local wage, income taxes, state sales taxes, and Social Security. Consult with your accountant from the beginning so she can advise you about your tax requirements, quarterlies, and so forth.
+ Consult with an independent insurance agent for advice about insurance needs for your: health, liability, disaster, disability, and so on.
+ Insist on having contracts with suppliers, independent contractors, and with your customers. Also have your lawyer write a waiver if you fear lawsuits could result from the type of business you do.
+ Legalize your name. If you do not want to concern yourself with a fictitious name, you can use your legal name in the designation of your business. If your name is Jane Smith, you can title your business Jane Smith Janitorial Services. However, if you call your

business Executive Janitorial Services, you will have to register your name with your state's business office and county clerk's office.

This business registration requirement is also called "doing business as" (DBA) and will be printed in your paper so people will know you are conducting business under another name. Your state will also let you know if that name is already registered. You can go to your local courthouse and register the name yourself, or you can have your lawyer do it.

Choose your name carefully because it will be a constant marketing tool. Here are some considerations in choosing the best name for your business:

❖ Your business name should tell potential customers who you are and what advantages they will have by patronizing your business. Names like "Smith Enterprises" or "ABCD Specialties" do not really describe what service or product you provide or how it will benefit your customers. Jane's "Sweet Endings" aptly describes her mouth-watering, specialty cheesecake and desserts business, as does professional organizer Shawn Kershaw's "Time Matters Organizing Services."

❖ Avoid names that are associated with well-known corporations to avoid confusion and even lawsuits.

❖ You can include the geographical location of your potential customers—town or county, for example—in your name. If your customers are across the country or even the world, you could include such terms as American, United, Pacific, National, or State to express the extent of your business market.

❖ Add a tagline (a short sentence summarizing your services or products) to your business name in five words or less. Two examples, "Computer Medic: The Housecall Specialists" and "The Cruise Palace: Personalized Cruise Travel Service" have taglines that imply their customers are going to receive a little extra service than they would from competitors like "Smith's Computer Consulting" or "Smith's Tours & Cruises."

❖ Make a list of names you like and then compare them to your competitors' and ask others their opinions.

The ideal name is the one that will help your customers associate better quality and service over your competitors.

For More Information:
Books
Names That Sell: How to Create Great Names for Your Company, Product, or Service by Fred Barrett (Portland, OR: Alder, 1995).
Trademark: Legal Care for Your Business and Product Names, 4th ed., by Kate McGrath and Stephen Elias (Berkeley, CA: Nolo Press, 1999).

How to Determine Who Is an Independent Contractor
Many home-based business owners work as independent contractors; therefore, it is important that you understand who is and who is not an independent contractor. The IRS has a list of criteria defining this type of employment status. Basically, the distinguishing factor between who is an employee and who is an independent contractor is one of control. If you are in control of your hours and business operations, you are an independent contractor; but if your client sets the guidelines of your business time and procedures, then you would consider being an employee. Talk to your accountant and/or an IRS representative *before* you ever sign your first contract as an independent contractor!

For More Information
Books
Choosing a Legal Structure for Your Business by Stuart A. Handmaker (Upper Saddle River, NJ: Prentice Hall Trade, 1997).
The Legal Guide for Starting and Running a Small Business, Vol. 1 by Fred S. Steingold, Mary Randolph, and Ralph E. Warner (Berkeley, CA: Nolo Press, 1998).
Let's Go into Business Together: Eight Secrets for Successful Business Partnering by Azriela Jaffe (New York, NY: Avon Books, 1998).

Independent Contractor Concerns

❖ Have insurance to cover general liability, professional liability, and perhaps an errors-and-omissions policy.

❖ As your business grows, consider incorporating to help protect you from liability and foster more credibility with clients.

❖ Work with your lawyer to come up with a standard contract that best fits your business and that you can vary according to each project for which you are contracted.

❖ If you are going to work for a company for the first time, ask other independent contractors who have worked for them for feedback about their experiences. If you get a bad feeling when negotiating terms of a contract with a company, trust your instincts and politely decline to do business with them.

Government/IRS Sources

To obtain free copies of IRS documents and forms, call 1-800-TAX-FORM or download from their site: < www.irs.ustreas.gov >. You can also write to the IRS Forms Distribution Center nearest you. Check your tax package for the address.

Independent Contractor or Employee (Section 530, Relief Requirements).

Circular E: Employer's Tax Guide (Publication 15) contains all the IRS's legal definitions and guidelines.

Employment Taxes (Publication 937) includes twenty criteria used to determine proper independent contractor classification.

Internet Sites

< www.corporate.com > "Corporate Agents, Inc.," provides information on incorporating your business.

< www.nolo.com/ic/ > Nolo Press's site has "FAQs for People Working as Independent Contractors," plus articles, books, and software helpful to independent contractors.

• SUCCESS SECRET 17 •

Get the training and education
you need for your home business.

If you worked in the corporate world before, most likely you had to attend ongoing training sessions and seminars. With your home business, keeping up with the training you need to stay competitive in your business or even to get your business going is *your* responsibility. One woman was turned down repeatedly when she approached medical offices to start a medical transcription service business. "They looked at me like I was crazy when they found out I had no training, so I enrolled in local classes at a local business school. After I completed my course, every medical office I solicited contracted with me!"

Where to Get Training and Education
Needed for Your Business

✤ First, ask yourself what skills or training you need to help you improve the quality or production of your services—basic business management? marketing? computer software training?

✤ Match your needs to the resources available to you that you can afford. Here are some suggestions:

- Small Business Development Centers and Women Business Centers offer seminars, conferences, small business management certificate programs, workshops, etc.
- Community Colleges and adult evening schools may offer computer and business classes.
- Industry trade shows offer speakers and demonstrations.
- Chambers of Commerce and other relevant business organizations design many learning opportunities for business owners.
- Other resources include home study programs, online courses, video and audiocassette tapes, CD-ROMs, and instructional manuals.
- For "free training," get a job or volunteer in the industry in which you would like to have a business.

Also subscribe to at least one industry publication which will help you keep abreast of the latest advances in your field. Maryanne Burgess, author/publisher of the *Designer Source Listing* and lifelong learner, says: "Savvy entrepreneurs never stop learning. Whatever your plans, be assured that information is developed today for the one-person operation just as it is for big business. Knowledge of your subject always give you the (competitive) edge, so go for it!"

For More Information
Internet Courses and Sites
< www.california.edu > California Virtual University (CVU).
Also type in major search engines (online courses; business) to find a number of virtual courses.

• SUCCESS SECRET 18 •

Know how to prepare yourself for a home business.

Preparation Considerations
You will want to prepare yourself ahead of time to get a home business started. Here are some considerations:

❖ **Make a list of the resources** (including names of contact persons, addresses, and telephone and fax numbers) for home businesses in your area: business organizations, government agencies, schools and colleges, state legislators' offices, newspaper editors, printers, and office supply stores.
❖ **Designate a room or corner for your office** that works best for you in running a business and home life.
❖ **Start surfing the Internet** for information sites and home-business sites that offer home-business networking with chats and message boards.

❖ **Find your business experts:** lawyer, accountant, insurance consultant, business coach, and others pertinent to your business.

❖ **Enroll in classes** for any training you need or see what home study programs are available for your business and business management.

❖ **Pay down** as much of your debts as you can to lower your monthly expenses.

❖ **Find a mentor or support person,** preferably another woman business owner that you can call on for practical advice and support.

❖ **Decide the basic equipment** you will need for your business and learn how to operate it.

❖ **Find a bank that is "friendly"** to small businesses and discuss the banking programs and loan procedures with the manager.

❖ **Write down your business and life goals** and decide when you will work toward achieving them.

• SUCCESS SECRET 19 •

Learn to tell the truth in business.

With so much information and talk these days, it is hard to know what is fact and what is fiction. Your potential customers feel this way, too—about businesses. They receive so many telemarketing calls and direct mail advertising, and are so bombarded by radio and TV ads, that they rarely even take note of what is being sold and who is selling it. This is because so many businesses lied to them by promising quality service and products then treating them with shoddy merchandise and rude service.

   You can get and keep customers by being honest, truthful, and forthright. Here are some tips.

❖ **Give an honest price** for your product and service, and don't tack on fees without consulting with your customer.

❖ **Treat all your customers with equal courtesy and respect,** no matter how they dress or what car they drive.

❖ **In turn, do not accept rudeness,** verbal abuse, calls after hours, or unrealistic demands from your customers. Set the tone from your first meeting with firmness and confidence, and do not be afraid to tell customers when they are overstepping the boundaries.

✤ **Be professional in your dealings.** Respond promptly to your customers when they leave a message, be on time with meetings, and meet your deadlines. If customers call at inappropriate times, politely tell them you are not available at the moment but will be happy to talk to them at a time convenient for you both.

✤ **Listen to what your customers want,** then ask them for honest feedback about your product or service. Take their criticism seriously and ask for their ideas on how to improve your business service or product.

✤ **Offer, in turn, suggestions to help others improve their businesses.** Two home-business owners who publish newsletters for their customers proofread one another's newsletters for content and typos before printing. The women say their newsletters have improved in appearance and quality as the result of one another's input.

✤ **Do not promise your customer what you cannot deliver.** If you already have a full workload or feel you may lack the skills or resources to handle a job, tell the customer right away. Keep a ready list of other business owners you can refer customers to (who may return the favor by referring customers to you). Being truthful with your clients will help you establish a fair and trustworthy reputation in the business world.

3

Home-Office Essentials

To work from your home, you will have to consider the necessary space, technology, software, and telecommunications you'll need to start and run your business. Besides the physical and technological considerations, you will have to think about your office in relation to your family and your own preferences in order to create the ideal working environment for yourself. If your office is dark, too isolated, inefficient in use of space, or detrimental in some other way, you will be less likely to want to work. This could negatively affect your production and eventually your profits.

You will most likely change your office setup and equipment as you develop a working routine and your business grows. Therefore, you will want to think ahead and prepare for future expansion and additions. One woman with a home-based, office-support services business says: "My first office was in an upstairs bedroom of our older home. When I first started a business, I was making handcrafted potpourri dolls. After I purchased a computer, I began to get requests to do office overflow work. Between the two businesses, I had papers, cloth, and dried ingredients all over. It was

71

so bad that I forgot I had sunflower seeds in a can; suddenly moths hatched and were flying everywhere!

"Then during the process of remodeling our kitchen, we ended up with a space above it. I was able to plan specifically for an office setup with better lighting, more windows, modern wiring, access for multiple phone lines, a door that I could close at the end of my work day, and no moths!"

These next Success Secrets can help you plan—maybe not your "dream office," but one with which you can work with the most efficiently to help you achieve your business goals.

• SUCCESS SECRET 20 •

Thoroughly analyze all your home-office options before you set up your workspace.

Home-Office Safety

Since you do not have a regulatory agency monitoring the safety of your home office, you will be responsible for monitoring yourself, your family members, and even your pets. As mentioned in a previous chapter, some mothers have a Dutch door, with the bottom half locked and the upper half open for communication and visibility of other areas of their home. Here are other common-sense safety tips:

✤ Be careful of wires, electrical outlets, and phone lines. Have them away from office traffic areas and avoid having too many hook-ups on one outlet.

✤ Keep objects such as paper clips, discarded staples, sharp pencils, rubber bands, and cleaning chemicals out of reach from small children and pets who can do harm to your equipment as well as to themselves. One home entrepreneur stepped out of the office for "just a minute" and her three-year-old pushed an entire box of paper clips into her computer's disk drive!

✤ Watch for equipment that can fall and injure children or even you—copiers, typewriters, even filing cabinets (which can hurt fingers when slammed shut).

❖ When children begin to understand, teach them what is touchable and untouchable in your office. Then make up their own desk nearby, complete with an "office supply box" containing writing materials, perhaps an old keyboard, and educational toys so they can "work" also.

❖ During their waking hours, spend some time with your children or family each hour or so. If possible, do this when they are *not* demanding your attention rather than when they are crying. You will help reinforce "good" behavior and let them know that spending time with them is as important as your business matters. One mother sets a timer for 45 minutes, and when it rings, spends the next fifteen minutes or so with her children.

❖ If possible, arrange your office where you can supervise children's indoor and outdoor play areas. Michelle's home office, which is attached to her kitchen, also has a window that looks out on their deck and swimming pool and backyard. Her children can play in the pool and yard with their friends or do homework and fun projects on the kitchen table—both within earshot and eyesight of their mother.

❖ When a project needs your full concentration, then arrange for child-care coverage by a spouse, part-time sitter, or trusted neighbor.

❖ Have voice mail or some other answering system to take calls if you are busy with your children—giving them baths or cooking hot foods, for example. When the phone rings, some children take that as their "signal" to head to the "forbidden" place or object because they know you are preoccupied.

❖ Patricia Gallagher suggests this: "Borrow a few classic children's movies from the library. Don't feel guilty about letting them watch them when you have deadlines to meet."

Preventing Repetitive Impairment and Other Job-Related Injuries
It is a given physical fact that joints and muscles used repetitively will develop pain and/or related injuries. You must be aware of possible injuries related to your specific business—such as burns from cooking, animal bites with pet businesses, or eye injuries from lawn mowing—and take precautions to prevent them from happening

to you. Cheryle had a thriving handcraft business that involved a constant wrapping of twine. After several years, she began to experience a numbing sensation in both her arms and extreme pain at night that prevented her from sleeping. She had developed carpal tunnel syndrome in both wrists that required operations to correct.

You need to keep yourself (and family) safe in your business activities or you will lose time running your business, profits, or worse. Here are some recommendations:

❖ Warm up and stretch (just as you would for any physical warm-up) all your muscles. Yoga, which is currently resurging in popularity, is an excellent way to stretch your body and your peace of mind.

❖ Look for a comfortable and ergonomically designed office chair, desk, keyboard, computer mouse, and any other equipment that you will use repetitively in your business. Your comfort and efficiency is more important than the equipment cost.

❖ Keep your forearms horizontal as you type and your wrists raised over your keyboard (much like playing the piano).

❖ Read all manuals that come with the equipment you purchase, follow the safety recommendations and cautions, and do not allow children to operate machinery without proper supervision.

❖ Practice good posture when you sit and stand and good body mechanics (using the legs and not the back) when you lift, to prevent backaches.

❖ Periodically take breaks and do stretches, walk around, and vary your office activities (just like cross-training) to give muscles and tendons a break.

❖ With your doctor's approval, keep your abdominal muscles fit. This will help prevent strain on your lower back.

❖ Use a phone headset or speaker-phone to prevent neck and shoulder cramping from holding the phone for long periods.

❖ Have a general first aid kit in your home and in your vehicle if you use it in your business, plus enroll in a basic first aid course.

❖ Sit approximately 20 to 24 inches away from your monitor. Whether or not you believe the effects of radiation are harmful, you receive far less radiation at this distance from your computer.

For More Information
Associations
Association for Repetitive Motion Syndrome (ARMS), P.O. Box 471973, Aurora, CO 80047-1973. "The International Clearinghouse of Information about Repetitive & Upper Extremity Injuries." For information about this association, send $1.00 for postage (no envelopes, please).

Books
The Repetitive Strain Injury Recovery Book by Deborah Quilter and Robert E. Markison (New York, NY: Walker & Co., 1998); Also visit Quilter's informative Web site about repetitive strain injury (RSI), < www.rsihelp.com >.

Internet Sites
< www.cdc.gov/niosh > National Institute for Occupational Safety and Health (NIOSH).
< www.ergonet.net > Links and resources about office health.
< www.workspaces.com > WorkSpaces. Information on ergonomic home-office equipment and other home-office tips.

Setting Up and Organizing Your Home Office
Find a Space
Finding a place for your office may be difficult, depending on your circumstances. Ideally, a spare bedroom or even a room specifically designed for a home office would be nice, but this is not always possible in the "real world." There are home-office deductions to consider, too. Home-office space is to be used primarily for office operations—thus cannot double as a bedroom, playroom, or laundry room, nor be used for any other purposes if you intend to deduct this space. Check with your accountant if you have questions.

Home offices are located in remodeled closets, basements, attics, laundry rooms, pantry rooms, mud rooms, breezeways, garages, corners of dining rooms, kitchens, and even remodeled chicken coops. Business experts advise that you not have your office in your bedroom or family room—but sometimes these are the only options. When one woman's oldest son got married, she turned his bedroom into her office. After he divorced two years later, however, he moved back into his bedroom (along with a pet ferret). She then had no choice but to put her office in her own bedroom. When her son remarried, she moved her office back into his bedroom, gave away the ferret, and told him to make his marriage work because she was not giving up her office again!

Shed Some Light

Some people like dark, cozy spaces; but you will need adequate lighting to conduct whatever business you have. Consider the natural light you have already entering your office, then supplement it with artificial light that will give you the adequate amount you will need. Note whether the sun will affect visibility of your computer screen. If you are prone to slight depression during the darker winter hours, make sure you have plenty of natural and/or artificial light to help cheer you, as well as light-colored walls. If you suffer from the more serious ailment, Seasonal Affective Disorder (SAD), also known as winter depression, consult a qualified health-care professional familiar with this disorder. The good news is that SAD is relatively easy to treat—via various light contraptions.

Make It Personal and Inviting

Your office must be functional, of course, and if you have customers come to your office, you will need space and adequate seating to meet with them. However, one of the advantages of a home office is your option to decorate it the way you wish. One woman has bulletin boards on almost all the walls so she can post sayings, photos, etc. and has installed bird feeders just outside her windows so she can enjoy her hobby of bird-watching. If you find your office setup is not working for you, try changing the arrangement of your furniture and equipment or look for another space in your home (or attached buildings). If you do not like working in your office, going "to work" will be more difficult.

Organizing Tips

Shawn Kershaw, professional organizer, advises this for setting up your office: "Designate your office or office area as sacred space: no kids, toys, catalogs. Make it appealing by painting the walls, hanging pictures, and displaying mementos. Give the area *value*." She also notes that "Women are notorious for setting up an office in the basement or the corner of a room. They need to treat it with respect and as a place that generates income or runs the household."

Here are some additional tips:

✤ At the end of the workday (or night) or periodically, straighten up your office. One woman says: "My office is a mess, but I (generally) know where everything is; but if it gets to the point that I cannot find something in a minute's time, then I know I have to take a few minutes to put my office in some semblance of order again." Every six months or once a year, clear out your files.

✤ Keep your supplies in one area, drawer, closet, or shelf. It will save you time when looking for supplies. Have a list posted in your office to write down when a certain supply is low. You do not want to unexpectedly run short of needed supplies—which seems to happen with a deadline or rush job!

✤ If you are short on space, look into vertical wall units, under-the-desk cabinets, stacking file crates, and even "fold-up" desk units. If you or someone else is good with woodworking tools, design your own setup. One woman's husband made standing shelves with plywood, covered them with hardboard, and fit the whole unit to cover a corner and two walls—all at a very reasonable price.

✤ Purchase a multifunctional piece of equipment (such as those made by such companies as Canon, Dell, Hewlett-Packard, or Xerox) that combine a scanner, printer, copier, modem, and fax machine into one peripheral unit. Make sure you try these units before you buy one and that you understand the warranties if one of the components malfunctions.

✤ Use office and drawer organizers, stacking trays, filing boxes, etc. Scan office-supply catalogs or walk through office-supply stores to see what new innovations for storage or space are available.

✤ Have daily planners, wipe boards, or notebooks to help you plan your business week and days.
✤ Use a combination of filing systems or what is the most efficient system for you.
✤ Shawn Kershaw recommends this: "Buy a huge trash can. You are much more likely to throw things away if a big trash can space is readily available."

For More Information
Books
Books by Lisa Kanarek, home-office organizing expert: < www.everythingsorganized.com >.

✤ *Everything's Organized* (Franklin Lakes, NJ: Career Press, 1996).
✤ *Organizing Your Home Office for Success*, 2nd ed., (Dallas, TX: Blakely Press, 1998).
Home Office Design: Everything You Need to Know about Planning, Organizing, and Practical Home Office Solutions by Neal Zimmerman (New York, NY: McGraw-Hill, 1998).

Companies
Visit your local office supply and technology store or contact the companies directly for their current catalogs.

Internet Sites
< www.ideasiteforbusiness.com/org.htm > Tips on organizing your office.
< www.quicken.com/small_business/ > Equipping your office and other information.
< www.canon.com > Canon.
< www.dell.com/dell4biz > Dell, P.O. Box 224588, Dallas, TX 75222-4588.
< www.hp.com > Hewlett-Packard.
< www.xerox.com > Xerox.

Office Furniture
Anthro Corp., Technology Furniture, 10450 S.W. Manhasset Dr., Tualatin, OR 97062. Economical computer carts and workstations.

Business & Institutional Furniture Company, Inc., 611 N. Broadway, Milwaukee, WI 53202-0902, < www.bi-furniture.com > .

Flexy-Plan Distinctive Office Furniture, 69 W. Ridge Rd., P.O. Box CC, Fairview, PA 16415-0829, < www.fyp.com > .

Sauder Wookworking Co. < www.sauder.com > , (419) 446-2711. Space-saving computer workstations.

Low-Cost Ways to Furnish Your Office

You need not spend a "fortune" furnishing your home office. Here are a few economical suggestions:

❖ Visit your local office-supply stores such as Staples and Office-Max for sales on office equipment.

❖ Read your local newspaper's display and classified ads for bargains on good, used office equipment; details about individuals or companies who are upgrading their offices; yard sales; public school auctions; and going-out-of-business sales.

❖ Some consignment shops carry previously owned office furniture and equipment.

❖ Put up your own ads around town or network within a business organization, announcing that you are looking for basic office furniture.

❖ At the end of college semesters, visit off-campus houses where many students who are moving out just "dump" their furniture (of course, the condition of such pieces could be questionable!).

❖ Look for store sales of slightly damaged pieces, many at a considerable lower price.

Securing Your Home Office

As your home office is usually part of your home, you may not need the same type of surveillance or security as a retail establishment, but you will want to consider some common-sense measures.

❖ Personal safety—If you are home alone or with just your children, do not open your door to strangers or clients unless they are expected.

❖ If you have an office that receives clients, make a separate entrance so people will not have to walk through your house.

❖ Back up important documents and information and store these in another place away from your home office.

❖ Have secure windows and lighting around your entrances and walkways.

❖ If you are on a business trip, have someone check on your home and pick up your mail and other deliveries.

❖ Have a dog—not for attack, but as a "mobile" alarm system.

❖ Plant bushes like pyracantha (fire thorn), barberry, cactus, and other spiny plants under windows to discourage people from climbing through empty windows.

❖ Have a home and business security consultant make some recommendations if you feel you need a professional's opinion.

For More Information
Items

bluVenom™ Computer Anti-Theft Device. For protection of your desktop or laptop computer (movement-activated). Call (888) 326-3388 or visit their Web site at < www.bluVenom.com >. BluVenom™ Anti Theft Devices Inc., 3873-C Airport Way, P.O. Box 9754, Bellingham, WA 98227-9754.

When You Do Business Away from Home

There are many reasons you may want to have your office in your home, but sometimes you need to take your business out of the home—and keep your home office as well. Here are some tips for anyone whose office is not professional enough to use for meeting with clients (or not quiet enough because of the kids, TV, or barking dog, for example).

❖ Contact the Executive Suite Association whose members rent rooms by the hour, day, week, or year. Contact them for a listing of an office near you (see next page for address).

❖ Schedule a community room at a local business association headquarters or a local bank.

❖ Meet at your clients' offices.
❖ Meet at a local public library.
❖ Meet over lunch.
❖ Barter a product or service with another woman business owner who has a free office you can use for your meeting.
❖ Contact a small business incubator near you to see if they have office space available.
❖ Be creative! For example, according to a magazine article, an elementary school music teacher let go because of budget constrictions subcontracted with several school districts to give music lessons to their students. She had a large, carpeted van that she parked at each school and gave music lessons to students inside it.

For More Information
Associations
Executive Suite Association, 438 E. Wilson Bridge Rd., Suite 200, Columbus, OH 43085, < www.execsuites.org >.
National Business Incubation Association, 20 E. Circle Dr., Suite 190, Athens, OH 45701, < www.nbia.org >.

• SUCCESS SECRET 21 •

Get the best technology to operate your business.

"Home-based women business owners are technologically savvy. In fact, home-based women-owned businesses are just as technologically savvy as other businesses with over half (56 percent) having at least one computer and nearly 4 in 10 (39 percent) owning more than one." —(National Foundation for Women Business Owners- NFWBO)

If you are starting a business, you may wonder what equipment you should purchase first. It is because of the affordable technology today that many of us can have our businesses at home! Business experts recommend you start with the basic pieces you need to get your business running and then purchase and upgrade your technology as you can afford it or need it. Joanne started her wallpapering business with some brushes, buckets, and a ladder that she strapped to her compact car!

Here is a list of a few tools a home-office owner can use for her business (not to mention any industry-specific technology you might need!), along with some of the companies that make these technological products. *This listing does not constitute any endorsement!* Realize that thousands of companies, worldwide, cater to home- and small-business owners.

To get more information on these products, visit several office supply and equipment stores, browse companies' sites on the Internet, and talk to others in your business field to learn what technology they use and prefer. Also read home-office publications such as *Home Office Computing* and *Working at Home* on a regular basis; these publications give reviews of the latest in home-office technology.

Computers

There are brand name computers (see the following list) and less expensive "clones," which can both be adequate for your business if you have done your research and know it is of the quality you want. You will need five major components of the hardware in computerizing your business:

❖ **The CPU (Central Processing Unit)** contains the main memory and microprocessor and area where the main functions occur. Memory is also called RAM (random access memory). Data is measured in bytes (one byte equals one letter, and the number of bytes determines memory capacity). Computer experts recommend that business owners get as much memory capacity as possible.

❖ **The Workstation** consists of a monitor and keyboard. Other devices you can purchase are the electronic mouse, microphone, camera, and light pen. There are also new advances with touch screens and keyboardless computers (voice-activated). Keyboards, similar to a typewriter, are changing to be more ergonomically comfortable.

✤ **Desktop Videoconferencing System.** These usually include a video camera, a video capture card, speakers, microphone, and a software suite—and are another option for home-business entrepreneurs to communicate with clients and other business associates. It helps to cut down on out-of-town business trips, increase joint ventures, and encourage virtual face-to-face meetings.

Other options besides the desktop videoconferencing include TV-based systems (no PC required) and e-mail programs with basic video capabilities. This video technology is still developing, so if you are considering this home-office system, do your homework, view demonstrations, and decide whether it is an option that can enhance your business.

For More Information
Internet Sites
(This listing does not constitute any endorsement.)
< www.3com.com > *3com*
< www.cvideomail.com > *CubicVideoComm*
< www.intel.com > *Intel*
< www.logitech.com/us/cameras/ > *Logitech*

✤ **The Monitor.** Also called a visual display terminal (VDT), this component is either connected to the CPU or built into the computer console. Of course, the various portable computers have these components compartmentalized into one compact unit for travel. Size, color, resolution and glare, sharpness, and clarity are all features to consider when shopping for a monitor.
✤ **Printer.** You will want to be concerned with speed, quality, paper feeds, and ability to print graphics, charts, and photos.

The following is a listing of major equipment components and business software along with the names of several manufacturers of the computer-related hard- and software that you may use with your business operations (this listing does not constitute an endorsement).

Future Trend: Home Networking

With the increase of husbands and wives working under one roof, dual entrepreneurs, multiple businesses, and family members doing Internet research and homework, many homes are beginning to look like a small office center (but a much more personable one). Some homes feature desktop and portable computers, photocopies, scanners, several kinds of printers, videoconferencing equipment, fax and answering machines, and a telephone line in every room! To serve all these needs, more home offices are turning to *home networking*—the interconnection of this equipment and technology.

This sharing of peripherals, phone lines, files, modems, and Internet accounts will help save on additional phone line costs and equipment and enable several people to work on the same or different projects simultaneously. According to experts, as innovations in the wiring and technology are developed, this trend of home inter-connections will also continue to grow as the new century begins. Note: If you are building a new home, some local phone companies offer to do wiring for present and future technology.

For More Information
Core Applications
❖ Contact management programs—*GoldMine Software, Symantec*
❖ Databases—*Lotus Development, ProVue Development*
❖ Integrated Software—*Claris*
❖ Office Suites—*Microsoft*
❖ Organizers—*Day-Timer Technologies, Adobe*
❖ Reference (books on CD-ROM)—*Microsoft*
❖ Spreadsheets—*The Novell Applications Group, Microsoft*
❖ Utilities (virus protection, disk repair, file searching, etc. in one program)—*Central Point/Symantec, Borland, Symantec, Now Software*
❖ Word Processing—*Microsoft*

Internet Sites
< www.phonelan.org > The Home Phoneline Networking Alliance.

Notebook Computers
❖ Notebooks—*IBM, Apple Computer, Inc.*
❖ Subnotebooks (next smaller size)—*Apple Computer, Inc., Toshiba*
❖ Palmtops (smallest notebook)—*Hewlett-Packard*

Publications
Entrepreneur's HomeOffice, "The Power of Many," February 1999, (p. 48).

Communications
❖ Answering Devices (multiple voice mailboxes)—*Bogen Communications*
❖ Communications Software—*Digital Communications Associations, Software Ventures*
❖ Fax/Modems—*Advanced Image Communications, Practical Peripherals, Global Village*
❖ Fax Software—*Delrina, Symantec, SmithMicro*
❖ Pagers—*Notable Technologies*
❖ Plain-Paper Fax Machines—*Hewlett Packard*
❖ Thermal Fax Machines—*Brother International*

Money
❖ Accounting—*Peachtree Software, Bestware*
❖ Personal Finance—*Intuit, Aatrix Software*

Peripherals/Office Equipment
❖ Backup Drives (store data)—*Iomega*
❖ CD-ROM Drives—*NEC*
❖ Color Printers—*Epson America*
❖ Copiers—*Canon, Sharp Corporation*
❖ Flatbed Scanners—*Canon Computer Systems, UMAX*
❖ Input Devices (mouse devices)—*Alps Electric, Kensington*
❖ Keyboards (ergonomical)—*Lexmark*
❖ Midsize Monitor—*Nokia*

Making Your Business Technologically Competitive

✤ Review competitors' Web sites to compare their products and services with yours.

✤ Check out Internet newsgroups in your industry where you may get opinions on your competitors (or your products or services!).

✤ Offer to host a message board, chat session, or online forum if you have experience in your industry.

✤ Keep your own Web site "active" with daily or weekly helpful business tips to keep customers returning to your site.

✤ Use a digital secretary that connects your phone to your computer and tracks and stores client data, which makes it easier for professionals to bill their phone consultations.

✤ Increase your availability so customers can readily reach you with voice mail, pagers, and cell phones.

✤ Laser Printers—*Lexmark, Hewlett Packard*
✤ Multimedia Upgrade Kits—*Creative Labs, Inc., Apple Computer, Inc.*
✤ Sound Cards—*Creative Labs*

DTP/Graphics

✤ Business Graphics—*Shapeware, Adobe*
✤ Desktop Publishing—*Microsoft Publisher, Adobe, CorelDraw, Quark, Inc.*
✤ Illustration—*Macromedia, Adobe*
✤ Image Editing—*Micrografx, Adobe*
✤ Presentation Graphics—*Software Publishing, Gold Disk*

Computer Purchasing Tips

Just a few years ago, some small business publications were still publishing articles debating whether or not you needed a computer for your business. Now with the affordability of computers, a business *must* have at least one (if not more) computer for business functions. A computer for your business can automate sales; create professional-looking promotional materials; allow you to communicate with your customers via e-mail, faxes, and voice messages; keep your business records and accounts; work with others on projects in "virtual offices"; build your Web site; and send e-mail messages and documents.

Before you purchase a computer for your business, you need to know the following:

* **The business function(s) you want your computer to do.** You will not need the family games, or the video or audio capabilities (unless you can use those in your business) that are often included in packages. (Consider buying a new or good used "family" computer for your children to use for games and schoolwork.) Look instead for packages that include business office suites. Save money by getting only the capabilities you require, but be sure that you can upgrade easily in the future.
* **The software you will be using** (and if you will need training to use it) and what each requires of a computer to operate.
* **What peripherals you'll need**—tape back-up? printer? oversized monitor? online operation?
* **What price you should pay.** You can start with a good, used computer, but have a computer expert help you evaluate its capabilities before you purchase one. There are good, new computers today that sell for less than $1,000 and come with guarantees in the event they malfunction.
* **Whether to buy retail or through mail order.** If you are knowledgeable in computer operations, you can do quite well buying over the Internet, or through mail order; or you might even buy the components and build your own. You'd better know what you are doing, though. One woman's husband purchased a computer and the peripherals at different stores when he found them on sale. Trouble was, he spent hours trying to get everything programmed so it would operate together.
* **Who or what course will help you learn the basic operation of the computer and/or software.** Some stores offer free classes

Upgrade or Buy New?

With technological advances in computers and software being announced daily, it can make you question whether you should spend the money to upgrade your computer or buy a new one with all the latest advancements. Here are some tips to help you make that decision:

❖ Know why you want to upgrade. (Faster modem? more memory to run new software? faster or new operations?)

❖ Find out if your computer can be upgraded. Contact the company or retailer you purchased it from, or a computer consultant, and explain your needs and ask if upgrading is possible.

❖ Think about future needs of your business. If you are able to upgrade, you can save time and money by getting a little more upgrade all at once for the future.

❖ Weigh the pros and cons and the expense of the upgrades you need. Also consider the cost of purchasing a new system (with warranties), which might save you time and money. Depending how out of date your old computer is, you could donate your old system, sell it, or use it for a backup or other work. One home-business owner went for a new system and is having her husband help her do the accounting and research with the old one—" 'His and Her' computers," she says with a laugh.

for customers, and occasionally computer consultants make house calls.

Common Computer Problems

One of the benefits of purchasing a new computer package is the guarantee and warranty that comes with it, which you can also get extended for a small price. Before you call for customer sup-

Tips for Checking for Trouble

❖ Read all operating manuals and keep them handy along with customer support telephone numbers.

❖ Back up all important information—use disks, hard drive, tape drive.

❖ Check that all power cords and plugs are connected correctly and power strips are turned on.

❖ Make sure all your peripherals—printers, speakers, and any others—are in the correct ports and are programmed correctly to work with your computer.

❖ Keep all your boxes and customer warranty and receipt slips in the event you have to return any equipment for returns or repairs.

❖ Only call technical support when you have eliminated all the probable causes.

❖ If your children were the last to use the equipment, ask (if they remember) what functions they were doing.

❖ Prevent computer equipment failure from dirt and dust buildup by keeping it clean, using the proper supplies.

❖ If your hard drive seems slow, delete unnecessary files and documents, remove software programs (use uninstall features on Windows 95 and Windows 98) or use programs that defragment your hard drive and improve its efficiency (*Symantec* < www.symantec.com >, *Cyber-Media* < www.cybermedia.com >.

❖ If nothing else works, call for support and advice. If you will have to replace a part or piece of equipment, get an estimate of the cost of both the item and the labor!

port or service, though, make sure you read your operating manuals of *all* your equipment and check to see whether you (or children or pets) inadvertently loosened your power cord. Also be aware of your software "Help" that may assist you. For example, one writer was printing out the copy of her latest book from her floppy disk, when one of the files that contained valuable information would not open.

In a panic, she clicked on her "Help" and found the category "fixing a disk." She said, "I followed Help's directions, 'fixed' my file, and retrieved all my information. To me, it was a 'miracle!' " (*Note:* The moral here is to back up all information you don't want to lose!)

For More Information
Books
Business @ the Speed of Thought by Bill Gates and Collins Hemingway (New York, NY: Warner Books, 1999).
Making Money with Your Computer at Home, 2nd ed., by Paul and Sarah Edwards (New York, NY: Putnam Publishing Group, 1997).

Computer/Hardware/Software Through the Mail
CDW™, 200 N. Milwaukee Ave., Vernon Hills, IL 60061. < www. cdw.com >.
Dell, P.O. Box 224588, Dallas, TX 75222-4588. < www.dell.com >.
Gateway Computers < www.gateway.com >.
Global® Computer Supplies, 11 Harbor Park Dr., Dept. GS, Port Washington, NY 11050. < www.globalcomputer.com >.

Computer & Technology Publications
(Look for others in your local bookstore, newsstand, or large library.)
Home Office Computing/Small Business Computing, Scholastic, Inc., 411 Lafayette, New York, NY 10003; < www.smalloffice.com >.
Smart Computing, Sandhills Publishing, 131 W. Grand Dr., P.O. Box 85380, Lincoln, NE 68501-2545; < www.smartcomputing.com >.
Windows® magazine, Box 420215, Palm Coast, FL 32142; < www.winmag.com >.

Cleaning Supplies
Kensington Technology Group < www.kensington.com >.
Perfect Data Corporation, 110 W. Easy St., Simi Valley, CA 93065. < www.perfectdata.com >.

Home-Based Business Technology Battles: Who Is Your Computer Expert?

"I always say, 'Technology is great . . . when it works,'" said one home-business owner with a laugh. "My two computer 'experts' are my son, who is a medical grad student, and my brother, who is an aeronautical engineer. They are usually able to help me when I have a computer problem, but I do have online tech support should I need it; and there is a computer consultant in our area whom I call on from time to time. I have also surprised myself a number of times by figuring out operations through trial and error—or reading the manuals!"

• SUCCESS SECRET 22 •

Obtain the best software suited for your business.

Software is what "powers" your business. Before purchasing software, business experts recommend you know what outcomes you want to achieve with your software (perform accounting? produce a newsletter? do graphics? set up a Web site?) It is also good to personally try the software out before you buy.

Here are some options home and small business owners prefer in their business software, and which you'd do well to consider when making your selections:

❖ User-friendly software saves time. It takes time and training to learn complicated software, which most people do not want to do, so software that is easy to use is naturally a hit.

❖ Office Suites are good investments. They offer a combination of operations like database, presentation graphics applications, word processing, spreadsheets, and more.

❖ Comprehensive graphics programs and desktop publishing software enable home-business owners to do their own professional-looking promotional materials.

❖ Multi-task database applications help track customer spending, job records, and other business records.

❖ Accounting and bookkeeping software enable you to keep track of customer accounts, taxes, and business finances.

❖ Easy Web site directions allow many home-business owners to design their own business sites.

❖ Internet browsers enable home-business owners to conduct business and do research over the Internet.

Popular Home-Business Software

The few manufacturer names listed below do not constitute any endorsement—you have to determine the best software for your business.

❖ Accounting—*Intuit, M.Y.O.B., Peachtree*

❖ Database/Filing—*Microsoft, Claris, Goldmine, Symantec*

❖ Internet Browsers—*Microsoft, Netscape*

❖ MailManagers—*MyMail List, Mailer's Software*

❖ Organizers/Management—*Day-Timer*

❖ Personal Finance/Tax—*Intuit, Microsoft, Turbotax*

❖ Personal Information Managers—*Lotus, Microsoft*

❖ Presentation/Graphics—*Adobe, Corel, Quark, Microsoft*

❖ Software Office Suites—*Corel, Lotus, Microsoft*

❖ Spreadsheets—*Corel, Lotus, Microsoft*

❖ Utility—*Norton*

❖ Word Processing—*Corel, Lotus, Microsoft*

Visit your software stores, read business publications reviews, talk to those who use these software programs, visit manufacturers' Web sites, and try sample versions before your buy software products for your business.

———

For More Information

Internet Sites

< www.cc-inc.com > MacMall & PCMall.

< www.pacbus.com > Club-Mac & Club-PC.

< www.warehouse.com > MacWarehouse, PCWarehouse, & Micro-Warehouse.

< www.zones.com > MacZone & PCZone.

———

Learning Your Software

You cannot achieve the full potential of your software if you do not have the knowledge of all its functions. Take time and/or invest the money you need to learn how to use your software. Take courses at schools or colleges or computer centers; hire a computer consultant; and contact tech support available for your software. It will take energy and hands-on use for maybe as long as six months until you fully understand how to translate your new knowledge of your software into computer results. The time you spend mastering your software, however, will result in more efficiency in your business operations.

Anti-Virus Software

Thousands of computer viruses exist today, and with the Internet, the exposure is increasing the danger. Viruses can destroy information, files, and wreak havoc on hard drives. Any time you open a transmitted file or use someone else's disk you are putting your computer at risk. To prevent a virus attack, use anti-virus software like the ones listed here:

❖ *Network Associates* < www.mcafee.com > .

❖ *Symantec,* < www.symantec.com > .

❖ Speech Recognition Software: Safe Computing, 2059 Camden Ave., Suite. 285, San Jose, CA 95124; speech recognition technology and other ergonomic computer products; < www.safecomputing.com > .

If you use a good printer and quality paper, and have a personal computer that can run desktop publishing software, you can generate such materials as business stationery and envelopes, business cards, brochures, newsletters, labels, and much more.

Desktop publisher Michelle Clevenger uses page-layout software (Adobe PageMaker or QuarkXpress) and publishing software (Windows or Mac versions of Microsoft Word).

Four other popular desktop publishing software programs are:

❖ *Corel Print Office* < www.corel.com > .

❖ *Design Intelligence ipublish* < www.design-intelligence.com > .

❖ *Microsoft Publisher* < www.microsoft.com/publisher.

❖ *Publish It Deluxe (PID) 3.02* desktop publishing software, < www.notalentrequired.com > , < www.macdigital.com > .

Other Related Equipment
Scanners
These bridge the gap between the computer and the printed page. They are used in the home office to scan documents, direct them into your word-processing program, and make changes; serve as an input device for your fax modem if you use your computer to send and receive faxes; and scan clippings to save on your hard drive or use in conjunction with your desktop publishing program. Here are some scanner companies:

✤ *Hewlett-Packard*— < www.hp.com >.

✤ *Logitech*—(800) 231-7717 < www.logitech.com >.

✤ *Microtek*—(800) 654-4160 < www.microtekusa.com >.

✤ *Tamarack Technologies, Inc.* (714) 744-3979 < www.tamarack. net >.

✤ *UMAX* (800) 562-0311 < www.umax.com >.

Digital Cameras
With these relatively new cameras, you can take a picture and download it to your PC and send it via e-mail to someone, use in your promotional materials, or place on your Web site. The technology and prices are both improving each year. Higher-resolution cameras give the better-quality images. Here are some of the manufacturers:

✤ *Canon* < www.canon.com >.

✤ *Epson* < www.epson.com >.

✤ *Kodak* < www.kodak.com >.

✤ *Nikon* < www.nikonusa.com >.

✤ *Olympus* < www.olympus.com/digital >.

———

For More Information
Books/Booklets
The Desktop Publisher's Idea Book: One-of-a-Kind Projects, Expert Tips, and Hard-to-Find Sources, 2nd ed., by Chuck Green. (New York, NY: Random House Reference, 1997).

Michelle Clevenger's booklet, *"Low Budget, High-End Results for the Self-Employed Desktop Publisher"* 1999. Cost-saving tips; $9.95

(PA residents add 6% sales tax) to 522 Race St., Perkasie, PA 18944. (Will also individualize booklets and provide tips/ short-cuts in specialized dtp areas, such as software, silk screening, or pre-press, upon specified mail requests.)

Internet Sites
< www.desktopPublishing.com > Many pages of helpful tips.
< www.ideabook.com > Chuck Green's Web site, which includes tips and free info.

———

With the right combination of hardware and software, your business has unlimited potential to be successful!

• SUCCESS SECRET 23 •

Equip your office with the best telecommunications for your business.

Choosing a Phone System

As you start your business, you may just have your home phone (though most homes these days have more than one line). It is important, however, to have at least a business line and/or line that is used for a fax machine. Sharon, who has a crafts wholesale business, started with one phone line—and had her telephone company designate a certain number of rings for her business. "My three children learned to distinguish the business rings as opposed to the household rings faster than I did," she says with a laugh. As Sharon's business grew, she added more business lines.

In choosing a phone system, again analyze the needs of your business and research thoroughly what is available within your budget. You will need the right mix of equipment and services to meet your customers' needs. Here are some tips that should help you in your selection.

❖ Know how many phone lines you need to receive calls, faxes, and access the Internet if you work online.

❖ Decide whether your business is going to receive many faxes; if so, you will want a dedicated phone line. If your fax and PC share a phone line, you can see whether your local telephone company has a fax-receiving service, or you can purchase a fax machine that can store faxes and print them later.

❖ If you take orders over the phone and most of your customers live out of your area, you might want to get a toll-free number.

❖ Decide how you will take business calls when you are unavailable. The new systems allow you to designate different extensions to leave messages and conveys a professional image. You can also use voice mail from your local telephone service, or use a combination.

❖ Decide if you need to screen phone calls. Caller ID allows you to pick up the phone before it goes into an answering machine or voice mail.

❖ Decide whether your customers will need to reach you if you are out of the office. Call forwarding, pagers, and cellular phones can keep you in touch.

If customers tell you they have had difficult time reaching you, then it may be time for you to update your telephone system.

For More Information
Items

Sprint and *Inc.* magazine are helping their businesses and new customers by providing "Sprint Performance Tools," three toolkits that offer software, instructional videotapes, planning templates, and how-to guides tailored to the needs of each business. Call (888) 877-4020 for more information.

Pagers and Cellular Phones

You may think home businesses do not need pagers or cellular telephones, but many do work at times in clients' homes—particularly those with service types of businesses. With more affordable prices,

added features, greater coverage, and smaller sizes, pagers have become more appealing to businesswomen. It is especially helpful if
you are a mother and are away from home when your children need
to reach you. Whether you rent, lease, or purchase a pager, make
sure you have checked the reliability of the paging vendor; use
quality equipment; and have reviewed the terms of service, and the
contract, and all the costs involved.

Cellular phones are also used by home-business owners who
find themselves away at times from their home offices. These
phones are increasingly popular in that they enable the owner to be
out in with their customers or doing business errands yet remain
in touch with their customers. One woman said her cellular phone
gave her clients a sense of her being available to them and their
concerns. Before, she had to play "phone tag" trying to return calls
or telephone in the evenings.

Voice Mail and Answering Machine Tips

Here are some tips for you to ensure you do not miss regular customers and potential customers' calls.

* Purchase a telephone/voice-mail system with voice mailboxes.
  Designate each box with a department, such as sales, marketing,
  or accounting.
* Sign up with a local answering service.
* If your answering machine is less than professional-sounding,
  you may want to sign up for voice mail with your local telephone
  company's voice-mail service. Check to see their rates and how
  many sub-mailboxes their service can handle.
* Have it arranged that your phone company can signal your
  pager when you have a call so you can promptly get in touch
  with your customers.
* Give your callers call-forwarding or pager numbers, or your
  e-mail address or fax number, so customers can reach you at
  other offices.
* Change your message daily and leave times when you will be
  available to return calls.

• SUCCESS SECRET 24 •

Explore the option of leasing your office equipment.

Leasing equipment is a popular alternative for many businesses. It may be a viable option to get your home business up and running. Here are some pros and cons to help you decide whether leasing is right for you:

Pros:

❖ Enables you to use very expensive equipment for your business you normally would not be able to afford or would prefer not to take out a loan.

❖ Makes it easier to update your equipment when your lease is up.

❖ Saves your line of credit for other business expenditures.

❖ Allows you to change your equipment if your business goes in another direction or more diverse directions.

Cons:

❖ Beware of hidden costs, interests, and constricting contracts you sign, and of being sold more options than you need.

❖ The equipment you lease may become obsolete or outdated before your lease agreement is over.

❖ You may not be able to take advantage of some business tax deductions (check with your accountant *before* you sign a contract).

In your efforts to find your essential home-office equipment, take your time to research all these areas. Talk to vendors, salespersons, telephone representatives, other women business owners, members of local chambers of commerce, women's business centers, and others in your industry for recommendations and referrals for companies that offer quality products and service. Other research can be done on the Internet and at your public library. Making the right decisions about what your home office can have is critical to the future success of your business.

4

Insurance for You and Your Business

If you are going to play the game, you'd better know every rule.
—Barbara Jordan (first African-American congresswoman
to be elected to the U.S. House of Representatives
from the deep South in 1972)

Today millions of Americans operate full- or part-time businesses from their homes (and the numbers continue to increase). It is important that these entrepreneurs realize that having a home-based business does not mean they can forget about the insurance their business needs to operate or about their own personal insurance concerns (if they are not covered under any other plans).

Insurance experts advise that you separate your home insurance coverage from your business insurance—even if your business is based in your home. You also need to be concerned about your auto, health, and life insurance policies. These chapters will help give you some tips on selecting the best insurance for you and your business, plus some resources to help you find out more information.

Note: The information supplied here is a general overview of insurance concerns for the home-business owner. Realize that insurance information may vary from year to year, state to state, and from company to company. Only insurance agents currently licensed in your state are qualified to provide you with the answers you need to make informed decisions in purchasing the best insurance for you, your family, your home, and your business.

• SUCCESS SECRET 25 •

Protect your business with the proper insurance plans.

Why Your Home Business Needs Insurance

Having a home business has definite advantages, but some disadvantages as well. Too many home-business owners do not investigate what types of insurance their business needs until it's too late. Most home-owners insurance policies do not adequately cover your business's needs or other important issues such as liability—even for deliverypersons who bring mail and packages to your door!

Joan K. McPeek, who is President of Lehigh Valley Insurance Services, Inc. in Easton, Pennsylvania, and an independent insurance agent, says: "Many women do not think about home-based business insurance. They assume their home-owners policies will cover all their equipment and liability exposures—and most policies do not. They generally offer little business property coverage and *no business liability coverage,*" she says. "It's very important that liability concerns—whether they have to do with the result of a product injuring a client or bodily injury or property damage caused by your business—are covered by insurance. If you do not have this coverage," McPeek continues, "and you are sued and cannot pay, a lien will be put against your assets—starting with your home!"

McPeek recommends the home-business owner first sees her home-owners insurance agent, who can help find a company that may be able to attach an endorsement onto the home-owners policy. An endorsement could, for example, cover the loss of equipment and structure as well as provide liability coverage for certain eligible business types. These endorsements are usually much more affordable than commercial insurance policies, but if your business specifically requires a commercial policy, your independent agent should also be able to help you or refer you to other agents who handle that type of insurance.

Even though more insurance companies are recognizing the specific insurance needs of home businesses, presently not as many are prepared to help home businesses as you would think. For that reason, researching and finding the best company to adequately insure your business may take some time. Understand that though you may never need it, the right business insurance coverage is the policy that addresses the specific needs of your in-home business and guards against the risks that could bankrupt you and/or your business.

The Kinds of Insurance You Need
Property Coverage
This type covers your building and structures, signs, office equipment and furniture, and supplies against loss or damage caused by certain risks such as theft and fire. Business inventory may not be included under property insurance and may need to be covered under a commercial business, especially if you do most of your work on-site and out of your home office.

If a vehicle is part of your business, you need to also have coverage for accidents and damage done to your vehicle by persons or weather, for example. Check with your auto insurance agent for more information concerning the business use of your car, truck, or van and to learn whether you need a business endorsement to your Personal Auto Policy or a Commercial Automobile Policy.

Liability
Three major kinds of liability insurance are:

1. **Product liability**—which covers you in the event one of your products causes injury or damage caused by the use of your product.

2. **Professional liability**—also called malpractice or errors-and-omissions insurance, this type covers suits that claim your advice or professional services were not performed as agreed upon. To help protect against such suits (and to prevent being sued by unsatisfied customers), you can consult with your lawyer and draw up a waiver or agreement that can be included in all your client contracts.
3. **General liability**—covers you in the event someone is injured when they come to your home for business reasons.

Packy Boukis, owner of "Only You Wedding and Event Consulting," located in Cleveland, Ohio, says: "I have an endorsement on my homeowners policy for my wedding consulting business in my home. This is basic liability and costs $50 a year. It would be considerably more if I had a storefront."

Business Interruption

This type of insurance covers your net profits and expenses should a fire, flood, tornado, hurricane, earthquake, or other misfortunes occur and you are unable to operate from your home office. Rates are usually calculated by figuring out an average of your business's income over the previous 12 months before the catastrophe. If your business income is the sole or main support of you and/or your family, this is an especially important type of insurance to have.

Determining How Much Insurance Your Home Business Needs

Before you make an appointment with an insurance agent, you need to know some specifics about your business so you and your agent can decide the best coverage for your venture. Here are some considerations:

❖ Do you have any employees or plan to hire any in the future?
❖ What is your business product or service and what impact does it have on your customers?
❖ Are you a consultant or professional who provides knowledge-based services, giving advice that can affect clients personally or their business decisions?

❖ Do you see clients in your home office?
❖ How many business deliveries do you average a day or week to your home?
❖ Do your customers require a certificate of commercial insurance from you?
❖ What is the value of your business-related equipment?
❖ Do you have clients' property at your home?
❖ What certifications and training have you had in your field?
❖ If you do work at a client's home or business site, what equipment of yours do you use and what of the client's do you use?
❖ What security, fire prevention, and other safety features do you have for your home office and/or equipment?

These are just a few of the issues you will want to discuss when assisting your agent in helping find a policy to fit the specific needs of your business. When choosing an agent, make sure he or she is reputable and recommended by more than one person or business.

Several Policy Options
Several types of insurance policy options are available for your home business. Here are some:

Incidental Business Endorsement
An "incidental business endorsement," depending on your type of business, is attached to your existing homeowners policy to cover other structures or equipment on your property that you use for business. This endorsement can also be modified to include your business liability.

Business Owners Package Policy
If your business does not qualify for "incidental business endorsement," a business owners package (also known as a BOP) can be purchased to provide property and liability coverage for your in-home business.

In-Home Business Owners Policy

Some insurance companies offer policies that combine to provide coverage for both business and home-owners property and liability. These policies offer coverage that is more affordable and inclusive than commercial policies. You and your agent will have to determine whether your business meets the qualifications for this type of policy, which are set by the companies that offer it.

Commercial Business Policy

A standard commercial policy may be the only option for your home business. This is not necessarily bad in that the rates may not be as high as you feared and may offer a fairly broad coverage on both loss and liability. Though home businesses are not as uncommon as they once were, some brokers may not be as familiar in dealing with in-home businesses needing commercial policies.

How Much Insurance Should You Have?

You want to strike a balance between how much insurance is ideal and how much you can afford. Decide with your agent which coverage you *must have* and make sure your potential risks are covered. Realize, too, that as your business expands, or changes direction or customers, your policies may also have to be updated. A good time to do this is when your renewal payment is due. Review your policy with your agent and make necessary adjustments so you will have peace of mind to operate your business. (See information on preventing lawsuits in chapter 12.)

Other Considerations

If your business grows to the point you need to hire employees, you are required to provide all your workers with workers compensation insurance should an employee become injured or ill due to a work-related injury or condition. If your business is incorporated, *you* may be eligible for workman's compensation should you personally suffer an injury.

Choosing an Insurance Company

The adage "Hope for the best, and prepare for the worst" can very well apply to purchasing insurance of almost any kind. No matter what happens, you need your insurance company there in the event of a loss or lawsuit. Here are some tips for finding a good company:

❖ Go by the recommendations of your insurance agent and other experts in the industry.
❖ Talk to owners of businesses similar to yours—especially those who have had to file claims.
❖ Deal with a company that is familiar with home-business owners' needs.
❖ Check a company's complaint history and record with your state insurance commissioner's office.
❖ Check the rating of the company to make sure it is solvent (can pay its claims and is not likely to go out of business). Contact insurance rating companies or read reports (available in your library) by companies such as Duff & Phelps or Standard & Poor's Insurance Rating Services. Or contact one of the two listed below to see if they have affordable reports available.
   A. M. Best, Ambest Rd., Oldwich, NJ 08858.
   Weiss Research, 2200 N. Florida Mango Rd., West Palm Beach, FL 33409.

• SUCCESS SECRET 26 •

Have a business disaster restoration plan.

Several years ago in a nearby small town, a fire broke out behind some old deserted buildings and spread quickly to others in the same few blocks. When the smoke literally cleared, a hotel, hair salon, a 5&10-cent variety story, a funeral home, an antique store, a travel agency, and several other offices were reduced to ashes and rubble. It was a catastrophe for both the businesses and the small town.

A fire, flood, or other unexpected disaster could happen to any home or business. Should the "worst" happen unexpectedly, you will more likely be able to rebuild your business if you have a disaster restoration plan. Here are some tips to guide you in setting up a plan:

✤ Have the numbers of your insurance agent, your customers, suppliers, and others you'd need to contact, in a safety deposit box or some other safe location.

✤ Make sure the *replacement value* and not the value of your used equipment is what your insurance covers.

✤ Keep accurate records of the equipment and other assets you have insured—in a safe place outside your home. Hire an inventory specialist to catalog your equipment, products, and other items if your insured property is large (many of these specialists sell inventory kits for you to do your own cataloging). Some provide a videotape of your protected property and contents.

✤ Have business interruption insurance (also called Business Income or "BI" coverage).

✤ Ask many "what ifs?" of your insurance agent when you first get your policy. *Do not assume anything.* Make sure the details are written clearly as to what is and what is not covered in the event of a disaster.

✤ Contact your agent as soon as any changes in business occur— such as the purchase of new equipment or a new building—to update your coverage.

✤ If you will be dealing with the public, make sure you are covered against liability or negligence suits.

For More Information
Books/Publications
Insuring Your Business—What You Need to Know to Get the Best Insurance Coverage for Your Business by Sean Mooney (New York, NY: Insurance Information Institute Press, 1992).

Disaster Recovery

Several years ago when Hurricane Andrew devastated whole communities in Florida, scenes of those destroyed homes revealed that home and business owners had scrawled in large letters the names of their insurance companies so that the claims adjusters could assess the damages and get insurance checks to them as quickly as possible. Here are some guidelines to remember in a crisis time:

* Notify your insurance agent as soon as possible.
* Depending on how bad your home or building is ravaged, make sure no further damage will occur by boarding up windows, covering exposed roofs, and so on. Some companies produce special "shrink" wrap to keep out rain and moisture.
* Secure your home and buildings from possible theft of undamaged items if you are forced to stay elsewhere.
* Take photos of the damage (auto insurance experts advise that you have a disposable camera in your vehicle's glove compartment to validate any claims should an accident occur).
* Notify your telephone company of where to forward your home and business calls.
* Take care of yourself and your family. Get help from family and friends and professional help if the trauma has affected you and your loved ones' emotional and mental health.
* Make a step-by-step plan of how you will rebuild your business and home. Use your business network of associates to help you.
* Notify your accountant, as he can tell you about tax deductions for damages and other relevant information.

Protecting Your In-Home Business (brochure). Independent Insurance Agents of America, 127 S. Peyton St., Alexandria, VA 22314. Send a LSAE for information.

Internet Sites

< www.iiaa.org > Independent Insurance Information Institute Press. Check their consumer section for information on protecting your home business.

• SUCCESS SECRET 27 •

Avoid risks and make your home business secure.

Chapter 4 discussed protecting your home-business site. This section will cover other threats to your business so you can take steps to prevent them from happening to you. Here are some simple tips to help you:

✤ Safeguard your equipment from unexpected power surges and lightning strikes with special power strips and surge protectors. Use anti-static mats, and keep your office temperature moderate and humidity levels appropriate for equipment operations.

✤ When you have a large printing job completed, instruct the shop assistant to give you any misprinted copies so they will not inadvertently be given to other customers or used as scrap paper. Because you never know in whose hands they could end up, it's important you eliminate the possibility of classified or incorrect material being read.

✤ Just as with personal credit cards, be careful to whom you give out your business credit cards numbers over the phone or Internet. Do not fill out credit card applications and place them in your mailbox to be picked up by your mail carrier. They can be stolen and your information taken and used. Drop them directly into a U.S. postal box or office.

✤ If you receive regular package deliveries at your door, have some method of protecting them from the weather or theft. Build a covered box outside your door that can be locked by the delivery-person simply pushing it down then opened only by you with your key.

❖ Ask your lawyer to draw up a non-compete clause for subcontractors, independent contractors, and consultants to sign if the work they do for you could be sold to your competitors.

❖ Have an umbrella policy to cover your liability for lost items such as valuable computer files or records of your customers' or your own concerning a current project.

❖ If you go outside for a break, lock your house doors. In many suburban neighborhoods, burglars have entered homes in the daytime and stolen valuables while the homeowners were out in their backyards. If you are home alone, make sure your doors are locked, but keep a car in the driveway or have a radio on so intruders will know the house is occupied.

Talk to other home-business owners and see what security measures or tips they may have to share. A little forethought and common sense will help keep you and your business protected.

• SUCCESS SECRET 28 •

Get the best health insurance plan for you and your family.

With the growth of self-employed individuals and home-business owners, health insurance providers are now offering more health insurance policies to both individuals and their families and to home and small business groups. That is the good news; the bad news is that it almost takes a background in insurance to fully understand the details of the plans available. It is not uncommon to have a sales representative spend a minimum of two hours explaining the different plans her company offers—and that is just one company!

Still, if you persist, you can find a health plan that will meet you and your family's needs. Here are some tips.*

---

*Ask your accountant how much of your insurance payments are tax deductible (according to the most recent IRS guidelines).

✤ If you have been downsized out of your job or you quit, you should sign up for COBRA (Consolidated Omnibus Budget Reconciliation Act of 1985). This federal law states that if you were a full-time worker for a company with 20 employees or more and received health benefits, your former company must offer you continued health coverage for 18 months. Of course, you have to pay, but signing up for this extended coverage can give you some "research time" to find another policy.

✤ Talk to health insurance agents recommended by other self-employed individuals.

✤ When talking to a health company's insurance representative, *you* control the discussion by asking a specific list of questions about the company's benefits that you want to know. *Do not* depend on just what the representative wants to tell you.

✤ Ask the agent for names of several people who have signed up for their plans.

✤ Know specifically the following: Can you use your health insurance around the U.S.? What is covered—prescriptions? medical tests? medical equipment?

✤ Join the chapter of your chamber of commerce (most of which have group health insurance plans). In addition, you'll benefit from networking in a community business organization.

✤ Join your industry's trade or special interest association. Artists and craftspersons have crafts and artists alliances (as do other professions and trades).

✤ Join national working associations like the National Association of the Self-Employed (NASE) that have different levels of plans from which you can choose. (See Associations on the next page.)

Realize no plan is perfect and that it may take some thorough research and pointed questions to get the answers you need, and to know *exactly* what health coverage will be available and at what cost.

If you reconsider after signing up for a plan, remember you have a certain number of days (depending on your state) to cancel and have your check returned.

For More Information

Associations

(See Resources on page 398 for addresses of these associations that offer group health plans to members.)

* ❖ American Association for Home-Based Business Owners
* ❖ National Association for the Self-Employed—(800) 232-6273
* ❖ National Small-business United—(800) 345-NSBU (6728)
* ❖ Small Business Service Bureau—(800) 222-5678
* ❖ Working Today—(212) 366-6066

Internet Sites

< www.insuremarket.com > Quicken's InsureMarket also allows you to get insurance rates.

< www.quotesmith.com > Quotesmith Corporation gives you access to compare rates and products offered by over 300 insurance companies.

Disability Insurance

Being self-employed, you do not have workmen's compensation to fall back on if you should be injured on the job. Some people do not believe it's beneficial to have this type of insurance, but even computer-related businesses have their hazards, such as repetitive motion syndrome—a condition that could prevent them from working. Again, discuss disability insurance with your insurance agent. Together you can make the decision best for you.

Here are some things you will want to consider in getting disability coverage:

* ❖ **Cost of living rider.** This guarantees that your disability benefits will stay in line with the rises in cost of living rates.
* ❖ **Own Occupation Clause.** This stipulates you cannot be made to work in a job in another industry if your injury or illness keeps you from doing your own.

✤ **Waiting Period.** If you became incapacitated, this is the length of time you would wait until your disability benefits would begin. The longer the waiting period you choose, the lower your premiums. Insurance experts seem to most frequently recommend a period of 90 days.

✤ **Benefit Period.** This is the time period the insurance company must pay benefits.

Depending on your insurance carrier, you may have more or fewer options. Choose your coverage carefully.

• SUCCESS SECRET 29 •

Know the benefits of life insurance.

Whether you are employed at a regular job, a stay-at-home-parent, or a home-business owner, you are important to others who would suffer—both personally and financially—from your death. Maintaining a life insurance policy that pays death benefits if you should die can help your beneficiary(ies) sustain living costs and possibly continue to run your business after your death, should they choose to do so. In some circumstances, borrowing money from a life insurance policy has helped fund business start-ups (check with your agent about what types of policies allow you to do this).

Determining what kind of life insurance policy is best for you can also be an overwhelming task. Here are some purchasing tips:

✤ Work with an agent you trust who is knowledgeable in this area and has dealt with other women who are home-business owners.

✤ Decide what amount you need for your purposes and then determine what you can afford.

✤ From there ask your agent to find quotes from as many companies as possible so you know the averages of the best prices.

✤ Realize you can ask your agent to negotiate with companies in an attempt to get the lowest premium payments that give you the best coverage possible.

✤ Periodically, review your life insurance policy to account for changes in your life and business. You can have your agent look

Getting the Most Insurance for Your Money

Insurance is a necessary expense if you want protection from potential risks to yourself and your home business, but you do not want to pay for insurance you do not really need. Here are some cost-saving tips:

❖ Compare the rates of different companies. Look for agents familiar with businesses in your industry who will know what options you do and do not need for your specific type of venture.
❖ Have a higher deductible and set your coverage level near the actual value.
❖ See if your trade association has insurance companies that give better rates to association members.
❖ Find out whether the companies you're considering give better rates if you carry more than one type of policy with them, or if other entrepreneurs in your family also go with your carrier.
❖ Notify your insurance if you add safety measures to your vehicle, home and business property—for example, a sprinkler system, electronic home security devices, anti-theft auto device—or if you quit smoking. Such changes can often lower your insurance premiums.

at new policies in the event they may be more beneficial than your present one, as well as discuss such things as annuities and your life insurance.

———

For More Information
Organizations
Independent Insurance Agents of America, 127 South Peyton St., Alexandria, VA 22314-2803; <www.iiaa.org> *Protecting Your In-Home Business* brochure, as well as other publications about

insurance coverage for your small business, home, auto, etc. Send an LSASE (long self-addressed stamped envelope) for information or check the consumer section of their Web site.

Insurance Information Institute, 110 William St., New York, NY 10038; (212) 669-9200; <www.iii.org> Write for a listing and prices of insurance publications. This institute also sponsors the National Insurance Consumers Hotline: (800) 942-4242.

5

Your First Business Plan: A Blueprint for Success

The woman who can create her own job is the woman who will win fame and fortune.

— Amelia Earhart, U.S. aviator and author

• **SUCCESS SECRET 30** •

Know how to do the preliminary research for a business plan.

Why a Business Plan?

Even if you are starting a business on a part-time basis, it is worth your time to write a business plan. Business experts say that the amount of time spent in planning and researching a business is directly related to its success. It is not uncommon for a person contemplating entrepreneurship to spend a year or more in the planning process, so you do not want to rush the research process.

Depending on the type of business, your plan can consist of only a few pages to a complex document of many pages and

115

supporting documents. Without one, your business can flounder and end up going too many directions for it to succeed. Here are some reasons why you should not skip this step:

✤ It will force you to take an objective look at the feasibility of your proposed business idea.

✤ It is like a road map or blueprint in that it can provide direction and structure for your venture.

✤ It is a document you can literally "take to the bank," or provide for other potential lenders with the purpose of aiding you in getting start-up or expansion funds.

✤ It is an organizational tool that can coordinate your thoughts and establish a clear vision of what goals you would like to achieve.

✤ It can reveal and solve problems before they occur.

✤ It can be used as a persuasive tool to gain support from lenders and advertisers.

Who Can Help You?

Where and how do you start to write a business plan? The following list suggests various types of sources that can help you write a business plan.

Your Accountant

He or she may have some good tips, especially in figuring the financials of your plan. Some have pamphlets and tip sheets helpful to their clients who want to start a business.

Banks

Some local banks have personnel willing to take the time to explain to you what they look for in a business plan when a potential business owner applies for a loan.

Business Plan Consultants

Some people help write the plan for you (see sidebar on page 118).

Business Schools and Local Colleges

Call to see if they offer college credit courses and/or continuing education courses on business start-up. They may also have business graduate students who will help you write plans.

College and Public Libraries

Look for business plan books, and in some reference sections, the *Business Plans Handbook* (updated periodically) published by Gale Research, Detroit, MI. Web address: < www.gale.com > This collection of actual sample plans of entrepreneurs comes with a template, glossary, and updated bibliography.

Government

Check with your local state legislators for state departments concerned with women's economic issues to see if they sponsor conferences or workshops. The SBA also has its Women's Business Centers < www.onlinewbc.org >, Small Business Development Centers (SBDCs), and the Service of Retired Executives (SCORE) < www.score.org >.

Women's Business Organizations

Some local chapters of chambers of commerce and local women's business organizations and chapters of larger state and national women's business ownership associations are comprised of both women who work in business and business owners who may be willing to help other women write their plans.

Preliminary Research

Before you sit down to write your plan, you will want to do some preparatory study. Here are some tips:

❖ **Consider the audience** who will be reading your plan and emphasize their specific interests. For example, bankers will be interested in your cash flow and tangible assets; investors will be concerned with your stability and marketing strategies to increase the growth of your business; and, if a large company is

Business Idea: Business Plan Writer

In this business, you will write business plans for beginning entrepreneurs and existing business owners who wish to get financing for start-up and loans for expansion. You can type up the plan or use one of the many computer software programs available. Your fee will be based on the complexity and length of the plan your customer needs.

Recommended Background
Training, experience, and background in banking, financing, and business development is essential. You should understand components of business plans and financial statements, be able to make sales and income projections, and write the plan in a clear format. You may also have to assist your clients with market research and alternative strategies. Contacts within your business community are important in helping your clients find support and possible financing.

Essential Equipment
Computer with modem, business planning software, laser printer, telephone, fax machine, answering machine or service, photocopier, and basic office furniture that is suitable for receiving clients in your office.

Start-Up Costs
$1,000 to $6,000 to start, depending on whether or not you have a computer with software.

considering you as a supplier, they will want a performance record and assurance of stable production of a quality product.

❖ **Compose an informal start-up business plan for your own review before you do a complete business plan.** This will help tell you if your business idea has the *potential* to be a business

Pricing Guidelines
Can range from $500 for a simple review of plan to $2,500 to $5,000 for writing the plan, depending on the complexity of each plan.

Income Potential
Depending on your clients and location of your business, this type of business service can make between $20,000 to $100,000 a year.

Marketing Tips:
❖ Network with local business organizations and Small Business Development Centers and Women's Centers.
❖ Teach business plan courses at local adult evening schools, community colleges, and business groups' workshops.
❖ Write articles in trade and business publications.

Success Tips:
❖ Look for areas with business growth and those "friendly" to home and small businesses.
❖ Network with local home and small business organizations, business incubators, and Women's Business Centers for referrals to entrepreneurs just starting out and established businesses seeking funding for expansion.
❖ Meet potential customers at women's entrepreneur conferences often sponsored by Small Business Development Centers.

and whether it is worth a further investment of money and time. For this start-up plan, write a *vision statement* that explains why this business should exist and how its benefits will entice potential customers; identify your business's *essential factors* that will enable it to succeed; identify whether there is a sufficient number of *potential customers* to warrant further planning of this business idea; and whether the *profit margin* of this business (after expenses) is enough to make a living.

• SUCCESS SECRET 31 •

Know how to write a complete business plan that you can "take to the bank."

In writing a business plan for a home business, the first one who will be reading it will be you, not a banker or investment company. Your plan probably will not need to be more than one to three pages in length. However, it is no less important than a complex plan because it will be an ongoing guide for your advertising and marketing strategies, for finding your target customers, for determining costs, and for setting goals for future growth for *your* business.

Here are explanations of the essentials of a business plan. Remember that not all sections may apply to your plan. For a home business, the most important sections usually are the *description of the business, the designated work space* for your home office or workshop, an analysis of your *competition*, your *advertising and marketing plans,* and your *financial plan*. Concentrate on these and update your plan as the need arises.

Description of Business Plan Sections
Following are the ingredients of a typical business plan.

❖ **Cover page:** Business's name, address, telephone and fax numbers, e-mail address, and Web site.

❖ **Executive Summary:** Condensation of your business plan—and the most important part, because it clearly explains the entire concept and purpose of your venture and is the first thing readers will see. Though listed at the plan's beginning, write it after your plan is finished for a more comprehensive summary. Keep this section as concise as possible.

❖ **Table of Contents:** Your business plan's format.

❖ **Statement of Purpose:** Your plan's purpose—a guide? to secure a loan? to attract investors?

❖ **Mission Statement:** Reasons for your business's existence and its customer benefits.

❖ **Business Description:** Specifies business operations, products, and/or services; legal structure; goals; objectives; and key success factors. Here you should approach your service and/or product from your customer's point of view in that how will they benefit from patronizing your business? Also list whether and how you will be expanding your product line or services.

❖ **Location of Business:** States where you will have your home office and/or workspace. Will your business services or production be primarily in-home (computer-related, at-home child care, mail order, raising plants, etc.), out-of-home (professional organizer, landscape consultant, cleaning, etc.) or half-and-half (bookkeeper, party and event planner, sign-painting, etc.)?

❖ **Operating Requirements:** Necessary equipment and facilities, business hours, legal structure.

❖ **Your Qualifications:** The education, training, experience, and other qualifications you have to run this business.

❖ **Competitor Analysis:** Lists competitors, their operations, strengths and weaknesses, and profiles their customers. Detail how your business will stand out from theirs.

❖ **The Product or Service:** Describes exactly what will be sold, the unique features, and your ability to meet the timely demand for products or services.

❖ **Advertising and Marketing Plan:** Profiles potential customers' likes, dislikes, and expectations. Explains sales strategies: pricing and sales terms, selling methods of products or services, and advertising plans. You will need to do important research in determining who your target market is (age, sex, income level, etc.). Then decide on the "4 Ps" of marketing: Product/or service? Price? Promotion? and Placement (distribution methods of goods and services)?

❖ **Financial information:** This is the most critical section of your business plan, so consult with a professional if you need assistance. Include start-up costs, a cash flow statement, a balance sheet, a profit and loss statement and a *break-even analysis* (the number of units you need to sell to cover all your fixed and variable costs without generating any profit or loss). *Note:* The break-even analysis can put an unrealistic idea in perspective, make you raise prices, or expand or contract your products or services. Add a cash flow prediction.

❖ **Summation:** Brief tabulation of your goals and objectives, plus a statement of your commitment to the success of your business.

❖ **Appendices:** Related information—supporting documents, quotes, estimates, articles, market research data, and so forth.

Writing the Plan

Talking about starting a business is one thing, but putting it in "black and white" can be intimidating. Here are some tips to help you overcome your fears of the actual writing of your plan:

❖ When you start, fill out first the sections that you feel the most confident doing and think you would enjoy most.

❖ Realize that no one else needs to view your plan (or second or third drafts!) until you feel it would be helpful or necessary. Write it for *yourself* at first.

❖ Write it through first *without* worrying about grammar and sentence structure, correct business terminology, correct math, and so on. You just want to have a first draft and something you can re-work and revise. Make use of business plan books, software, and articles in business publications to guide you.

❖ See whether your plan answers the questions you want answered—Did you figure out the basic financials? Were you able to have an estimated predicted cash flow? Do potential customers exist for this business? Do you know your break-even point (when your profits equal your expenses and you begin to actually make money)? Follow formulas listed in business plan books or use software to help you determine your break-even point.

Note: The most dangerous time for a new business is during its first two years because of inadequate working capital. You will need to have your business on a budget (see chapters 10 and 11). Remember, too, it may take two years or more before you will be able to earn a living with your new business.

❖ When you are ready, get another objective opinion—from a mentor, another woman business owner, a SCORE counselor, or someone else you have confidence in.

❖ Review and rewrite or revise your plan until you are satisfied with it and believe that it is complete. Do not rush the process! A thorough plan should take you a few weeks or even months to gather all the necessary information.

The main objective is to get a plan written. Later on, if your business is successful and you need to expand, *then* you can write a more extensive plan. Follow your completed plan's guidelines as you start up (or expand) your business to monitor marketing plans, expenses, and profits; to focus the direction of your business; and to anticipate potential problems with preparation of fall-back plans. Refer regularly to your plan, but realize it will change with your business's growth and diversity.

This crucial planning process will direct your business to focus on its future growth and stability. Remember: Businesses don't plan to fail; they just fail to plan. A business plan is the most important step you can take toward making your dream of owning a successful business a reality!

Business Plan Samples

Here is a sample business plan (see figure 5.1) by Tracey Lowrance who says, "My business plan and business objectives have helped me tremendously in the 18 months of my business. I have watched the list grow in the number of and depth of the goals I'd like to achieve. It is such a motivational tool when I look at the number of items I've crossed off my to-do list over the months! I would suggest this format for anyone who doesn't feel the need to write a long, wordy business plan. In addition, they must have the stick-ability to make things happen without identifying each avenue to take for each goal. I envision what has to take place and start putting those things in place. I know when I've reached my goal intuitively! They will too!"—Tracey Lowrance, OutSource ConneXion, (404) 299-7549; e-mail: Tracey@OutConneXion.com; or visit her Web site at < www. OutConneXion.com > .

OutSource ConneXion

1335 Cavendish Court
Stone Mountain, Georgia 30083
(404) 299-7549 Office
(404) 299-8346 Fax

**Business Plan
as of
December 1997**
* * *

This business plan has been prepared solely for the confidential use of selected individuals, groups, companies, and organizations. It is intended only for the use of the person or entity to whom it is given and may not be distributed in part or in whole to any other person or entity without permission of OutSource ConneXion.

Table of Contents

Figure 5.1. Sample of Tracey Lowrance's Business Plan for her home marketing business, OutSource ConneXion.

EXECUTIVE SUMMARY
COMPANY DESCRIPTION

OutSource ConneXion is a marketing communications firm that specializes in developing marketing programs for small-to-medium sized businesses. Our mission is to provide our clients with effective marketing programs and innovative advertising resulting in positive feedback that propels their business forward. It is our goal to exhibit a high degree of professionalism, integrity, and exceptional service in each project we undertake.

Located in Stone Mountain, Georgia, OutSource ConneXion was founded in October 1997 by Tracey Lowrance. It is a home-based business operated as a sole proprietorship. Our license to operate is issued by DeKalb County, Georgia. Our license number is _____.

It is our goal to incorporate the business by third quarter 1998 to eliminate the inherent personal liabilities associated with a sole proprietorship structure.

Currently we sell our service in the local market focusing on four (4) counties: DeKalb, Fulton, Gwinnett, and Rockdale. These counties were chosen due to the proximity to the office and the growth of new business in these counties. **(Put statistical information here.)** In 1999 we will begin marketing our services throughout the State of Georgia. Year 2000 will mark our entry into the Southeastern states of Florida and North Carolina.

According to the *Atlanta Business Chronicle* 7% of their 28,645 paid subscribers operate a business. Additionally, 44% operate a home-based business either full- or part-time. Lastly, 43% plan to select a new provider for advertising/media services in 1998. This includes ad agencies, public relations, printing services, etc.

It is evident by this information that the marketing communications industry is in great demand and headed for substantial growth. As such, OutSource ConneXion will strategically position itself to be the small-to-medium sized business's marketing communications partner.

The marketing communications industry provides various outlets for businesses to promote their product/service. This includes, but is not limited to, printed materials, image development, logo design, print advertising, audiovisual/broadcast production, direct mail, publicity, promotional items, etc.

There are several mediums to obtain the aforementioned products/services. However, we will review only the following: graphic designers, full service printing centers, advertising agencies, and public relations firms.

(continues)

(Figure 5.1, continued)

- Graphic designers take their client's idea(s) and create a literal piece of art—an ad, a brochure, a newsletter, etc. Effective graphic design determines whether the document captures the reader's attention and gets the desired action—or becomes just another throwaway.
- Full service printing centers not only provide printing services, but they also provide typesetting and graphic design/layout services. An in-house graphic designer works with customers to aid them in designing materials, etc.
- Advertising agencies develop campaigns that encompass print advertising, audiovisual, and broadcast production. They will write copy, design and layout, select media vehicles, and negotiate pricing and placement. The larger the company the more likely they will hire an ad agency.
- Public relations firms aid businesses in gaining "free" media exposure—news articles about the company, quotes of its officials, by-lined articles by company executives in trade journals, interviews on radio and television, and speaking engagements. While there is a tendency to consider news media exposure "free" there is a cost associated with getting articles and interviews. The cost may come in the form of executive or their employee time given over to public relations or from fees paid to a PR firm.

Each of these entities provide a key component of the marketing communications mix. However, an effective marketing program must incorporate each of the components. Just as personal selling requires the support of advertising, advertising requires the support of the entire marketing communications mix.

OutSource ConneXion provides each component of the marketing communications mix. In essence, we are a **one-stop shop** for the marketing needs of small-to-medium sized businesses. We determine the needs of our client during our initial consultation and through continued dialogue. We learn our client's industry, their marketplace, and their competition to ensure that we understand their challenges, concerns, and opportunities. In addition, we review their past and present marketing strategy and communication tools to devise a plan of action to secure and strengthen their position. Once the plan is agreed upon we provide the resources to implement it through the use of our network of subcontractors. The client works solely with Out-Source ConneXion throughout the process. Our network of subcontractors will provide the services required, and if necessary, attend meetings with OutSource ConneXion, under our umbrella, to discuss the project to ensure complete understanding to get the work done correctly the first time.

OutSource ConneXion provides the small-to-medium sized business with the same resources afforded larger companies at a fraction of the cost. In addition, we focus on the entire marketing aspect, not just one area, to ensure our client's marketing program is effective.

Although OutSource ConneXion has a network of subcontractors we must ensure that we do not rely on any one supplier. To combat this potential problem we have selected a minimum of three (3) suppliers for each of the following areas: graphic design/layout, printing, photography, writers, illustrators, local courier service, express delivery, and service bureaus. Therefore, if one supplier cannot handle any additional work we have the capability to contact another supplier to handle our client's needs.

Another potential weakness is the lack of an in-house staff. This could pose a problem when working on several projects. This is combated by not taking on more projects than can be handled according to our guidelines. If we do not feel that we can provide the client with 100% professionalism, provide the services on time and within budget we will not undertake the project. Our foremost concern is to provide our client with the service they deserve and expect.

MANAGEMENT

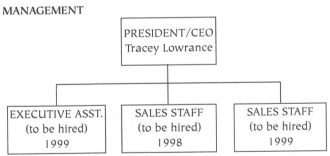

OutSource ConneXion is owned and operated by Tracey Lowrance. Ms. Lowrance's title is president/CEO.

President/CEO

Responsible for all company objectives, planning and operations. Functions covered by this position include, but are not limited to:

- setting company policies and objectives, including marketing objectives

(continues)

(Figure 5.1, continued)

- coordinating divisions & departments and establishing responsibilities and procedures for achieving objectives
- overall coordination of all projects
- all marketing activities including public relations, community relations, event planning, employee relations, and media advertising
- planning and directing sales programs including hiring additional help and attendance at trade shows/conventions
- financial recordkeeping, including bookkeeping, billings, payables, taxes and so forth
- reviewing activities and financial reports to determine progress in attaining objectives, revising objectives, and plans in accordance with current conditions
- directing and coordinating funding for operations
- conferring with clients to evaluate and promote improvements in service

Ms. Lowrance has over 9 years in the marketing field working with the marketing departments of several Fortune 500 health insurance companies. In addition, Ms. Lowrance successfully started and operated three (3) businesses from 1992–1997 ranging from a bookkeeping firm to a day-care center. This is her fourth company.

Executive Assistant (to be hired)

Responsible for overseeing the management of the office in conjunction with the president/CEO. Functions covered by this position include:

- provide administrative support to the president/CEO which includes planning & conducting research, recordkeeping, coordinating travel arrangements, market surveys, special event planning, coordinating all meetings, conferences, trade shows/conventions
- facilitate handling of accounts receivable & accounts payable, negotiate pricing for all office supplies, furniture and equipment
- office management: ordering office supplies, equipment, and furniture; open, sort, and deliver incoming mail & fax transmittals; file maintenance and destruction; database maintenance; answering and proper distribution of incoming calls
- conferring with clients to evaluate & promote improvements in services; customer calls unrelated to services
- address media in president/CEO's absence and schedule news conferences for major developments

Sales Staff (to be hired)

Functions covered by this position include:

- finding and following up on client's leads
- attendance & participation at sales meetings, conferences, trade shows/conventions
- routine sales calls
- servicing appropriate client needs related to services requested, e.g., providing advice on marketing tools for appropriate activity

OutSource ConneXion's 90–180 DAY OBJECTIVES

- Develop corporate sponsorship packet to submit to potential sponsors for at least two seminars—Sept./Oct. and Feb./Mar.
- Develop outsourcing brochure and mailing kit
- Develop marketing partnerships with various companies (accountant, lawyer, banker, printing firm, graphic design, Web site designer)
- Develop e-mail monthly newsletter
- Begin submitting articles for publication and payment to national magazines, e.g., *Home Office Computing, Self-Employed Professional, Business Start-Ups,* etc.
- Develop name recognition in niche area (writing articles for both local and national business periodicals and magazines, message boards, online discussion groups, e-mail marketing, Web site, etc.)
- Prepare and submit qualification packages to associations and organizations for speaking engagements (audiotape and video)
- Join local organizations, associations, serving the niche (PRSA, WCOC, GSA, Atlanta Press Club, Institute of Management Consultants)
- Begin writing a marketing column in at least 2 business periodicals/ magazines (*Atlanta Small Business Monthly, Atlanta Living, Atlanta Tribune, Atlanta Business Journal,* national magazines)
- Develop/acquire database capabilities (ACT, Bacon's, MediaMap)
- Upgrade Internet marketing strategy with new Web site, hosting online seminars, conferences, submitting articles, etc.
- Develop advertising campaign in local business magazines to get potential clients to inquire about services and request consultation
- Develop PR campaign strategy
- Develop community relations campaign with Dunwoody High School, Henderson Middle School, PRISM, and through member associations and organizations
- Obtain 4–6 solid clients

(continues)

(Figure 5.1, continued)

OutSource ConneXion's 6-MONTH OBJECTIVES

- Enhance image and reputation of firm
- Expand present client base to clients with revenue of at least $1–10mm
- Improve net profit on each project
- Ensure survival/profitability of firm with investors
- Set up profit centers (speaking engagements, book, seminars, workshops, etc.)
- Provide more recurring sources of new business through networking
- Develop a set of resumes that feature various skills sets, i.e., technical writer, marketer, marketing communications, public speaker, and trainer and instructor
- Acquire large fee clients through PR, advertising, and public speaking
- Expand base of high potential clients through public speaking, seminars, online forums, etc.
- Transform market from diversified to concentrated (authors, non-profit organizations, artisans)
- Transform client base from a volume to a cluster firm
- Identify and develop working relationships with others in niche (editors, politicians, etc.)
- Obtain 6–10 solid clients

Action Plan

Once you have your plan, now comes the task of putting it into action. Here are some tips:

❖ Using your plan, define the major issues your business is facing—getting the equipment you need? financing? getting the word out to potential customers?

❖ Decide which issue you will tackle first and determine your strategy to address it.

❖ Now implement your strategy—make 10 cold calls, write your ad, shop for a computer, etc.

❖ Concentrate on one strategy at a time—moving in too many directions too fast can be overwhelming. Give yourself some time to work on each strategy and then take some more time to evaluate its effectiveness.

✤ Realize that not every decision you make while putting your business plan in writing will be the right one and that you will have to take a certain amount of risk to succeed.
✤ Let your plan guide you as you grow your business, but do not be afraid to rewrite as you go. What looks good on paper is not always practical, but at least a business plan gives you a good base from which you can start your road to success.

Business Plan Software

Business plan software can help you write a polished and professional-looking business plan, but make sure you personalize it by adding specific marketing strategies and other details that make your business stand out from the competition.

Here are just a few of the many software programs designed to help you prepare business plans.

✤ BizPlanBuilder Interactive by Jian, 1975 El Camino Real, Mountain View, CA 94040. (800) 346-5426; <www.jian.com>.
✤ Business PlanPro by Palo Alto Software, 144 East 14th Ave., Eugene, OR 97401. (888) 752-6776; <www.palo-alto.com>.
✤ The Business Planning Guide, Dearborn Multimedia, 155 N. Wacker Dr., Chicago, IL 60606. <www.dearborn.com>.
✤ Business Resource Software, 2013 Wells Branch Pkwy, Suite 305, Austin, TX 78728. <www.brs-inc.com>.
✤ The Learning Company (was named Softkey International), 1 Athenaeum St., Cambridge, MA 02142. <www.learningco.com>.

For More Information
Books/Publications
Anatomy of a Business Plan: A Step-by-Step Guide to Starting Smart, Building the Business and Securing Your Company's Future, 3rd Ed., by Linda Pinson and Jerry Jinnett (Chicago, IL: Upstart Publishing Co./Dearborn Trade, 1996).
All-in-One Business Planner: How to Create the Plans You Need to Build Your Business by Christopher R. Malburg (Holbrook, MA: Adams Media Corporation, 1997).

"Business Plan for Home-Based Business," SBA Publications, P.O. Box 46521, Denver, CO 80201-46521.

Business Plans for Dummies by Paul Tiffany and Steven Peterson (Foster City, CA: IDG Books Worldwide, 1997).

Model Business Plans for Product Businesses by William A. Cohen (New York: John Wiley & Sons, Inc., 1995).

The Start Up Guide: A One Year Plan for Entrepreneurs by David Banks, Jr. (Dover, NH: Upstart Publishing, 1998).

Internet Sites

< http:www.sba.gov/ > The U.S. Small Business Administration offers an extensive description of business plan text.

< www.morebusiness.com > "The Business Resource Center" site, from Khera Communications, Inc., has business start-up information, including tips on business plans.

< www.bplans.com > A variety of sample business plans (from Palo Alto software).

• SUCCESS SECRET 32 •

Plan to set business goals and develop the methods to achieve them.

Succeeding *"Against the Odds"*

Why do some people with few resources overcome obstacles to become successful business owners while others with greater assets never get beyond talking about doing it? By reading profiles of women such as those highlighted every year in *Working Woman* magazine's top women-owned businesses in the country, you begin to glean from their successes some common threads. Here are just a few of their success tips:

Cultivate Strong Networks

Business experts say that women who have a strong network of business friends and family support are more likely to succeed.

They tend to team up with others to help achieve their goals. Chris Carroll, who is her comedian husband's agent, uses her mother to help her manage two weekend comedy clubs (and baby-sit her two little girls) while her husband is on the road; other friends in the entertainment business help her book acts for her clubs.

Dr. Donna Brooks—who co-authored the book *Seven Secrets of Successful Women* with her twin sister, Lynn—says that women who succeed in achieving their goals "set a goal and then follow up on it. Then they set about to develop a support network of advocates to encourage them, whether it be face-to-face, through e-mail, telephone calls, or letters."

Brooks also advises women "to expand their network to reflect upon the goals they want to achieve. Find someone else who has gone through it—the experience—and can give you some advice to help you reach your goal, too." For example, your goal might be to lose 20 pounds, but if no others in your network have experienced this, you will not be able to get the kind of support you would from someone who has been through the trials of losing weight. Thus you need to expand your network to include someone who has dieted and succeeded."

Translate this advice into goals for your home business and network with other women business owners, as well as those in the same business industry as you—whether cleaning, business support, computer services, or another—to learn from and support one another.

Immerse Yourself in Your Industry
Successful women test their products and services before they go solo. As was discussed before, the majority of home businesses are started part time while the woman is working full time at another job. By the time their business is ready to be a full-time venture, they have put in the hard work and long hours necessary to learn business management and survive the many trial-and-error experiences that happen in a new business.

Know Why You Are in Business
Successful women have embraced entrepreneurship for the independence and the purpose it gives to their lives. They go forward,

Secrets to Achieving Business Goals

For entrepreneurs, goals are essential for achieving success. Goals give direction and purpose to your business. A well-known stained-glass artist and entrepreneur advises: "Set goals for yourself—long-range and short-term—then you'll have a plan of action." Here are some suggestions:

❖ **Match your business's goals with your lifestyle.** You may wish you could start a sideline to your business doing cross-country seminars or consultations, but you may not want to leave your young children. Instead, teach one-night seminars at a local evening school or community college. One woman who sells herbs from her backyard teaches at several local high schools once a week. She gets to share her love of herbal lore while learning how to teach and make presentations.

❖ **Give yourself deadlines.** One woman sells her horse art at tack shops and equestrian shops. She says she sends out so many brochures a week and then makes herself do as many follow-up calls to see if the stores are interested in carrying her cards and other products.

❖ **Set the end-result of your goal then work backwards** to detail the steps you will have to take to reach the final goal.

working toward their goals, but also with a passion for their work and a desire to use it to help others.

Kimberly Stanséll says: "I set my goals based on what it is I want to achieve in the short and the long term. My goals all tie into my life's purpose, which is to help people realize their dreams with little or no money." < www.kimberlystansell.com >.

❖ **Write your goals down and post them** where you will see them every day to remind you in which direction you need to be headed.

❖ **Evaluate and review your goals each week.** One entrepreneurial couple "meets" every Monday morning at breakfast to discuss which goals they will be working toward that week.

❖ **Be realistic.** Know the difference between a dream and a goal. You may dream of being the owner of a multimillion dollar business, but first you have to achieve the goal of being a profitable business.

❖ **"Start off with small goals."** This advice comes from Jennifer Basye Sander, co-author of *The Millionairess Across the Street*. She continues by defining small goals: ". . . something that you can achieve in a short period of time. Once you quickly accomplish that small goal, you can move to setting larger goals that will take months or years to accomplish. If you just start out with big goals that will take forever to reach, it is all too easy to get discouraged and quit. But the boost you get quickly achieving a few small goals will help you keep going for the long term."

❖ **Treat yourself** (and your family or spouse) if you accomplish an important goal. Eat out; go on an outing.

For More Information
Books

The Millionairess Across the Street by Bettina Flores and Jennifer Basye Sander (Chicago, IL: Dearborn Financial Publishing, 1999).

Seven Secrets of Successful Women by Donna Brooks, Ph.D., and Lynn Brooks (New York, NY: McGraw-Hill, 1999).

6

Financing Your Venture

It is not how much money you have. It is what you do with it that makes a difference.

—A common saying

• SUCCESS SECRET 33 •

Start your business economically.

"Home-based women business owners are much more likely than other entrepreneurs to use private sources and credit cards to finance their businesses than they are to depend on business loans, leased equipment, or vendor credit," according to the National Foundation for Women Business Owners. Business experts say one of the major financial mistakes new entrepreneurs make is to under-finance their home venture. But women ask all the time: "How *do* I finance a home (or small) business start-up if I have little or no cash?"

Hopefully, this chapter will give you some helpful suggestions on obtaining funds for your venture.

"One-Tenth" Rule

Eight years ago, Sue Harris and a good friend started a very successful consignment shop on a shoestring. Sue used her "One-Tenth Philosophy" to ensure the success of her shop and also for a second one they opened later on. Harris says: "The basic idea is that we made a list of all our start-up expenses, including equipment, attorney fees, advertising, liability insurances, business licenses, etc., and came up with what seemed a huge number of dollars. But before we asked for the money, we put the budget on a 'diet' and slashed everything by 90 percent. Think, instead, of these words: smaller, cheaper, resale, handmade, and used."

Harris and her friend applied the "One-Tenth Philosophy" in setting up their shops using the following methods:

❖ They did their business's accounting on paper until they felt comfortable with all the ins and outs of their financial management and they had a solid profit and could afford a computer and the appropriate software.

❖ They used family to help them build shelves, racks, and dressing rooms. They add: "Yes, we paid them for their time and materials, but did not hire some fancy construction company to remodel our space."

❖ They looked in newspapers and on the Internet for ads featuring equipment and supplies sold at warehouse sales and company going-out-of-business sales, as well as searched the Yellow Pages for used furniture and equipment shops.

❖ Borrowed from their children's savings accounts! However, they created a monthly coupon pay-back system and treated these loans as seriously as any bank loan.

Harris says: "Assuming your business is taking some months to get a sound footing in your community, how are you going to pay the bank some huge monthly loan balance and take care of all your other expenses? Using this philosophy will help you to have a tiny start-up balance so that you can (possibly) manage without getting the bank involved at all."

For More Information
Publications
The Consignment Workbook by Sue Harris, 1995; $23.00 (prepayment). Order from Scandia International, 133 Olney Rd., Petersburgh, NY

12138, < www.consignment.org >. Based on the author's eight years' experience starting and managing two very successful Vermont consignment resale shops.

———

The Frugal Mindset

Kimberly Stanséll, bootstrappin' expert and author of *Bootstrapper's Success Secrets: 151 Tactics for Building Your Business on a Shoestring Budget*, defines a "Bootstrapper" as "a person who starts a business with inadequate capital and manages to build it up relying more on creativity or resourcefulness rather than a checkbook balance." She says if you came from a job where you did not have to make cost-effective decisions, you are likely to have developed spendthrift habits that can now kill your new business. Stanséll knows this fact well because nine years ago she left a corporate job to launch two businesses; published independently a national newsletter, *Bootstrappin' Entrepreneur;* and currently facilitates a traveling workshop and seminar program before audiences worldwide as an entrepreneurial author and trainer.

Stanséll says: "Your survival as a bootstrapper will depend on your ability to distinguish between your needs, wants, and absolutes. Make it your business to know the difference, so you don't indulge in your wants while ignoring your needs and end up too broke to handle your absolutes!"

Here are some other ways to prepare your "frugal mindset:"

❖ **Downsize your cost of living expenses—not your quality of living.** Save money by borrowing videos from your public library instead of renting them; brown-bag your lunch; shop at an upscale clothing consignment shop; when your lease runs out on your vehicle, buy a good used one instead and eliminate a monthly payment; do not buy a second vehicle (unless your home business requires it); and save on insurance, gas, parking, and maintenance costs.

❖ **Monitor your office supply usage.** Recycle discarded paper by cutting for notes and using the blank side for personal photocopying. Look for sales at your local office supply store or print shop.

❖ **Save money on phone bills.** Call in the evening when rates go down if your clients are located in the West (or before rates go up if your clients are in the East). Use e-mail when it is appropriate. Write down a list of items you want to discuss during your call, then you will not waste time or have to call again because you forgot something.

✤ **Save auto gas bills.** Cluster all your errands or appointments on one day a week.

✤ **Read Boardroom Inc.'s money-saving information packed publications.** To get either *Bottom Line/Business* or *Bottom Line/ Personal and Bottom Line/Tomorrow,* write to Boardroom, Inc., Box 2614, Greenwich, CT 06836-2614.

You do not need to live a Spartan existence to be a start-up entrepreneur, but if you start thinking like a frugal entrepreneur in the early years of your business, it may just make the difference between running a business that thrives and one that folds.

___

For More Information
Books
Bootstrapper's Success Secrets: 151 Tactics for Building Your Business on a Shoestring Budget by Kimberly Stanséll (Franklin Lakes, NJ: Career Press, 1997), < www.kimberlystansell.com >.
The Frugal Entrepreneur: Creative Ways to Save Time, Energy, & Money in Your Business by Terri Lonier (New Paltz, NY: Portico Press, 1996).

___

• **SUCCESS SECRET 34** •

Determine how much money you will need for your home business start-up.

Before you start your business, you will want to thoroughly analyze all of your financial needs. Do not forget to include expenses of your personal and cost of living expenses—such as mortgage or rent, medical and insurance costs, utilities, food, clothing, transportation, and leisure activities.

As mentioned before, if you are the sole supporter of your family and plan on starting full time, you will need *at least* six months to two years of living expenses saved up.

Estimating your Business Expenses
These are *suggested* lists of home-business costs and will vary according to your personal needs and the specific needs of your business. Their totals will help give you an idea of the *approximate* amount of money you will need. These expenses will be figured out when you write your business plan. Consult with your accountant or other business expert qualified to help you with this financial projection.

One-Time Start-Up Costs
   Furniture
   Office supplies
   Telephone–answering and services
   Computer
   Peripherals
   Fax machine
   Scanner
   Pagers/Cell phone
   Software
   Additional equipment related to your specific business idea
      necessary for start-up
   Decorating/Remodeling
   Inventory (if product-oriented)
   Utilities
   Professional fees (lawyer, accountant)
   Licenses/Permits
   Printed promotional materials
                    Total Start-Up Expenses:_____

Monthly Expenses:
   Mortgage/Rent
   Subscriptions/Dues
   Your earnings (many owners put these back into their business
      to purchase more equipment or pay off loans)

Advertising
Supplies
Telephone
Insurance
Taxes, including Social Security
Postage
Utilities
Maintenance
Lease/Rent (equipment, etc.)
Miscellaneous
                    Total Estimated Monthly Expenses:_____

Total Estimate of Your Business Expenses
(Start-Up Expenses + Monthly Expenses):_____

Setting Financial Goals

It may be difficult to set financial goals at the onset of a business, because you will not have any sales to review (unless you started your business on the side), but you can start with a basic financial strategy by having a concept of what you want to accomplish. Here are some suggestions to help you plan a financial strategy for your home business:

❖ Make sure your own personal finances and affairs are secure, because you will need to use your business resources mainly toward growing your venture.

❖ Get help from a professional such as your accountant, a business consultant, financial services professional, or a volunteer such as those from SCORE or other SBA offices. Make sure the professional is experienced with assisting home and small businesses by asking for references. Another option is to gather a group of other women business owners periodically to support and help one another's businesses with their problems.

❖ Make a list of your financial needs and prioritize them and ask questions such as these: What is the minimum amount I need to get started? What equipment or supplies do I need to buy first? Which method of advertising will I try first?

❖ With your financial consultant, next determine some possible solutions for your financial needs.

❖ During the first year of your business, it will help you to review quarterly or even monthly your financial statements and business progress with your financial advisor. It is a good investment because you may avoid some costly mistakes. You will want to measure your progress and analyze your strengths and weaknesses to see if you need to change directions in strategy.

As your business grows, you can use your financial strategy to make the most of tax advantages, develop retirement plans, and prepare for future expansion. Your financial strategy can influence whether or not your home business will be successful and is a factor that you should neither put off nor fear tackling on a regular basis.

• SUCCESS SECRET 35 •

Explore all your financial options.

Raising Capital Tips

Money—in one form or another—is needed to start, sustain, and expand a business. A home business has the advantage in that it is less expensive to start because you do not need a storefront. If is a service-oriented business, then *you*—your expertise, skills, experience—are the business, and it will generally be less to start than a product-oriented business. The knack in finding the money you need is finding the source(s) that best fit your business's needs and have requirements for which you qualify and terms that you can handle.

Take your time to investigate the financing options available to all businesses, because you never know when the circumstances of your business will change and you'll need a different kind of financing than those you used previously. If you do the research now, you will already be aware of a number of financing options from which you can choose.

Subscribe to at least one general home-business magazine and one publication in your industry, and be aware of what small business support programs your state may offer. Ask your local legislators to put you on their state news mailing list. Keep in touch with other local women business owners in your area. Through this reading and networking, you will be able to take advantage of the latest programs, awards, grants, and such as they become available.

When you do get money through one method or another, the trick is to do the most with it. This comes from having the right knowledge and tools—your business management skills. Enroll in business management courses if you feel you need more know-how.

There are many options you will want to explore in getting financing for your home business start-up and (hopefully) expansion. Here are some common (and some not-so-common) options you will want to investigate.

Sources of Funds

Recent surveys of small business owners found that a majority of them relied on their personal savings to provide their start-up financing. Using your savings may help you obtain a bank loan in the future because banks generally require that you, the loan appli-cant, contribute 30–40 percent of the total investment. The entre-preneurs surveyed expressed that raising start-up capital was their biggest challenge. Fortunately, many home-based entrepreneurs meet this money challenge with both traditional and "creative" financing methods. Here are a few of them:

Savings

Make the most of money you already have. Negotiate with your bank for less costly services tailored to the financial situation of your business. Look for mail-order bargains for supplies. Learn how to do some of your business's tasks yourself.

Credit Cards

Use credit cards for fast cash and to borrow from the future. Com-pare cards for the lowest rates but pay off the balance before the interest rates go up substantially (as many do). If you are still work-ing at a job, pay off that credit card balance. This will move your credit limit up to the maximum so that when you start the business, you will have an available line of credit.

Other Jobs

Moonlight or work at a part-time job for extra cash. It will be a double benefit if you get a job related to the business you want to start—you'll get first-hand experience and money to help you live or save for your venture.

Corporate Sponsors

If you are creating new products and technology, you may be able to find a larger company that offers money or access to a distribution network in exchange for licensing rights to new products.

Personal Assets

Do you have an antique or jewelry you really do not need? Sell them for needed funds.

Home Equity

If you own a home, you can take a home-equity line of credit, a second mortgage, or refinance your original mortgage (check to see if the state you live in permits this). Just make sure you pay back the equity or you could lose your home.

Other Assets

Consider borrowing from insurance policies, IRAs, pension plans, stocks, and securities. Check with your insurance agent, or look into the policies regarding borrowing from your mutual funds or retirement account. Before you borrow, though, make sure you are aware of the pay-back terms, penalties, and taxes you will be required to pay.

Internet Sources

Entrepreneurs are now using the Internet to find information on funding and investors. "Angel Investors" are individuals who like to buy into businesses to help fund start-ups. They are often willing to take risks that venture capitalists and other investors are not because many are entrepreneurs themselves. Of course, before signing any contract, make sure you know something about the investor's background and what they expect in exchange for their money! Sometimes investors demand they have some input as to the direction of your business, which would lead to conflicts in business decisions. Also, do consult with a lawyer knowledgeable about securities regulations and laws to see whether your home business is to the point that you would like to sell your company's securities online.

Two Web sites are the Angel Capital Electronic Network (ACE-Net) and America's Business Funding Directory < www. businessfinance.com > (see #40: Take advantage of the financial sources available online).

Specialty Loans

Local banks now offer specialty loans for women, where a one-page application can land you an unsecured credit line or loan ranging from $2,500 to $50,000. (See also "Government Sources" under *For More Information* on page 148.)

You can get information on such specialty loans by contacting organizations such as the following:

✤ Wells Fargo/NAWBO Program (800) 359-3557, ext. 120.
✤ Bank of Women/America, Inc. (213) 680-3375.
✤ Other National Associations dedicated to helping members who are *women entrepreneurs* (some have local chapters) include:
  • American Women's Economic Development Corporation (AWED) (212) 692-9100.
  • Women Incorporated (WI) (800) 930-3993 < ww.womeninc. com >.
  • Women's Growth Capital Fund, 1010 Wisconsin Ave., NW, Suite 600, Washington, DC 20007, (202) 342-1431. A private organization that funds expansion capital for successful women-owned businesses (not for start-up businesses).

Suppliers, Customers

If your suppliers will agree to accept payment in 90 days instead of 30 days, and if your customers make advance payments, you

SBA Women and Minority Loans

❖ Office of Women's Business Ownership (OWBO) has the same address as SBA. Its Web site is < www.sba.gov/ womeninbusiness >. This is the only office in the federal government specifically targeted to facilitate the growth and development of women-owned businesses. It *does not* provide direct funding or loan guarantees to women business owners, but *does* help them achieve financial success through pre-business workshops, management/technical information, and guidance on how to access capital.

   OWBO also has a listing of Women Business Development Centers across the U.S. that provide workshops and programs for women entrepreneurs and established women-owned businesses. Write or visit the site < www. onlinewbc.org > to see if there is a center near you.

❖ SCORE. The Service Corps of Retired Executives is a volunteer management assistance program of the SBA that provides one-on-one counseling, workshops, and seminars. SCORE chapters exist throughout the country. Many work in conjunction with local chambers of commerce. SCORE and Visa have also joined forces to help home-based and small business owners. Contact your SBA office, local chamber of commerce, or the Web sites for more

have some leeway to pay and some cash to use. Just make sure you make your payments as agreed and deliver the "goods" as expected to your customers. This is not a good means for long-term financing.

Factoring

Many businesses sell their goods and services without any advance payments. Accounts receivable (the money owed to you by your customers) are sold to a third party called a *factor*, which pays you a percentage of your invoices (depending on how large or small your invoices are), sometimes within 24 hours. This type of financ-

information. SCORE: < www.score.org > ; Visa's small business resources: < www.visa.com\smallbiz\ > .

+ IRS. Internal Revenue Service, (800) 829-1040, < www.irs. ustreas.gov > . Call for listing of helpful publications such as *Business Use of Your Home* (publication 587), *Your Business Tax Kit: Starting a Business & Keeping Records* (publication 583), and others.

+ U.S. Department of Agriculture (USDA), Rural Business-Cooperative Service, 12th St. and Independence Ave. SW, Washington, DC 20250; Rural Information Center: (800) 633-7701 (301-504-5547 in Washington D.C. area and outside the U.S.). Provides information about federal rural development programs. Free information: *A Guide to Funding Resources & Federal Funding Sources for Rural Areas.* (See also your local USDA Cooperative Extension Office in your county.)

+ SBA Publications: For 50 cents, order a copy of the SBA's *Resource Directory for Small Business Management,* which contains a listing of publications on small business start-up and management, such as *Financing for Small Business and Business Plan for Home-Based Business.* Order from SBA Publications, P.O. Box 46521, Denver, CO 80201-46521, < www.pueblo.gsa.gov > .

ing is more commonly seen in manufacturing-type businesses instead of service businesses. It helps companies growing quickly and/or those who do not qualify for typical bank loan and who need money quickly.

Venture Capitalists

This financing method (and factoring) are generally not used by new home businesses, but they cannot be ruled out in all circumstances. Venture capital firms buy part of a start-up business to help it expand and hope for big returns if the business should ever go public and sell stock. Money invested here is at least $250,000, with many deals in the millions of dollars. A downside to venture capital is that you may experience loss of control because venture capitalists typically want to play a major role in the decisions and operations of the business.

Another form of this is the *private placement market,* which instead provides cash to a business as a loan. These investors generally deal with businesses that are already earning a profit and do not request the level of control in a business that venture capital investors might.

Contests
Awards, Honors, and Prizes is a library reference guide by Gale Research that lists awards in every field of endeavor (some are cash awards). Check also entrepreneurial publications such as *HomeOffice Computing, Income Opportunities, Success,* and *Entrepreneur's Business Start Ups* for occasional business contests that offer cash awards, prizes, or in-kind products and services.

Government Sources
Federal
The U.S. Small Business Administration (SBA), (800) 827-5722, 409 Third St. SW, Washington DC 20416; < www.sba.gov >. Contact for the telephone number of SBA offices nearest you. The SBA works through banks and non-bank institutions, as it guarantees rather than makes business loans to small businesses. The three classifications of lenders through which it works are Certified Lenders, Participant Lenders, and Preferred Lenders. Discuss the differences with an SBA consultant. These offices can give you more information on guaranteed loans to small businesses such as Low-Documentation Loan (LowDoc), FA$TRAK Loan, Micro-Loan Program, Women and Minority Prequalification Pilot Loan, and Certified Development Company Programs. It also has a mentor program, WNET—Women's Network for Entrepreneurial Training— which operates nationwide, matching women business owners with women just starting out.

Government Funding and Assistance from Your State
There is a primary state government agency (commerce department, the finance authority, or the economic development agency)

More SBA Women and Minority Loans

The SBA offers assistance to new entrepreneurs with its Minority and Women's Prequalification Pilot Loan Programs. This program focuses primarily on the applicant's character, credit, and apparent ability to repay the loan from earnings. Loans under this program are limited to $250,000. To be eligible for the Women's Prequalification Loan Program, a business must be at least 51 percent owned, operated, and managed by women; have average annual sales for the preceding three years that do not exceed $5 million; and employ less than 100 persons, including affiliates. The women's program uses nonprofit intermediaries, and the Minority program uses both nonprofit and for-profit intermediaries.

❖ **The Micro-loan Program** provides start-up capital of $25,000 or less to businesses considered too small by many commercial lenders. Administered by nonprofit intermediaries who will often help you in formulating your business plan, this program is available in forty-six states. The SBA says it gave over half of these loans to women-owned businesses and a little less than a third to minority-owned businesses.

❖ **SBAExpress (formerly FA$TRAK)** now makes unsecured revolving lines of credit up to $25,000 more readily available to small businesses.

❖ **The LowDoc Program** loans money for amounts less than $100,000 and requires only a single-page application if your request is for less than $50,000. Your business's cash flow and your personal credit rating is important in being granted this type of loan.

❖ **The 8A Program** helps minorities with loans for business start-up and expansion, plus guidance in getting contracts with the federal government.

There are other loans and funding available through the SBA. Talk with a person from one of the SBA offices to determine which one is best suited to your and your business's needs.

or office *in each state* that provides one-stop guidance on financial programs and services offered to small businesses, including minority/women's opportunities at the state level. Contact the office of your local state senator and/or state representative for referrals and information, and especially ask for *your state's financial incentives to meet the needs of new businesses.* Also check your state office of economic development for available funding and possible grant sources—usually found under "Economic Development" in the Blue Pages of your telephone directory.

Local

Besides the federal, state, and national offices concerning small business in your area, contact your local business groups and associations for any existing entrepreneurship support programs.

Check also to see if your local and/or county government has any funding programs such as the Community Development Corporations (CDCs). These programs receive both federal and state grants to fund businesses in areas of low employment in order to create employment opportunities.

Also, foundations, colleges, and local schools may have various programs and continuing education programs to help entrepreneurs with start-up information and information on funding.

Grants, Awards, and Contests

Grants are not as easy to find for business start-ups as some sources would have you believe. Neither the SBA nor the Economic Development Administration offers grants to individuals—just their federally backed loans. However, federal block grants are given each year to state economic development agencies, and nonprofit groups and universities. These, in turn, award grants to businesses that are disadvantaged, owned by women, researching and producing high-tech products, and others contributing to their community's development or job potential or education that qualify for local or state grants.

Some business associations and/or nonprofit foundations also help with loans or give cash awards. You will have to do your research to learn what is available.

Grant Money—Fact or Myth?

Dr. Robert Sullivan, author of *United States Government: New Customer*, says in an article in *Spare-Time* magazine (February 1999—See Resources on page 398) that grants of any type are increasingly harder to come by, though they are still available. Kimberly Stanséll, author of *Bootstrapper's Success Secrets*, says: "Truth be told: 'Free' money is a myth. There are few government agencies and private organizations that give individuals money to finance a start-up.

"The research for my book led me to Norton Kiritz, president of The Grantsmanship Center in Los Angeles, who said the majority of grant money is really targeted at nonprofit organizations and government agencies. He said these groups use the money to fund a variety of special projects such as community revitalization, job training, or research, with a limited amount of money to individuals for scholarships and financial aid or to fund artistic activities or fellowships."

For More Information
Books
Business Capital for Women: An Essential Handbook for Entrepreneurs by Emily Card and Adam Miller (New York, NY: Macmillan General Reference, 1996).

Commerce Business Daily, issued by the U.S. Department of Commerce, contains information on contracts, procurements, and needs of agencies. Found in some public libraries, or write to: United Communications Group, P.O. Box 90608, Washington DC 20090-0608, or visit their Web site: < www.cbd.savvy. com > .

Finance and Taxes for the Home-Based Business by Charles and Bryane Miller Lickson (Menlo Park, CA: Crisp Publications, 1997).

Finding Money: The Business Guide to Financing by Kate Kister and Tom Harnish (New York, NY: Wiley, 1995).

Free Money from the Federal Government for Small Business & Entrepreneurs by Laurie Blum (New York, NY: Wiley, 1996).

Free Money from Uncle Sam to Start Your Own Business (or Expand the One You Have) by William Alarid and Gus Berle (Santa Maria, CA: Puma Publishing, 1997).

From Gale Research. Check your local library or a college library near you or call (800) 877-GALE. *Grants on Disc* is a library reference guide providing electronic access to information on 30,000 grants per year; and Gale's *Awards, Honors, Prizes* lists awards in every field of endeavor.

Launching Your Home-Based Business: How to Successfully Plan, Finance, & Grow Your New Venture by David H. Bangs and Andi Axman (Chicago, IL: Dearborn Trade, 1997).

Other People's Money by Harold R. Lacey (Traverse City, MI: Sage Creek Press, 1998).

Note: Chapter 2 of Lacey's book discusses government funding along with the advantages and disadvantages of this type of financing.

Starting and Operating a Business in . . . (one compiled for each state) by Michael D. Jenkins, (Oasis Press, Grants Pass, OR). You can order one for your state through your local bookstore. See also state and local chapters of chambers of commerce, SBA district offices, Small Business Development Centers (SBDCs), which are listed at < www.smallbiz.suny.edu > and Small Business Investment Companies (SBICs), which offer services and investments for and in small businesses. Your SBA district office can give you their office locations in your state.

The States and Small Business: A Directory of Programs and Activities. Published by the SBA's Office of Advocacy, this directory gives the details on many of the programs and services available in U.S. states. The book is available from the Government Printing Office by calling (202) 512-1800. The GPO stock number is 045-000-00266-7.

United States Government—New Customer! by Robert A. Sullivan (Great Falls, VA: Information International, 1997). Available in bookstores or by calling (703) 450-7049 or visiting < www. isquare.com > .

Venture Capital Handbook: An Entrepreneur's Guide to Obtaining Capital to Start a Business, Buy a Business, or Expand a Business by David J.Gladstone (New Jersey: Prentice Hall Trade, 1988).
What No One Ever Tells You about Starting Your Own Business by Jan Norman (Dover, NH: Upstart Publishing, 1998).
Where's the Money? Sure-Fire Financing Solutions for Your Business by Art Beroff and Dwayne Moyers (Irvine, CA: Entrepreneur Media, Inc., 1999).

Federal Government

The Catalog of Federal Domestic Assistance. Published annually, this is a comprehensive listing of federal grants that are awarded. Contact your local SBA–affiliated office or visit < www.gsa. gov/fdac > .
Commerce Business Daily (listed on page 151). Also lists the recipients of block grant monies.
The Federal Registrar. This daily publication of procurement information is found at larger public libraries and many state offices; also contains a listing of grants and contact sources.
The Foundation Center, 79 Fifth Ave., New York, NY 10003-3076 (has three other offices: San Francisco; Washington, DC; and Cleveland, OH). Write for their latest catalog of specific guides to nonprofit funding, including the book *The Nonprofit Entrepreneur* and two resource books it publishes: *The Foundation Directory* and *Grants to Individuals.* < www.fdncenter.org > .

Free Publications

Access to Credit: A Guide for Lenders and Women Owners of Small Businesses, Federal Reserve Bank of Chicago, Public Information, P.O. Box 834, Chicago, IL 60604. A free, 41-page guide offering advice to entrepreneurs and bankers.
The Credit Process: A Guide for Small Business Owners. A free, 26-page workbook offering guidance to entrepreneurs seeking first-time financing. Order from the Federal Reserve Bank, Public Information Dept., 33 Liberty St., New York, NY 10045.
The Small Business Financial Resource Guide: Sources of Assistance for Small and Growing Businesses, MasterCard International and The

National Federation of Independent Business. Write to 600 Maryland Ave. SW, #700, Washington, DC 20024 or visit their Web site: < www.nfibonline.com >. A free, 150-page book discussing various funding options and sources.

Internet Sites

< www.businessfinance.com > American's Business Funding Directory. A search engine that matches entrepreneurs with potential funding sources.

< www.lowe.org/smallbiznet/index.htm > Offers books, information on entrepreneurship, and links to other small-business sites.

< www.moneyroom.com/ > The Moneyroom, a national talk-radio show for home business hosted by Michael Lamb.

< www.nvst.com > Venture capital opportunities.

< www.sbsn.com > American Institute for Financial Research (AIFR). Helps you assess your financial needs, and sells a related software package, *Small Business Start-up.*

< www.toolkit.cch.com > CCH Inc.'s business start-up information including "Small Business Financing."

< www.village.com > Part of the Women's Network, which also has a section for home-business questions and regular articles on home-business management.

< www.visa.com/smallbiz/ > Financial information sponsored by Visa.

Creative Financing

Kimberly Stanséll* says: "When you're working on a shoestring budget, you need the following characteristics to be successful in coming up with solutions to your financing challenges:

------

*Kimberly Stanséll, a Los Angeles-based entrepreneurial trainer and author of *Bootstrapper's Success Secrets: 151 Tactics for Building Your Business on a Shoestring Budget* (Career Press) and the forthcoming *Witty Workin' Woman.* Her consulting and training firm specializes in producing programs, materials, seminars, and workshops aimed at entrepreneurs and working women.

Her Web site < www. kimberlystansell.com > is dedicated to helping people realize their dreams with little or no money. For your free subscription (subscribe @kimberlystansell.com) to the "Bootstrappin' Tip of the Week and Success Library" of articles and information for shoestring entrepreneurs.

1. Creativity (in coming up with a laundry list of solutions to your cashless state).
2. Resourcefulness (in how you approach the challenge and work around your lack of cash).
3. Courage and boldness (in approaching others and soliciting their support and creating an alliance to advance your product or service into the market)."

Examples of "creative financing" women have used to help fund their ventures include everything from having garage sales to gambling. Besides splitting her paycheck in half and borrowing from her parents and husband, Joyce says: "As embarrassed as I am to say, I've even used winnings from the racetracks. On a good day, I've won several hundred dollars!"

Though betting at tracks is not recommended for your financing, once you begin to put your thought processes in the "creative mode," you will undoubtedly come up with ideas to finance your venture.

For More Information
Books
Finances & Taxes for the Home-Based Business by Bryanne and Charles P. Lickson (Menlo Park, CA: Crisp Publications, 1997).
Financial Savvy for the Self-Employed by Grace W. Weinstein (New York, NY: Holt, 1996).

Tips for Borrowing from Family and Friends
Many people have borrowed from parents or siblings or spouses to start their businesses. If you choose this method, make sure you have a contract to ensure you repay your benefactor to prevent hard feelings. Sally Silagy of Gardening Greetings says: "Believe it or not, my husband financed my greeting card business. An agreement was drawn up where I would pay back the borrowed amount after year one. I totally surprised him and reimbursed him after six months . . . now it's all mine!"

Certified financial planners offer these additional tips in borrowing money from a friend or relative:

❖ All loan agreements should be drawn up by one or all three of these experts: an attorney, certified financial planner, and a certified public accountant.

❖ It should be a formal agreement so that both parties will treat it as a "real" contract and help to avoid payback problems should one of the parties die.

❖ Have a payment timetable. Sue Harris borrowed money from her children's savings accounts to start her consignment shop and created "coupon books" similar to car and mortgage loans so she would not skip any payment and made it part of her weekly budget.

❖ Keep communications open before, during, and after the loan period.

❖ Tax concerns are a consideration if the loan is over $10,000. You should consult with your tax specialist and/or accountant for guidelines on these matters.

❖ It may be better to explore other financing sources and skip this option altogether because of the potential of harming a relationship.

For More Information
Software
"Smart Business Start-up," a four-module software package. To help you assess financial needs and find funding. For more information, write to Smart Online, P.O. Box 12794, Research Triangle Park, NC 27709.

• SUCCESS SECRET 36 •

Know how to be a successful bank borrower.

The March 1996 issue of *Working Woman* magazine featured an excellent article, "Smart Women, Foolish Bankers" by Clint Willis, which detailed the obstacles women had to face in overcoming financial institutions' assumption that women were poor credit risks.

Based on a poll conducted by *Working Woman* magazine and Dun & Bradstreet, which revealed that "small, women-owned businesses are just as creditworthy—if not more so—as other companies."

That was several years ago, yet women may still face discriminatory attitudes from banks and other legal institutions. Realize that it is illegal for these institutions to deny your loan just because you *are* a woman; but know, too, that:

✤ You can improve your chances of getting a bank loan by preparing a business plan.
✤ More networks are now available to specifically help women obtain business financing.

By joining national women's organizations like Women, Inc., the National Association of Business Owners, and others, you can learn more about loans, venture-capital pools, and other funding opportunities.

Sooner or later every business will need capital to start up, expand, and/or survive. Though the good news is that more loans are being given to women business owners, the bad news is that your loan application may still be rejected—not because you are a woman, but because bankers want to feel confident that you and your business are a good "investment." Here are some guidelines to help you:

Preliminary Steps to Obtain Loans
Assemble Necessary Materials
Your accountant can assist you putting together the following:

✤ A business plan (the most important tool for obtaining a loan)
✤ Your business's cash-flow projections
✤ Three years' company tax returns (if applicable)
✤ A personal financial statement

Do Your Research
✤ Talk to your own financial institution first. They are familiar with you and may be able to make some recommendations. Ask them to what kinds of businesses they give loans.

❖ Talk to other women business owners in your area or in your industry who may give you tips or leads on lending institutions with which they were successful in getting a loan.

❖ Check with community business associations such as the chamber of commerce, a home-business association, a local chapter of the National Association of Women Business Owners (www. nawbo.org) to see what micro-lenders exist in your town. They may also be able to inform you of the existence of "Angel Investors" (local businesses that invest in other local businesses).

❖ Ask your state senator or state representative if special state loan programs for women and minority business owners are available.

What Lenders Want to See

Jackie Ruiz, a former loan officer and now a Realtor with Century 21 Grosse & Quade, gives this advice to women preparing to go to a bank for a loan: "Have a business plan with facts and figures. Know what you need to get started, the expenses you will incur, and why you need the money. Have a qualified accountant do a projected income and expenses projection. This will demonstrate to the banker that you take this business seriously and that you understand how much time and money you will need to make the business profitable." When applying for a loan, be prepared with each of the following:

❖ **Your contribution:** A percentage of what your business needs in terms of tools, equipment, or money.

❖ **Your expertise:** The experience, knowledge, and training you have in your industry.

❖ **Your collateral:** Today there are no unsecured loans.

❖ **Your personal credit history:** If you have a blemished credit record, try to get it cleared before you start applying for new credit. Also note that if you have too many inquiries listed on your credit record or have a record of loan turn-downs, lenders are likely to be cautious.

❖ **Your payback plan:** Consult your accountant on this one.

❖ **Your honesty:** Ask for only the money you need (provide written cost estimates) and discuss anything that may jeopardize your loan. Your forthrightness will be appreciated.

Preparing to apply for a bank loan takes some effort but the pay-off will be worth it if it results in your getting the money you need and possibly developing a relationship with a lender who can offer you valuable advice on other financial services beneficial to your business.

For More Information
Books
Borrowing to Build Your Business: Getting Your Banker to Say "Yes," 2nd ed. by George M. Dawson (Chicago, IL: Dearborn, 1999).
How to Get a Small Business Loan by Bryan E. Milling (Naperville, IL: Sourcebooks, 1998).

Choosing a Commercial Bank
With so many banks "in transition" these days with mergers and buy-outs, choosing the bank with the best services and rates for your business's needs can be difficult. Not only has the percentage of women business owners with bank credit increased from 1996 to 1998, so has the amount of credit they have available. In 1998, 34 percent of women business owners who have bank credit have $50,000 or more available for use in their businesses, compared to 20 percent in 1996.

However, women still lag behind their male counterparts. In 1998, 58 percent of men business owners had $50,000 or more available bank credit (NFWBO). Here are some factors to help you choose a bank for your business:

❖ Instead of the typical services of deposits and loans, some banks are expanding their programs to be "financial service providers," to provide additional services to their business customers such as investments, equipment leasing, and employment benefit programs.
❖ Choose a bank that has kept up with technology for its customers—has the ability to access account data from your PC, telephone banking, accounts receivable financing, or Web sites with information, for example.

✤ Select a bank large enough to serve your business's needs but not so large that it does not give good customer service.

✤ Research to see what banks offer small businesses in terms of loans, free business consulting, and financial advice.

✤ Banking fees and rates can vary widely even within the same community, so shop around and compare. Then talk to the loan officers to learn what they require for a business loan application and whether they are participants in the SBA loan programs.

✤ Bargain with a banker and see if you can reduce any of your fees if you have personal or savings accounts with the same bank.

Making "Friends" with a Banker

No matter how tiny your venture is, it is important to have a good business relationship with your banker. Banking decisions are often made on the basis of how trustworthy you are, so you will want to present yourself with professionalism and proficiency. Let your banker know you are starting a home business and ask for any banking tips they might have for you. Visit your bank regularly so the tellers and bank managers associate your name with a face in the event you have to call them with a problem.

A good banking relationship can also help you:

✤ Get faster approval for bank loans or credit.

✤ Get referrals to other business persons and potential customers.

✤ Get references if you should need them in your business dealings.

✤ Get up-to-date financial information and banking trends as they relate to your business.

You, in turn, can help your banker and his or her bank by recommending them to other business owners. Just remember, too, how you conduct your business banking may affect a banker's opinion about other home and small businesses, so you will want to conduct your banking transactions like the CEO you are!

What to Do If Your Loan Is Rejected

If your loan is denied, here are some questions you will want to ask your loan officer or supervisor (you are legally entitled to a full explanation):

❖ Find out for what business reasons you were refused: Too much debt? Insufficient collateral? Business plan too vague? No cash flow? Other?

❖ Ask what you can do to rectify these business deficits so you can reapply again.

❖ See if you might qualify for a smaller loan or one from the SBA (may require less collateral).

❖ If the bank says your personal financial condition has too many liabilities (such as college loans or second mortgages), see if you can pay down some of your debt.

❖ Consider selling your products and/or services to governments. Despite the paperwork that is usually involved, if you obtain a contract, you are likely to have a long-time customer. This will make you less of a risk to a bank.

❖ Consider consulting with a business expert familiar with helping small businesses with their financial plans to get another professional's opinion of your proposal.

Being turned down may be an opportunity for you to concentrate on slower yet continued business growth, which will help you establish a solid track record of sales. The next banker will be much more likely to say "yes" to your loan.

For More Information

Internet Sites

< www.bankweb.com > Bank Web is a large listing of banks, state by state.

< www.barnett.com > Barnett Bank's Web site with information on questions to ask when applying for a loan.

< www.FinanceHub.com > FinanceHub supplies a range of resources and links to venture capitalists and banks.

< www.nvst.com > An Internet "hub" for the private equity indus-
try (venture capital).

———————

Once you have financed your business, draw up a business
budget, and examine every purchase carefully, and you may never
need to borrow money again.

• SUCCESS SECRET 37 •

Use financial-solution software
for your home business.

Just as you might have used software to help you write your business plan, you can also use software to help you prepare for applying for a business loan. Here are some recommended by financial
experts:

❖ *LoanBuilder* by Jian < www.jian.com >. Helps you do a financial
analysis for the groundwork for a loan application, including
preparation of documents, spreadsheets, forms, and an explanation of the SBA's loan offerings.

❖ *LenderPro* by Moneysoft < www.moneysoft.com >. Recommended for established businesses with its business cycles and
income statements.

❖ Internet Site Sources:
  • < www.filez.com > *Filez.*
  • < www.download.com > *Download.*
  • < www.shareware.com > *Shareware.*

———————

For More Information
Internet Sites
< www.accountingnet.com > This CPA link provides a nationwide
directory to help you find an accountant or specialist in business planning, technology, and small-business accounting.

Software
QuickBooks—Intuit, Inc. 800-446-8848.

_____

• SUCCESS SECRET 38 •

Learn how to avoid the biggest
financial mistakes.

Judith E. Dacey, CPA, says: "The most common and ultimately the biggest financial mistake women business owners often make is failing to maximize the power hidden in entrepreneurship. Instead of leaping joyously into all the possibilities of incredible success, we take little baby steps. I think we are imprisoned by our lifelong experience of being the responsible one."

Dacey continues: "By limiting the scope of our business to a local marketplace instead of national or global, we diminish our chances of significant financial success. By limiting our vision to an understandably affordable venture instead of seeking substantial funding, we nurture an adequate result instead of mind-boggling wealth. Just this one mistake causes forfeit of potentially unlimited rewards. The solution? The number one key to beating the odds is awareness. We cannot change it until we can conceive the problem and irrevocably commit to overcoming it. It does not matter how many ways it will not work, we only need one way it will."

Financial mistakes can literally "cost" you your business. Here are a few of the most common ones and some tips on how to catch them before it becomes too late.

❖ **Neglecting to set a financial plan for both your personal future and the future of your business.** Without written goals, you may overextend your business's finances in too many directions to be profitable in any one area.

❖ **Lack of planning for business expansion.** You may do a great job in marketing your business, but neglect to plan how to finance the ways to get your product and/or services to your customers. You could go to a wholesale craft show and take in

$5,000 worth of orders, but if you have not planned how to fill all those orders—with the equipment, packaging, and shipping that is involved—you could lose credibility with your present and any future buyers.

✤ **Overspending on equipment and supplies.** As mentioned before, be thrifty and cost-conscious in setting up your office and buying equipment until you can afford it and you see which direction your business will take.

✤ **Not putting your business on a spending budget.** The old adage that people spend up according to their income should not apply to your business.

✤ **Letting your business deplete your personal assets.** Even though you are your business, do not be tempted to use all your private funds to finance a slow business, or you could end up not only with a failed business, but with no personal financial resources as well. Look for funding sources other than your own money.

✤ **Neglecting to plan for your retirement.** Even though you may plan on working the rest of your life because you love your work, there may come a time when you will have to slow down because of health or age-related factors, and age sixty-five is not the time to start thinking about it! Sit down now with a financial planner to begin to set up the best retirement plans that fit you and your business (see chapter 14, "Planning for Your Business's Future").

✤ **Thinking you will recoup your investment if you sell your business.** For many service businesses, you are the entire business. Without you, customers may not want to patronize the business.

✤ **Not planning how to pass your business along to your heirs.** One man who worked with his father and brothers bought his father out with payment terms of his getting a monthly percentage of the business. Now the father has a steady income and the sons a larger percentage of the business's profits. You need to arrange how the business should be handled if you should die. For example, have disability and life insurance, buy-out agreements if there are any partners, make plans to hire others in your place, and plan selling procedures. Seek the appropriate legal and financial experts to help you prepare for any unexpected events.

A little planning and forethought now can ensure you peace of mind and a better financial future for your business, yourself, and those who depend on you.

• SUCCESS SECRET 39 •

Use bartering basics to help sustain and grow your business.

"Barter!" says Michelle Clevenger, who runs a home-based desktop publishing business. "I cannot say this enough," she continues. "Offer your services or products in exchange for the items you need. You will find many businesses will say 'yes' to bartering. Make sure you are offering something they need, and that it is fair trade for what you are asking. You will almost never be turned down."

Barter is the exchange of goods or services in lieu of money. A barter exchange is still taxable sale or income (keep careful tax records), but it can be a way to get a product or service if you are short of cash. It is best to consult with your accountant before you barter because state laws and reporting procedures vary.

Advantages of bartering include getting services or items you could not afford otherwise; giving your business other marketing opportunities as you attract customers who favor this way of doing business; and making contacts with other businesses that could be valuable sources of leads and information. Disadvantages are that you can overextend your trading and be in a cash deficit, you may have to wait a period of time until you get the good or service you want, and few cash-paying clients will accept bartering exchanges. You can barter in different ways:

✤ **One-to-one:** Involving an exchange between just two individuals or businesses.

✤ **Barter exchanges:** Clearinghouses and brokers arrange barter arrangements in return for a percentage of the exchange members' transactions.

✤ **Corporation Barters:** An exchange of unused goods and supplies between corporations.

✤ **LETSystems** (Local Employment and Trading Systems): Barter exchanges set up on a local basis where members pay a fee to join so they can trade goods and services based on a point system.

One community has a parents exchange that trades babysitting hours among parents who need child-free blocks of time—to work in their home businesses, go to college classes, or simply have free time.

While business experts recommend that you do not do more than 25 percent of your business in bartering trade, it is a method promoting your business with profit potential that you might want to think about for your home business.

For More Information
Assocations
International Reciprocal Trade Assn. (IRTA), 175 W. Jackson Blvd., Suite 625, Chicago, IL 60604, < www.barter.com/irta/ >. For a free list of barter exchanges in your state and information on how to start your own barter exchange, send a LSASE (long self-addressed stamped envelope).

National Association of Trade Exchanges, 27801 Euclid Ave., Suite. 610, Euclid, OH 44132, < www.nate.org >.

Publications
BarterNews. A quarterly publication; for subscription information, send a LSASE to BarterNews, Inc., P.O. Box 3024, Mission Viejo, CA 92690, < www.drmag.com/magazines/BarterNews.cfm >.

• SUCCESS SECRET 40 •

Take advantage of the financial resources available online.

It can be overwhelming with all the Web sites out there, but make a list of the ones that seem most promising and access their pages. Visit chats on women's sites that feature home-business chats with guest experts on small business topics and articles like those on iVillage, < www.ivillage.com >, or Women Connect, < www.womenconnect.com >. You can also go directly to many banks' sites for information on loans and applications.

Here are just a few you will want to investigate. If you do not have access to the Internet in your home, most public libraries will let you reserve time on their computers.

❖ < www.acenet.sr.unh.edu/pub/ > The ACE-Net (Access to Capital Electronic Network). Created by the SBAs Office of Advocacy to meet the expanding demand for a national small-business securities market.

❖ < WWW.BUSINESSFINANCE.COM >. American Business Funding Directory with business-financing information.

❖ < www.cashfinder.com > Quicken Business Cashfinder. Help in applying for a business credit card, a credit line, a lease, or loan. Includes software and assistance from ten leading financial institutions.

❖ < www.financeweb.com >. Finance Web. Gives a listing of links for home-based and small businesses.

❖ < www.ivillage.com/work/index.html > The Women's Network, iVillage.

❖ < www.keybank.com > KeyBank. Lets small business owners apply for cash reserve, line-of-credit, or term loans.

❖ < www.womenconnect.com > Women Connection

❖ < www.isquare.com > The Small Business Advisor. Informative small business site by Dr. Robert Sullivan.

❖ *Small Business Lending in the United States*. This is an SBA report that ranks the lending performance of more than 93,000 banks by state. Lists those that are "friendly" with micro-businesses. Read the report at the SBA Web site < www.sba.gov >.

7

Marketing Plan

To Market to Market
  the wise one did go
With questions for all
  coming to, going fro
Her queries would yield
  the knowledge to sow
the success of one
  who asked to know.©
  —Maryanne Burgess

• SUCCESS SECRET 41 •

Know how to do preliminary market research to find the best customers for your business.

One of the major purposes of writing a business plan is to determine the market potential for your business idea—to find out whether you will have the needed customers who will pay for your service and/or product and thus sustain your business. The goals of marketing are:

1. Find your potential customers.
2. Make them aware of the goods and services your business is offering.

Marketing plans can run from simple to complex with costs amounting to almost nothing to thousands of dollars.

The successful home-business entrepreneur is one who realizes marketing is an ongoing, and almost daily, process. To do anything less may result in your competitors passing you and even "stealing" some your customers. However, the goal for you is to discover the most economical and—even more importantly—the most effective marketing methods for your business.

The purpose of this chapter is to give you some tips and sources you can implement into your own marketing strategies. But do not be afraid to come up with "creative marketing" tactics of your own. Some businesswomen have told me marketing is one of their most challenging tasks, but originating new ways to get customer recognition is also fun.

Market Research

Statistics show that the amount of research an entrepreneur does *before* a business start-up correlates directly with the success of that venture! While corporations and large businesses may spend thousands of dollars to determine who will be the "ideal customer" for their new product or service, you may not have the financial assets like these "big guys." Polly, who started a home-based business painting sweatshirts with her daughter-in-law (and has since started two other businesses), says: "You've got to *research* your market *before* you invest large amounts of money and time into a product." Here are some low-cost resources you can "tap into" to do the market research for your business idea:

Community Sources

Start here because information is easier to access, and your business will most likely seek its first customers locally.

✦ **Public Libraries.** Look for listings of manufacturers (*Thomas Register of American Manufacturers* < www/thomasregister.com >); suppliers; business and telephone directories (to find competitors); local government agencies and associations; local newspapers; U.S. Census reports (which give the local demographics and details of defined populations in your areas and around the country); and specific and general how-to business start-up and management books.

✤ **Chambers of Commerce.** Contact local chapters for a listing of area businesses and a profile of area residents, plus additional relevant community demographics that may influence residents' buying decisions.

✤ **Home-Based Business Associations.** These organizations can offer networking and referral opportunities, plus give you some feedback on the success rates of the area's home businesses similar to your idea.

✤ **Government.** Federally supported sources include Small Business Development Centers (SBDCs), which are usually associated with local colleges; Women's Business Centers (there are over sixty across the U.S.); the SBA and the SBA's Service Core of Retired Executives (SCORE), who can give you some feedback on your idea. Look in your local telephone directories to see if SCORE is in your area.

✤ **Local State Legislators.** These elected officials may be able to provide you with information on goods and services that are being sought by your state government, as well as about business-support programs.

✤ **Potential Customers.** Friends, family members, and customers of the competitors in your community can give you their opinions about your business idea and answer to questions such as: Do they think such a business (or additional ones) is in needed in your area? What would they be willing to pay for your products or services? What do they like (or not like) about your competitors' products and/or services? What can be done to improve them?

✤ **Suppliers.** They often can give you some insight as to present buying trends and who is doing well in your industry. You can find them at industry trade shows or through referrals from other business owners.

✤ **Trade Associations.** Look for those with local chapters that you can join and gain useful information about the latest developments in your industry. Read their journals and newsletters, which give "insider" information and tips. Attending and later exhibiting at their trade shows can give you valuable feedback on your proposed business products and/or services.

+ **Media Sources.** Local cable and national television channels, and newspaper advertising directories can provide the latest trends and buying patterns of potential customers.

+ **Internet Sources.** Industry sites, online newsletters, magazines (e-zines), newsgroups, associations, online chats, and more can all help you gather statistics, network with others in your field, and reach potential customers from either having your own site or being listed on a business group's site.

+ **Test Marketing.** Start your home business (or businesses) on a part-time basis and get customer feedback through question-naires or follow-up telephone calls about your products/and or services, your prices, your handling of customer complaints, and most importantly, if they would use your services or products again. Test marketing may also help you discover untapped mar-kets or unique niches, and possibly motivate you to go into a dramatic redirection of your business resulting in larger profits.

+ **Books, Small Business Publications.** Those detailing future consumer and business trends like *Clicking* by Faith Popcorn, *Future in Sight* by Barry Howard Mink, or *Trends 2000* by Gerald Celente < www.trendsresearch.com > can all help to give you some valuable insight for the long-term potential of your busi-ness idea.

+ **Businesses in the Same Industry.** Seek out owners of businesses similar to your idea outside your competing area and ask them if they would share some practical "working" tips plus their opinions about your industry's future direction.

+ **You.** Is this business idea something you would really like to do? Your venture will generally take longer hours than a regular job plus will require your personal commitment to it for suc-cess. For that reason, your business had better be something to which you want to devote your passion and energies.

Also ask yourself whether you can work from home. Success-ful home-based owners are self-disciplined, self-starters, cre-ative problem-solvers, and people who thrive on overcoming obstacles.

❖ **A Review of Your Start-Up Business Plan.** This will help you determine if your business idea will be profitable by having you do a simple break-even analysis. This analysis will help you determine—realistically—how many sales you will need to make to realize a profit after paying all your expenses.

If you have concluded from your research that your business idea will not have the customer base in your area to support it, do not despair. Conduct similar studies in nearby communities on your business concept, and you may find a different market—customers who may be more receptive for your new venture.

If after all your research, you still cannot find customers who want your product or service, then you have to ask yourself again: "Do I really have a potential business idea?"

Again, do not be disappointed if you conclude that this venture will not prosper—be glad you did not waste money on something that might have failed. Take a breath and start the research process again, into other ideas that show more profit potential. Statistics show that entrepreneurs are characteristically persistent, and remember that it takes them an average of three business attempts before they achieve a successful venture. Polly Harr says: "Try a number of places or people for feedback on your service or product. If the response is weak, try another area or another business idea."

It may take time to find the business that best matches you—and customers' wants and needs, but if you are determined to become a successful entrepreneur, thorough market research of your money-making idea(s) will help you turn your home-business dream into a profitable reality.

For More Information
Books
Which Business? Help in Selecting Your New Venture by Nancy Dresher. (Grants Pass, Oregon: Oasis Press, 1997).
The Market Research Toolbox: A Concise Guide for Beginners by Edward F. McQuarrie (Newton, NH: Sage Publications, 1996).
Researching Your Market, SBA Publications, P.O. Box 46521, Denver, CO 80201-46521.

Preparing Your (Marketing) Plan

If you have reached the point in your home business start-up where you're ready to start marketing you product, you will want to devise a marketing plan—how to make that connection between you and your potential customers. Here are some tips:

❖ **Assess the present situation of your business.** Is it just beginning? Does anyone know about it yet? What were some of the positive and negative comments you received during your test marketing phase?

❖ **Where do you go from here?** Set some realistic goals and then work backwards, writing down the steps you need to take to reach that goal.

❖ **Look for a "niche."** Find those customers whose needs are not being met. Pam, who had a successful bookkeeping business, found that her best customers were seasonal businesses—concrete or masonry contractors—whose wives usually did the bookkeeping duties. "Larger bookkeeping firms did not want to have them as customers because they were too small," said Pam. "Most of the wives hated doing their husbands' books because it led to so much fighting, and they were happy to hire me to do it!"

❖ **Prepare your messages.** This is where you can try both traditional forms of advertising and those "creative" methods you wanted to try. List the media outlets—columns, talks, etc.—and then write the ones that you want to do and can afford first. (See chapter 8, Advertising.)

❖ **Plan to use a combination of low-cost and fee-based promotions.** One woman who decided to sell instructional videos of her specialized craft says: "Producing videos is very expensive, but it is very important to point out that quality does not cost; it pays. Because of the quality of our first tapes, they sold so well that we went on to produce over 60 videos, with our first one still outselling any others in the industry."

❖ **Start now.** You want to put your plan into action and persist to keep it going and growing. Jeanie Swisher, who started her publishing business on a second-hand kitchen computer, has a sign hanging over her desk that states: "You can't do this, Jeanie." Those words never fail to put fire in her spirit. If you dare to tell her that she can't do something, she will show you that she can!

For More Information
Publications

Making the Rules by Jeanie Swisher (1999). Spectrum Publishers Direct, making the rules, 35 S. High St. #4001, West Chester, PA 19382 ($16.95). "Focuses on the many facets of running your own business including direct mail, multi-level marketing, Internet tips, Web site development and much more."

Marketing Plan Pro. Step-by-step software guide to creating a marketing plan. Check in local software stores or call Palo Alto Software at (800) 229-7526; < www.palo-alto.com > .

Marketing Standards

All marketing of goods and services follows certain standards or codes in conducting business. Here are some of the most recommended that you might want to apply in your marketing efforts:

❖ Do not promote what you cannot provide your customers.

❖ Let the quality of your work and service speak for itself and customers will speak about it to others.

❖ Follow your marketing plan to save yourself time and energy in trying to locate the best markets.

❖ Make your customer your partner. Learn your customers' specialized needs and wants and provide the goods or services to meet those.

❖ Stay current with your industry. "Keep investigating new ideas, items, supplies, etc., advertised in trade publications to update or improve your product or service," says Polly Harr.

❖ Make an editor your friend. If a writer has written a nice article about you or a radio personality has interviewed you, send them a thank-you note. Also be generous in giving them tips or leads for other business owners' accomplishments.

❖ Define your own business. You can pick up and practice very good marketing and business tips from other business owners—but run your business in your own way, at your own pace, according to your business plans. You are your business and thus what your customers like. Do not try to be someone or something you are not, or your business will lose its uniqueness—what makes it stand out from your competitors.

Marketing Your Image

When Jerrie first opened her home-based gift-basket business, she spent a good amount on brochures that described each basket and its contents along with prices and other gift suggestions. She says: "I knew I would be distributing these brochures to companies in my area, and I wanted the brochures to look professional and high-quality so they would know my gift baskets were, too." In marketing your business, you will be marketing an image—and you want it to be one of quality and professionalism.

Evaluating Your Results

After doing your market research, you now want to use the information you gathered. Here are some suggestions:

❖ Analyze your information—who would be the best customer for your product or service? Which people are not being served?

❖ Based on potential customers' feedback, concentrate on developing the products and services they prefer.

❖ Design your promotional materials and advertising to this target market on the advantages your business offers over your competitors'. Use the advertising venues that they respond to the best.

Time for an "Image" Update?

As your business grows, you may want to consider "upgrades" such as the following so your customers know you are a serious professional:

❖ Use a quality voice-mail system instead of the "tinny" answering machine.

❖ Get a cell phone or pager so your customers can reach you wherever you travel.

❖ Set up an e-mail address specifically to receive your business messages.

❖ Periodically upgrade your software and hardware to produce better quality printed materials, such as invoices and correspondence.

✤ Research further any related spin-off services or products in which potential customers expressed an interest. It may turn into a lucrative sideline.

Market research is not a "once-and-done" task but an ongoing evaluation to determine whether you are supplying your target customers with the services and products they want.

For More Information
Books
Target Marketing by Linda Pinson and Jerry Jinnett (Chicago, IL: Dearbourn Trade, 1996).
Finding Your Niche by Lawrence J. Pino (New York, NY: Berkley Publishing Group, 1994).

• SUCCESS SECRET 42 •

Determine the best marketing strategies for your business.

Marketing is communication and making the connections with the right persons or companies—those who will be interested in buying what your business is offering. The one point to remember is that marketing evolves and is constant. Here are some marketing strategies from women business owners I've spoken with over the years. You may want to use these for your home business.

✤ "Be persistent in letting businesses (customers) know of your services, and look for more than one way to advertise. Start with a good press release and go from there."
✤ "Introduce yourself to your clients and customers. The customers are able to meet you ask any questions they might have."
✤ "Offer a good product/service at a reasonable price. Imagine yourself in your customers' shoes and ask 'Why would I want to do business with me?'"
✤ "I keep in touch with my customers with regular mailings about special promotions I may have."

Questions to Ask to Define Your Target Market

Ask yourself (and potential customers) these (and other) questions to determine who is most likely to buy your product or service and how many such people exist.

✤ Who buys services or products like mine?
✤ If I sell to consumers, what are their profiles? Men or women? Age? Average income? Education? Where do they live or work? How much education? Interests or hobbies? Marital status? Children? Parents? Grandchildren? Pets? Reading preferences? Other?
✤ If I sell to other businesses, what types purchase my services and/or products? What industries are they in? How many employees (if any)? Are they home-based, small, or large companies? Are they interested in quantity or quality?
✤ What businesses would I be competing against? What kinds of services and/or products do they provide their customers? What do their customers like or dislike about them? How could I make my services or products more appealing than theirs? What methods of advertising do they use to reach their customers? Are there people they are not serving?
✤ What type of slogan, image, or picture can I display for my potential customers to make them remember my business?

The answers to these questions and others of your own should help you to target your marketing and advertising efforts to the best customers for your business.

✤ "Listen to your customers and keep up with the latest innovations in the industry so you can offer your customers up-to-date services or products."
✤ "Enjoying what you do comes across in the way you do business and makes it more enjoyable for customers to do business with you."

❖ "If you make a product, try to get as many of the items as possible out in the public 'eye'—with samples, models, give-aways, etc."

❖ "Be courteous to your customers and business friends with whom you network information. Send cards and thank-you notes when appropriate. They will return the favor with refer-rals and more business."

❖ "Do not be afraid to do a little extra than the customer expected or to fulfill a special request (if you are able)."

For More Information

Books/Publications

Creative Ways, Marcia Yudkin, Ph.D., P.O. Box 1310, Boston, MA 02117. Yudkin is a marketing expert and author; write for more information about her books, publications, and audio tapes or visit her site at < www.yudkin.com/marketing.htm > .

Guerrilla Marketing for the Home-Based Business by Jay Conrad Levin-son (Boston, MA: Houghton Mifflin Co., 1995).

1001 Ways to Market Yourself and Your Small Business by Lisa An-gowski Rogak Shaw (New York, NY: Perigee, 1997).

Marketing Strategies for Growing Businesses. SBA Publications, P.O. Box 46521, Denver, CO 8201-46521.

Uncommon Marketing Techniques by Jeffrey Dobkin < www.dobkin. com > .

Internet Sites

< www.ideasiteforbusiness.com > Idea Site for Business—Market-ing ideas, including advertising on the Internet.

< www.timevista.com > Time Vista Boardroom by *Time* magazine where you can query business experts about marketing and other business topics.

Associations

American Marketing Association, 311 S. Wacker Dr., Suite 5800, Chicago, IL 60606 < www.ama.org > . For marketing pro-fessionals.

• SUCCESS SECRET 43 •

Practice frugal marketing methods.

In starting a new business, you will have the dilemma of how much to budget for your marketing and advertising. However, some of the lowest-costing marketing methods can be just as effective (if not more) than the expensive ones.

❖ Offer free evaluations, samples, or demonstrations.
❖ Give out your business cards. Doree Romett, who has a gift-basket business, gives out samples of her chocolates wrapped in clear cellophane with her business name and information on a printed sticker.

Sampling Your Wares

You can often gain new customers by offering free samples of your product or even your services. Here are some suggestions should you wish to try this effective marketing technique:

❖ Secure a booth at a community event—fairs, bazaars, local trade shows, and other events.
❖ Offer to speak at a meeting of a community group and give out samples with your business card.
❖ Join with another home-based business owner whose products complement yours, and distribute or display each other's products—for example, sell your plants in another woman's specialty pots.
❖ Give gift-wrapped double samples to friends, family members, and neighbors—one to keep and one to give away. (Make sure your samples include your business name and contact information.)
❖ When traveling on business or vacation, always have samples with you to give to people you meet on trains, planes, buses, or even on the beach!
❖ Offer coupons for free samples or services in advertising mailers.

❖ Encourage referrals. One Web designer gives a discount to regular customers for every new customer they refer to the business.

❖ Send press releases to the publications and papers that your customers read. Talk to the editor *before* you send the release to find out the right person who should receive your release and ask about the format.

❖ Michelle Clevenger, who does desktop publishing for schools and small businesses, says: "Cold call. Choose a business district in your area and visit every company, introducing yourself and your new enterprise. Leave a flyer or brochure."

❖ Offer yourself as the "expert" willing to present a workshop or class on your topic or speak on a business topic to a local business association. Do not come across as hard selling, but rather teach on your topic and have some brochures handy if those who attend are interested in your services. One woman who raises and sells herb plants offers an evening course on how to use herbs in your diet.

❖ Join with another business in a marketing promotion. One woman with a garden consulting business offered a children's class on how to plant flowers for Mother's Day gifts at a local garden center. The children were happy with their flowers, the garden center owner was happy with the sales, and the woman received some business from parents who brought the children.

❖ "Meet as many people as possible," urges home-business owner Rosalie Marcus. "Tell them about your business—give them your business card—and you take theirs. You never know when you can network information valuable to you both sometime in the future."

These are just a few of the frugal marketing tactics you use to "get the word out" about your business. (More marketing and advertising tips will be discussed in the next chapter.)

For More Information
Publications
Marketing Ink, Creative Ink Marketing Communications, 3024 S. Glencoe St., Denver, CO 80222; < www.marketing-ink.com >.

Features low-cost, high-yield marketing strategies for small and home-based businesses.

Marketing for Small Businesses. SBA Publications, P.O. Box 46521, Denver, CO 80201-46521.

Taming the Marketing Jungle: 104 Marketing Ideas When Your Budget Is Low and Your Motivation Is High (1998) by Silvana Clark. Order for $6, shipping included, from 2100 Birch Circle, Bellingham, WA 98226.

THE GUERRILLA *Marketing NEWSLETTER* published by Jay Conrad Levinson. To obtain free information, write Guerrilla Marketing, P.O. Box 1336, Mill Valley, CA 94942, < www.marketing.com > .

• SUCCESS SECRET 44 •

Learn what government contracts (local, state, and federal) may be available for your business.

According to Dr. Robert Sullivan, the federal government is the world's largest purchaser of goods and services—over $225 billion a year. Depending on your services or product, you might want to consider contacting the government as your customer. "The U.S. Government buys just about everything you can think of," says Sullivan, "so it's likely that the product or service being offered is being purchased by someone at some agency. What is helpful for women-owned businesses is that most (government) agencies have a women-owned business advocate who will assist in dealing with that agency."

Sullivan continues: "Most agencies have women-owned business goals. For example, The General Services Administration (GSA) increased procurements with women-owned businesses from $97 million in 1992 to $352 million as of August 1998. Find contacts using the Internet—all the major agencies have very useful Web sites."

Here is some additional information for you about selling to the federal government:

❖ Determine the Standard Industrial Code (SIC) for your product or services. You will need this code in filling out any forms. The SIC codes are listed in *The Standard Industrial Classification*

Manual, found in the reference section of larger libraries or from the Government Printing Office. For price and ordering information, call (202) 512-1800, or write Superintendent of Documents, P.O. Box 371954, Pittsburgh, PA 15250-7954.

You will need a D-U-N-S® number from Dun & Bradstreet. For free registration, call (800) 333-0505. (Also see chapter 9, *Resources for All Entrepreneurs*, for more information about Dun & Bradstreet.)

Next contact The Central Contractor Registry (CCR), which will help you with additional registration procedures in being able to do business with the government. These include a CAGE code (especially if you are selling to defense department agencies); a registration in ABELS (Automated Business Enterprise Locator System), a database to register minority-owned businesses; and a PASS (Procurement Automated Source System) registration, which, according to Dr. Sullivan, is going to be administered by pro-net, < www.pro-net.sba.gov >.

This is not as overwhelming as it sounds. Here are the steps to work your way through:

❖ Look in your local telephone directory under the U.S. Government section for SBA offices near you.

❖ Call whichever office is listed—Small Business Development Center, General Services Administration Centers, Women's Business Development Center, Business Information Center, or SCORE office—and tell them you are interested in doing business with the federal government, or call the SBA toll-free number: 1-800-827-5722.

❖ Read books like Dr. Sullivan's to get an idea of the terminology and what is involved in the procurement process.

❖ If possible, talk to other women business owners who do business with federal, state, or local government offices for tips.

Another avenue you may want to pursue with an SBA representative is a "Small Business Setaside." Currently, any large company that has a contract with the federal government is required to set aside a certain percentage of their contract to women- and minority-owned businesses. The NFWBO says that women-owned businesses that produce goods (such as manufacturing and construction) and those in transportation or communications are among the most likely to sell products or services to government agencies and large corporations.

You can find a listing of all the major corporations that have federal contracts by going to the site: < www.sba.gov/sbainfo/fapa/allsubs.txt > . Rosalie Marcus, who owns a home-based advertising promotions business, says: "I was able to get a very good subcontract, by finding and then matching my business products with a larger company's that had a federal contract to produce these items."

The possibilities are out there and the federal government wants to help you. It can lead to a good business partnership and steady customer—"Uncle Sam."

For More Information
Books/Publications
Successful Proposal Strategies for Small Businesses: Winning Government, Private Sector, and International Contracts, 2nd Ed. by Robert S. Frey (Boston, MA: Artech House, 1999).
United States Government: New Customer! by Dr. Robert Sullivan (Great Falls, VA: Information International, 1997).
Commerce Business Daily. Department of Commerce news on contracts, procurements, and needs of U.S. government agencies. Is available at SBA offices, larger libraries' reference sections, or visit it online: < http://cbd.savvy.com > .

Internet Sites
< www.isquare.com > "The Small Business Advisor."
< www.entrepreneurmag.com/entmag/contract > *Entrepreneur Magazine's*—Information on big businesses looking for subcontractors.
< www.womanowned.com > WomanOwned.com. Entrepreneurial information including "Government Section," about getting government contracts.

• SUCCESS SECRET 45 •

Explore the possibilities of local, state, and
nationwide markets for your home business.

Local and State Procurement

For getting contracts with local government agencies—city, town,
township, borough, county—visit their offices and get a copy of what
products or services they put out to bid for local businesses and the
procedures for putting in bids to be awarded contracts. Attend meetings of the agencies to see how the meetings are conducted. Talk to
other business owners and/or members of business associations
who have dealt with these governments to get some recommendations. Make sure you are registered legally as a business and have
the insurances and licenses required for your business.

For business with your state, check at the office of your state
representative or state senator for free information about agencies
that help promote women-owned, minority-owned, and small businesses. See whether they offer seminars or workshops on state procurement practices. Also check in your local library or bookstore
for the latest editions of *Starting and Operating a Business in* . . . (there
is one in each state) by Michael D. Jenkins. Also check to see
if free books are available, such as *Starting a Small Business in
Pennsylvania*.

State Conferences

If you think your business has a statewide market, see what state
publications and newspapers reach your target market and advertise in those, or attend state-sponsored entrepreneurial conferences. Small Business Development Centers and Women Business
Development Centers, through or with the SBA, also work in conjunction with state agencies to help entrepreneurs. The SBDCs are
listed in your telephone directory's white pages, and a listing of
the Women's Business Development Centers' locations can be
found on the Internet: < www.onlinewbc.org >.

Competing with Large Businesses/Chains

How can *you*, the home business, compete with larger businesses or chains? The answer for many entrepreneurs is *not* to compete *with* them but *on all sides* with them. Here are some suggestions:

❖ Offer personal service, better quality, better prices. Go to a chain store in the spring to get plants, for example, and you may get a lower price, but no guarantee that this plant will grow or (even worse) that it isn't diseased. But if you go to a local nursery or home-based grower, you will get plants native to your area with "friendly" advice and growing tips to make sure the plant survives. One couple who has a small farm outside several suburban communities runs a wholesale business raising and selling pansies and a lucrative perennial business offering home-grown plants.

   Their prices are so good that gardeners from all around come to load up the little red wagons this couple provides with pot after pot of sturdy stock. The woman owner says it gratifies her, too, to know that she and her husband have helped beautify so many yards when her customers bring her photos of planted flowers they purchased from the couple.

❖ Get an Internet site for your business. No one can "see" the size of your business but millions of customers *can order* your products! (See chapter 13, Going Online for more Internet business information.)

❖ Focus the advertising on your target market. Accentuate the benefits your business can offer them over bigger enterprises.

❖ If you have a product that could meet the demand, consider selling on local and/or national shopping channels.

Especially these days, when many people feel like "just a number," treating your customers with respect and courtesy and giving them the best service or product will help ensure customer loyalty, no matter what the "Big Guys" offer them.

• SUCCESS SECRET 46 •

Explore the possibilities of going global with your home business.

International trade experts say the number of small business exports is growing. Depending on your service or product, your business may have the potential for markets worldwide. Of course, the Internet has opened unlimited possibilities for this. Karen Sauter, who owns a small candy-specialties business, Ann Hemyng Candy, Inc.—Chocolate Factory—(< www.chocolateshop.com >) ships her handmade chocolate candies all over the world to customers who have discovered her business through her Web site.

To find out if there are worldwide buyers for your product or service, contact the U.S. Export Assistance Centers, (800) USA-TRADE, which will help you find markets and develop marketing strategies. Also check the sources in *For More Information* on the next page.

Best Foreign Markets

Check with your local SBA-related office to see if they offer any SBA-sponsored conferences and seminars on how to export your product or service, and which world countries are actively seeking your services or products. Statistics by the NFWBO and other research foundations show that women's entrepreneurship is growing in Mexico, Ireland, Argentina, and many other countries.

After attending such seminars, you can participate in SBA-sponsored trade conferences and missions to help you find a world-trading partner at a low-cost outlay of your time and money.

Visit the SBA's Internet site: < www.sba.gov/ > From there a person can link to the home page for the Office of International Trade to access information about export products in demand by selected countries, etc.

If you join a national trade association in your industry and/or a national women's business ownership association like the National Association of Women Business Owners < www.nawbo.org > or Women Incorporated < www.womeninc.com > , you can network with other women business owners who are involved in international trade.

Shipping Globally

As you gather information about exporting possibilities, you will want to consider how you will learn the rules and regulations of international shipping and transportation. More than likely, these, along with other important details, will be offered at any international trade seminars you attend or through one-on-counseling. Here are some additional sources to help you find the answers you need:

♣ The Export Hotline: To register for information on market data on many countries and industries; visit < www.exporthotline.com > or try the U.S. Department of Commerce International Trade Office at (800) USA-TRADE or visit < www.ita.doc.gov >.

For More Information
Books/Publications

A Basic Guide to Exporting—Helps entrepreneurs to decide whether to market internationally; available from the Government Printing Office at (202) 512-1800.

Breaking into the Trade Game: A Small Business Guide to Exporting by the SBA and AT&T. Available free at local SBA district offices nationwide.

Building an Import/Export Business by Kenneth D. Weiss (New York, NY: John Wiley & Sons, 1998).

National Export Directory—Lists organizations, trade offices, Department of Commerce offices that offer seminars and other global trade information. Obtain from the Trade Information Center (TIC), listed on the next page.

Internet Sites

< www.ciber.bus.msu.edu/busres.htm > The Michigan State University Center for International Business Education and Research's site providing international marketing information.

< www.earthone.com > The Association for International Business—Information about world business.

< www.sba.gov/oit > The SBA's Office of International Trade.
< www.tradeport.org > TradePort—Designed to help companies compete in the global market.

Business Guides

Import/Export Business Guide, from *Entrepreneur's* Small Business Development Catalog. Call (800) 421-2300 to order the guide or a copy of the catalog.

Government Sources

International Trade Administration, The U.S. Department of Commerce, Herbert C. Hoover Bldg., 14th St. and Constitution Ave. NW, Washington, DC 20230, (202) 482-2000. Offers export counseling, overseas market research, export financing information, and advice on licenses and controls.

The Export Opportunity Hotline: (800) 243-7232. Answers questions on overseas trade.

Trade Information Center (TIC): (800) USA TRADE. Provides export counseling. Has an automatic phone-to-fax service providing answers to exporting questions.

The U.S. Export-Import Bank: (800) 565-3946. Has information on its various programs for marketing products or services overseas.

Organizations

Forum for Intercultural Communication (Forum) is a nonprofit research and education organization, which among other things, seeks "to promote economical development and local-global partnerships." Its publication, *Global Woman,* 2400 Virginia Ave., NW, Suite 102, Washington, DC 20037-2601, "links local-to-global issues as a resource for organizations and individuals seeking opportunities for investment abroad."

———

8

Advertising

When business is good, it pays to advertise, when business is bad you've got to advertise.

—Anonymous

No offense to pro-football teams, but people now seem to look forward to seeing the television commercials as much as they do the Super Bowl. Still, as entertaining (and expensive!) as some of the commercials are, some are just that—entertaining—but when the commercial is over, you have no idea what the company was selling! Two lessons about advertising can be learned here: You do not need to break your business's budget on ads to get your sales message across, and do just that—make sure your message is clear!

A home-based entrepreneur has to "test" different methods of advertising to see which one or ones are the most effective. For service-type businesses, word-of-mouth referrals from satisfied customers result in the largest percentage of new customers. Michelle Halbsgut, a certified massage therapist, says she does not even have to advertise to get her new clients because of all the referrals from existing ones. However, you do need to explore other ways of advertising—especially with a new business start-up, to announce a new product or service, when existing clients move or go somewhere else, or when your goals include future growth and/or expansion.

The advertising methods presented in this chapter are listed with tips and practical advice for you to use; however, they are by no means the only methods available to you. You can try them one at a time or test several simultaneously. One woman who has had three home businesses "tracks" her newspaper and magazine business ads by adding a code onto each one. For example, she will have her address listed at the end of an ad as such: Jane Smith, P.O. Box 55 1-PH, Everywhere, PA 55555. The number "1" is her code for the first ad placed and her initials "PH" are the code for that specific publication. She then assigns different numbers and initials for ads placed in different publications. This way she can record which ads have the strongest customer response and which ones are not worth the investment.

Of course, this is a very simplified way of "tracking" your ad responses, and just because an ad has a poor customer response does not mean you should not try that publication again for future advertising opportunities. Some factors that can contribute to lack of response to your ads include poor writing, wrong timing, lack of product photo, or wrong publication—your potential customers may not even read that particular magazine or newspaper or listen to that radio station or watch that television channel. You may want to consult with an advertising specialist—but more often than not, studying the publication or media in which you plan to advertise will give you insight to help you determine whether this will be your best advertising avenue.

The advertising departments or persons in charge of the publication can give you the details on their readership, listeners, viewers—demographics and statistics (income level, sex, family status, age, etc.)—that can help you match your potential customers with theirs. When considering where to place an ad, request that they fax or send this information about their customers. This will help you avoid wasting valuable advertising money. Do not be rushed by overzealous advertising salespeople into placing an ad. Do your research, and look at or listen to the ads they are currently running.

If you see or hear ads repeated, study those so you can see what kind are getting results. Ads that are getting poor responses will not be placed again. Know the audience you want to reach and how much you can spend. Some of the advertising departments will even give you advice as to the appearance and wording of your ads. Do not be afraid to ask lots of questions. After all, advertisers help to pay their bills!

Here are some questions you can ask yourself to help decide where to place your ad:

❖ **Does the price of the ad justify the response?** What percentage of your target customers can you estimate will read this ad? One woman selling her booklets took a classified ad in a popular parents' magazine for $2,000 and got only 20 responses. She placed the same ad in a local parenting newspaper for $20 and received 100 responses.

❖ **How often does your ad need to be run?** If you have a seasonal business selling herb plants (depending on your climate), you will want to run your ad more frequently in the growing season than the winter—unless you can come up with an herb product that you can sell year round, such as dried herbs or herb vinegars.

❖ **Will this advertising avenue enable you to adequately list all the facts and details?** You need enough space and time to provide the sales points that will make your target customers want to contact you.

The purpose of all advertising avenues is to attract customers and increase your sales. If you have conducted thorough market research and targeted the potential customers who are looking for a service or product like yours, then you are ready to decide what kinds of advertising avenues you are going to use. In order to do that, you need to consider what results you are hoping to achieve through your advertising. Here are just some of the results your advertisements can achieve:

❖ Bring in new customers.
❖ Increase usage.
❖ Produce customer inquiries.
❖ Announce new or improved products or services.
❖ Report awards, special recognition that you or your business have received.
❖ Announce special promotional events, contests, or sales.

❖ Help increase service or product recognition.

❖ Produce sales leads with announcements of toll-free numbers, discounts, coupons, etc.

❖ Increase publicity with your community involvement.

• SUCCESS SECRET 47 •

Take advantage of low-cost and easy methods to grow your home business.

Advertising costs can quickly consume a large part of new businesses' start-up costs and existing small businesses' operating expenses; but without advertising you'll have few if any customers or continuing sales.

Low-Cost Ideas

Fortunately, there are low-cost advertising avenues requiring more of your creativity and time than your dollars. Here are some suggestions:

Business Cards

One of the most important marketing tools for your enterprise is your business card. It is a tiny "billboard"—an advertising method that must capture a potential customer's attention and then explain in a few *memorable* images and words the product and/or services your venture offers. The cost of having business cards produced by your local printer can range from $25 to several hundred dollars. You can minimize this expense by using pre-designed papers and desktop publishing software.

One woman who could not afford business cards for her custom-cushions business typed and designed her cards, then had her local photocopying center run them off and cut them to the size she wanted. As soon as she began to get customers, though, she had her card designs professionally printed.

Because your business card is often the first introduction to likely new clients, you want to make sure it motivates people to contact you and (hopefully) purchase your services or products.

Dissecting Your Competitors' Ads to Improve Yours

Whether your business produces a service or product (or both), you will want to know the following:

* Who is your competition?
* What advertising methods are they using?
* Are they competing for the same target market or have you discovered a "niche" market that you would want your ads to attract?

Here are some ways your ads can "beat" theirs:

* If their ads give their hours—your ad could offer business hours for unusual times, such as Saturdays, early morning, or evening hours one weeknight.
* If their ads target bigger businesses, yours could say: "No job is too small."
* If their ads say: "We will not be undersold," yours can emphasize quality.
* If they sell the same type of service as you, you can offer a free consultation.
* If they have a free catalog of items, but you can't afford to give yours away, request money for a catalog that will be credited to your customer's first order.
* If their ads make no mention of personal service or guarantees, your ads can offer "special orders welcome," or "personal satisfaction guaranteed or your money back."
* If their ad mentions their product or service, your ad can offer a different or improved product, or tout that you use the latest technology in the industry.

Just remember: You cannot be misleading with your ads, and you should follow through with whatever "extra" service or product you advertise or you will lose the trust of new and any future customers.

Here are some suggestions about what your business card should (and should not) include:

Your Business Card *Should* . . .

✤ Highlight a slogan, mission statement, or catch-phrase that sets your business apart from your competitors'.

✤ Be memorable and stand out (tastefully) through its statements, design, color, size, etc.

✤ Inform customers where they will purchase your product and/or services—your home office? A retail establishment? Their home or place of business?

✤ Include your name (or a contact person's) and also your street address (post-office boxes are often not acceptable for deliveries).

✤ Be given out to anyone (and everyone!) who may be a potential customer or who could give it as a referral. Look for business card exchange opportunities at local and national business associations' functions and industry trade shows.

Your Business Card *Should Not* . . .

✤ Use inferior paper or printing quality.

✤ Have incorrect contact information, such as old phone numbers, inaccessible e-mail or Web site addresses. (Crossed-out information looks "tacky" and detracts from the professional image you want to project on a business card.)

✤ Include a logo or clip art that does not relate well to your business. (If illustrations don't depict the proper business "image," are boring or mediocre, or give an unclear picture of the services and/or product you're offering, then clarify with a tagline or change to more appropriate and self-explanatory illustrations.)

✤ Be difficult to read. (Stick to 8-point or larger type and clear fonts.)

✤ Use a dark background color. Dark colors inhibit people from making notations about you or your business on your card.

Do not be afraid to use both sides of your business card for information. One writer has her editorial services and contact information on one side, and a listing of her publications along with 800-numbers for ordering on the other side.

Most cards are standard size (2 inches by 3.5 inches); however, odd sizes like a bookmark (6 inches by 2.5 inches) or a folded card with important statements printed inside can be effective. Many professional crafters use a combination of business card/ hang tags that include special features or a little "story" that make their product stand out (for example: "made from recycled materials" or "a well-known Bucks County artisan").

Design stand-out business cards (*Victoria* magazine issues highlight women's unique business cards). Hand them out to everyone you meet. Ask relatives and friends to do the same. A well-designed business card can be a crucial factor in the continuous growth of your business!

Giveaways and Advertising Specialties

Give away free samples of your product, or use advertising specialties (such as magnets or mugs). Rosalie Marcus has had a very successful advertising specialties business, Lasting Impressions (< www.lastimpress.com >) for over 20 years. She says, "Advertising specialties—pens, calendars, magnets, etc.—offer home and small businesses a low-cost advertising medium with the longevity of repeated exposure. People always know where to find you by seeing your name and address over and over again as they reuse the item with your business name and address on it."

How can you determine the best type of advertising specialty for your home business? Marcus recommends you consult with an advertising specialty counselor who can help you choose a product related to your business. "For example," Marcus says, "if you have a computer business, you can give away mouse pads, wrist rests, or calendars. Or if you have a catering business, you can give refrigerator magnets away every time you visit a client." She recommends, though, that you choose an advertising specialty counselor with a good reputation and who knows the business.

Special occasions and holidays offer a unique opportunity to show appreciation to your loyal customers and attract new ones. As you make out your Christmas list for family and friends, do not forget to include your respected customers. According to several surveys, over 50 percent of businesses use the holiday season to market and promote their businesses, strengthen client relationships, and extend good will in their communities. Here are some of the many ideas you can consider to let your customers know you appreciate their patronage:

Gift Item Suggestions
* *Office Supplies:* calendars, pens, paperweights, calculators, free-standing clocks, personalized pocket magnifiers.
* *Food and Beverages:* fruit baskets, chocolate/candy, cheese/food baskets, coffees, liquors/wine, special nut mixes, flavored popcorns, gourmet pancake mixes and syrups.
* *Miscellaneous Items:* personalized leather organizer, bookends, copies of favorite books, videos, music, calling card/business card combo, subscription to favorite trade publication, special plants suitable for office climates, desk ornaments in the form of games, commemorative pins.

Additional Ideas
* If it is appropriate and unobtrusive, you may want to put your business logo and/or address on your gift to help remind the recipient of your generosity. A candy company owned by a mother-daughter duo specializing in handmade chocolates replicated a historic restaurant's building in chocolate for the owners to hand out to diners during the Christmas season.
* Have a celebration! One woman with a home-based antique business has an annual open house the first weekend in December, inviting her customers to come for refreshments and see her decorations. Each person attending receives a free ornament.
* Contribute to a charity on the client's behalf.
* Give your favorite customers tickets to a sporting event or a theater show.

Gift-Giving Tips
* Make sure the gift is appropriate to your targeted customers by taking the time to learn their interests and what they would find useful. Record these preferences for future reference.

❖ Give something that relates to your business, such as a gift certificate for your services, calculators if you are a bookkeeper, and so on.

❖ Spend an appropriate amount on a gift—too much may appear as a bribe, too little may make you appear "cheap." Check with your accountant to see what gifts are considered tax-deductible.

Just a Card
If you cannot afford to give business gifts, business associates and patrons always appreciate holiday cards. Visit your local printer for prices of printed cards or create your own with special holiday card kits and software found in many office supply stores.

Using the holidays to choose unique ways to demonstrate customer appreciation is a valuable chance to show your thanks to the clients you value most—and a smart marketing move to keep them from going to your competitors.

Signs
Design a logo and slogan that will become identifiable with your business name. Display them on all of your business cards and promotional materials, as well as on magnetic vehicle signs, lawn and/or sidewalk signs, T-shirts, flyers, etc.

Teaching
Give free demonstrations at trade shows and community or store events. Teach courses at local schools and/or community colleges or conduct workshops at business conferences or expos.

For More Information
Companies Offering Pre-Designed Papers
(Call for current catalog.)
NEBS: (800) 225-6380.
Paper Showcase: (800) 843-0414.

Software for Business Card Design
Microsoft Publisher from Microsoft®. (800) 426-9400; < www. microsoft.com > .

MyBusinessCards by MySoftware Company. (800) 325-3508; < www.mysoftware.com >.

Copyright and Royalty-Free Design Sources
(for business cards, brochures, newsletters, etc.)

Artville, 2310 Darwin Rd., Madison, WI 53704, < www.artville. com >. Sells royalty-free illustrations related to business on CD-ROM.

Dover Publications, Inc., 31 E. 2nd St., Mineola, NY 11501-3582. CD-ROM advertising art. Write for a catalog.

Associations

Promotional Products Association, International. < www.ppa. org > This trade association serves over 5,000 manufacturers and distributors of imprinted promotional products and services. Visit their site for more business gift-giving tips.

Internet Sites

< www.promomart.com > Promotions Mall.

< www.lastimpress.com > Lasting Impressions. Promotional ideas, information, and products.

Additional Promotional Materials' Tips
Do-It-Yourself Ad Tips

Here are some tips and guidelines to writing the copy for your home-business ads:

❖ Look at advertising as an investment, not an expenditure for your business.

❖ Even in slow times, keep on advertising—your name will stay in your customers' minds.

❖ Know what motivates your target customer to purchase your product or service.

❖ Advertise your image—inexpensive or expensive, quality or quantity.

❖ Make sure before you pay for advertising that it is going to reach the target customers best for your business.

❖ Get feedback from your customers with survey cards, calls, etc.

Brochures

Brochures can be a considerable expense, though with software such as *Microsoft Publisher,* you can make a variety of sizes. Although business cards are certainly handy to carry with you at all times to post or hand out to friends, business associates, and potential customers, brochures provide the opportunity to describe in more detail your business and its products and/or services. Many brochures include an insert to place the business card.

For More Information
Publications
Publicity on Paper by Marcia Yudkin, Ph.D. For ordering information and availability, write to Creative Ways, P.O. Box 1310, Boston, MA 02117.

Why Ads Fail
Here are some reasons some ads do not "hit" their target market:

❖ Not running (or sending) the ad often enough. Some business experts say that a customer must see, hear, or read your ad between six or seven times *before* they will make a purchasing decision.

❖ Forgetting to specify what actions those who are interested in your service or product should take (no directions such as "Call for a free catalog" or "Write for a brochure about our services").

❖ Not asking for professional help if you should need it in designing or putting together your ads. Remember that if your ads are not effective, you will be wasting your time and money.

❖ Not emphasizing how your products or services will fulfill your customers' needs.

❖ Using graphics or photos that detract from your business's message.

❖ Having an ad that's too complicated or too crowded. Sometimes a simple and concise ad can attract more attention than one that tries to say everything about your business.

❖ Not setting a goal with each ad's placement—How long will it run? What kind of responses do you hope it brings?

What to Say (and Not Say) in Your Ads: Advertising Legal Concerns*

Unfortunately, in today's litigious society, if you are not careful how you word your ads, you could be liable for a lawsuit. Here are some tips to help you write "legal" ads for your business:

❖ Have others view, read, or listen to your ad to see if they clearly understand your message and to make sure there are no misleading statements that might make customers think they are receiving a benefit or price that is not really being offered.

❖ Make sure you are not selling "snake oil"—that is, you make no promise or guarantee that your product or service will "absolutely" make your customers earn more money, improve their lives, or any other misleading statements you cannot prove. You must be able to back up any claims you state about your business or product.

❖ Use tentative language like "could," "may," "might," or "help" when extolling the benefits of your products or services.

❖ Contact the Federal Trade Commission, which regulates false advertising, for current brochures and information containing advertising guidelines. Call (202) 326-2222 or visit < www.ftc. gov > .

Creating Effective Display and Classified Ads

Many home businesses start with the inexpensive advertising method of placing their business cards and flyers on community bulletin boards, then place classified and display ads in local newspapers and weekly shopper papers. One way to save money on display ads is to go in with several other women business owners and share the cost of a larger ad. Many papers have seasonal and annual business supplements in their papers that feature articles

---

*Consult with your insurance carrier to see whether advertising is covered under your liability. Also consult with an attorney familiar with your business if you need more feedback on the legality of your ads.

about local businesses. This is an opportunity to have your business highlighted, so be certain to contact your local or citywide papers to find out whether they publish these special editions and the rates.

Here are some classified and display ad tips to make the most of your advertising dollars.

Classified Ads

Many home businesses, especially service businesses for consumers—such as at-home child care, garden consulting, professional organizing—spread the word through classified ads. Weekly shopper papers free to consumers have a large readership. The drawback is that ads that are not surrounded by a border or in bold print sometimes get "lost" among the garage sale and auto ads. Some papers place ads in categories while others do not. Try your classified ads in several papers to see which one(s) get the most customer response. Here are some tips for writing the copy for your classified ads:

✤ Include "action" words and phrases that motivate potential customers to contact you. For example: "Call now before supplies are gone." "Send LSASE for more information."
✤ "Reward" the potential customer with a free tip sheet or brochure for their inquiries.
✤ If you can afford it, set off your ad with a bold border to make it stand out.
✤ If you have more than one ad in a newspaper, have it coded; or ask those who respond how they heard about your business.

Display Ads

These can be very expensive, depending on the publication. You may, however, want a display ad if you're announcing a special event such as an open house or a famous guest. Or, consider a display ad if a holiday or season is coming up that relates to your business (such as custom costumes for Halloween or an ad for tutoring services in August).

You can design the ads yourself, hire an agency, or have the in-house staff at the publication assist you with it. However, if you spend a little time and study other small business display ads (including your competitors'), you can come up with a creative ad that will hopefully capture the attention of your target customers. Here are some ideas:

✤ If you have a logo or trademark, make sure you include it in all your ads to make the visual connection between your business name and the logo.

✤ If you have a good photo or illustration related to your business, it can draw more attention than just lettering.

✤ Write down the objective of your display ad and make sure your copy is written to achieving that objective. After the ad is composed, ask yourself: Does it tell the reader who I am and instruct the reader about my business and what I want my customer to do—call, write, visit the office?

✤ Use copies of the display ad in your brochures, sales letters, and other promotional material.

✤ Be positive in your wording to emphasize the benefits of your business to your customers.

✤ Repeat ads that are successful.

✤ Unless you are running for political office, the biggest display ad is not necessarily the most effective—the design and wording is what makes it unique.

For More Information
Software for Designing Display Ads
Announcements 6.0 Deluxe < www.parsonstech.com > .
Microsoft Publisher < www.microsoft.com/publisher/ > .
Corel Print House < www.corel.com > .

Tips for Writing Sales Letters
If you decide to do direct marketing to your target customers, you will have to make your sales letters stand out from the other multitude of direct-mail pieces that people receive in their mail each day. Doree Romett says her best advertising has come from building off her existing customer bases. "I have a fax database, an e-mail

database, and a general all-around database. Keeping my name in front of those already existing satisfied customers seems to build the best foundation of repeat business for my gift-basket business."

Here are some tips to get potential customers to read your direct-mail pieces:

❖ Have your envelope correctly addressed—correct spelling of recipient's name, complete address—and include your return address. Labels are handy and convenient, but sometimes people see these and assume (sometimes correctly) that the piece is part of a mass mailing from someone they do not know.

❖ Use quality business stationery that will reflect the quality of your business.

❖ Just as in a press release, tell the letter recipient the *purpose* of your offer and *what* you are offering in the first paragraph.

❖ Highlight the benefits your potential customer will have by patronizing your business.

❖ Close with an offer and the contact information for interested persons. You can include a postcard response (postage included).

❖ If you have a deadline for a special offer or want to highlight some other specific point about your business, include it in your P.S., which experts say most people read.

❖ Keep the letter short—some pieces of direct mail go on and on, making you search for the information.

❖ Get feedback on your sales letter from marketing experts or other business owners.

❖ Evaluate your mailing to see what response you have and to determine whether (and how) you need to revise your letter and/or your mailing list.

For More Information
Associations
The Direct Marketing Association (DMA), 1120 Avenue of the Americas, New York, NY 10036-6700, (212) 768-7277; < www.the-dma.org > . This is the national trade organization for direct

marketers. Contact them for a catalog of their industry books or visit their Web site.

Internet Sites
< www.gmarketing.com > Guerrilla Marketing Online—Sales and marketing articles.

———————

Evaluating Your Advertising Methods
Advertising can cost from nothing to thousands of dollars (and more!), and of course, takes valuable time you need to put into running and managing your business. You want to get the best responses for your money. Here are some ways you can track your advertising methods:

✤ Put codes on your classified, display, and Yellow Page ads.

✤ Offer a free tip sheet or toll-free number if you are interviewed or you advertise on TV or radio.

✤ If you exhibit at a trade show or business conference, ask if people would like to be on your mailing list, or offer a prize that requires people to place their contact information on an entry form. These are potential customers for future mailings and you can see how well that conference "worked" for your business by their responses.

✤ Offer a coupon in a paper that people can redeem.

With each ad, assess the "worth" of the ad and its responses. You can afford to run some ads on a regular basis to get a better overall assessment of their value in bringing in new business; others may be a one-shot deal. The goal is to try to "hit" your target market with your ads and to get them to respond.

E-Mail Ads
Business experts say business e-mail promotions are becoming an increasingly used method of advertising; however, many people "trash" the unsolicited e-mails they receive. Here are some pointers to get yours read.

❖ Do not participate in "spamming" (sending unsolicited e-mails). Develop an e-mail mailing list of people who contact you for more information via your e-mail address, which you list on promotional materials, in the tagline of articles you have written, and so on.

❖ Follow the benefits rule (as with all your advertising) by answering this question: How will my product or service help my customer?

❖ E-mail a number of times to help motivate the recipient to respond.

❖ Let them know how to respond—via e-mail? A visit to your Web site?

More information on how a home business can benefit with the Internet is offered in Chapter 13, "Going Online."

Telephone Advertising
Maximizing Your Phone/Fax System

E-mail business correspondence is now competing in popularity with business-related faxes, but faxes are still a fast way of transmitting documents and other information. Here are tips to maximize your fax use for your business:

❖ If you receive a large number of orders or faxes, you should have a dedicated fax line to receive them. If this is not possible, find out whether your local or national telephone company offers a fax mailbox in case your line is busy.

Condense your information onto the first page of your document to save both paper and toll costs.

❖ If you must use a cover sheet, include some advertising on it—such as your logo and contact information. One writer had her books' images reduced and created a fax template that has her book covers and titles on the bottom of her cover fax sheets. She also includes her e-mail and Web site URL.

❖ Use a type size no smaller than 10 points. Sometimes 14 and bold is even better because, since all fax transmissions are different, the larger and bold type will make some easier to read.

♣ If you are sending a document to a large office, print a large-type attention line with the person's name at the top, so it will not get lost in a pile of incoming faxes.

♣ Avoid large graphics that slow faxes down.

♣ If you are doing a large fax broadcast, you might want to use a fax service. Check in your telephone directory or ask your long-distance carrier if they have this service.

Toll-Free Numbers: Pros and Cons

Bert has a toll-free number for her mail-order curtain business. She lists this number in her magazine ads for people to request a brochure or for ordering using credit cards. If you have a product that appeals to customers in a region outside your calling area, an 800-number is a convenience for your customers and a good way to encourage contact from potential customers. The drawback is that when local people use this number, you have to pay for every call. Again, know the target market you are trying to reach and determine whether a toll-free number will be beneficial to them (and thus to you). The easier you make it for your customers to order, the more likely they will be to patronize your business.

Cold-Calling Tips

Lisa is an artist who sells horse-related art products: greeting cards, T-shirts, drawings, etc. She has found that feed-supply stores and equestrian shops are some of her best customers. Lisa will send a brochure and a sample of her card and then follow up with a call and then a visit. Sally Silagy, with her "Garden Lady" greeting cards, has found that cold-calling works well for her, too.

Yellow Pages

It is widely accepted that a *Yellow Pages* listing can be expensive. The breakup of the Bell system brought the opening of companies that have their own directories. Bell Atlantic, for example, also has a *Business-to-Business Directory* < www.BABtoB.com >. Check whether your phone company has a similar listing just for businesses. The Philadelphia, Pennsylvania, area (and a number of other cities) has *Women's Yellow Pages*. Call (312) 294-6300 for advertising information. *The Yellow Book*™ (formerly *The Donnelley Directory*®) < www.yellowbook.com > competes with the typical *Yellow Pages* directory sections and offers other options for small businesses.

The question is—and continues to be—Will ads in these directories be worth the investment? Will you recoup enough in sales to warrant the expense? This will depend on the type of home business you have. If you think a large number of customers will look for your type of business in these advertising pages, then you may want to consider the cost and take a gamble that it will bring increased sales in the long run.

For More Information
Books

Do It Yourself Advertising and Promotion: How to Produce Great Ads, Brochures, Catalogs, Direct Mail, Web Sites and Much More by Fred Hahn and Kenneth Mangun (New York, NY: John Wiley & Sons, Inc., 1996).

Promoting Your Business with Free or Almost Free Publicity by Donna G. Albrecht (Upper Saddle River, NJ: Prentice Hall, 1997).

Software

Microsoft Publisher < www.microsoft.com/publisher >.

MyBrochures Mailers & More < www.mysoftware.com >, MySoftware Company, 1259 El Camino Real, Suite 167, Menlo Park, CA 94025-4227; (800) 325-3508.

• SUCCESS SECRET 48 •

Know the most effective
promotions for your business.

In addition to traditional methods of promotion, you might come up with your own unique ideas. The ideas to follow were used successfully by women business owners.

Community and Charity Work
❖ Sponsor a scouting troop's float in a community parade.
❖ Sponsor a booth at a local fair or carnival.
❖ Sponsor a local community sports team.
❖ Contribute to a scholarship at a local high school.
❖ Donate a product or a few hours of service to a charity auction or raffle.
❖ Support a nonprofit organization in your community.
❖ Donate to a public radio or television channel, and offer to meet a contributor's donation to a certain amount (the channel will announce your business's challenge).
❖ Donate a savings bond to a student group that is cleaning up the streets on Earth Day.
❖ Offer to have a program related to your industry at a local library. One woman with a storytelling business regularly makes a free visit to children's library programs.

Of course, once you have sponsored one organization and group, you may be inundated with requests for more contributions. To handle this, set your budget and guidelines for your giving. If you identify with one or two of these groups—the ones dearest to your heart—others will realize you have made your commitments through these affiliations.

Creating a Logo—Your Image
As you work from a home office, customers do not have as much opportunity to develop an image of your business because they do not see a building, a famous spokesperson, etc. Thus, reinforcing the image your business does develop is important. One way to do this is to have a logo on your professional stationery and other promotional materials. You can use copyright-free clip art, but for the going rate, which can be fairly inexpensive, you can hire an artist or graphic designer to design one for you. A clever and well-drawn logo can help your customers to remember your business and keep it in their minds.

Creating Positive First Impressions

First impressions really can have a positive (or negative) effect on your home business. Here are some tips to ensure your first impressions will *favorably* impress customers:

❖ Welcome your callers with good telephone answering techniques or voice-mail messages. Be sure to return any calls within 24 hours or less.

❖ Impress prospective customers with quality promotional materials—clear and succinct language with no typos.

❖ Be ready to say in approximately 12 seconds (around 50 words) what products and services your business offers customers and how they can find out more information about it. Write it as a script and practice it.

❖ Think of your business as an entity and that all the parts—products or services, customer service, community participation, promotional materials, talks—reflect the purpose of your business and translate that impression—good and bad—to those who approach you for business.

Self-Promotion

Marketing and advertising pertain to selling your service and/or products, but promotion is about creating consciousness about you and your business. Promotion helps customers to automatically "connect" you and your product or service—they think of you as the "giftologist" if you have a gift-basket business or the "bridal expert" if you are a bridal consultant. You will want to foster this association in any and all ways that you can.

You can promote yourself by establishing yourself as an expert on your business—through the many ideas featured in this chapter. From speaking at group functions to being interviewed online during a chat, there are countless opportunities for people to see your name. All will help potential customers recognize you and your business. The more times others see your business name, the more likely they are to remember you and increase the likelihood of their buying your goods and/or services. Promotion is an ongoing process, but if you are successful in gaining instant recognition of your expert knowledge and quality products or services, people will buy from you.

_____

For More Information
Corporations

EntrepreneurPR, "America's #1 Small Business PR Firm," 3050 Fite Circle, Suite 209, Sacramento, CA 95827-1807, (916) 368-7000, < www.EntrepreneurPR.com >.

_____

Media

❖ Be available for last-minute interviews on local radio and cable television shows as a "fill-in" guest to replace unexpected cancellations.

❖ Write how-to articles for industry publications.

❖ Host a local cable television show related to your business—perhaps on growing herbs, "handy woman," home fix-it projects.

❖ Place classified ads in free shopper papers.

❖ Send out *newsworthy* press releases (see figure 8.1 for an example of a press release). Use them sparingly. Here is how to get the media to select your press release:

Daily editors and producers of various media receive an innumerable number of press releases announcing the release of new products, new business start-ups, individuals' achievements, or the dates of upcoming events. *Effective* press releases can result in a feature article, radio and television interviews; increased sales and new markets, and unexpected opportunities for your business. Conversely, poorly written press releases waste everyone's time and are usually tossed.

To get your press release picked, not pitched, before you begin writing it, ask yourself :

• What is the purpose of this release and who do I want to reach with it?

- What publications or other media would reach the most of my target audience? Am I well acquainted with these publications or media?
- What are the *specific names* (not titles) of the persons (editors, producers, etc.) who should receive my press releases? How do they like to receive releases—e-mail, fax, or traditional mail?
- What makes this press release a *news* story? How will the information benefit my target audience? Will it pique their interest and motivate them to respond?
- What actions do I want my audience (and/or media contacts) to take as a result of reading this press release?—Send or call for more information? Attend an event?

In writing the release:

- Be familiar with the standard press release format (see *For More Information* on page 213). Study examples of press releases and practice writing them. Keep your typeface and design plain and simple to read.
- Include the most important information in the first paragraphs—who? what? where? when? why?—because editors cut from the bottom up.
- Make it interesting, credible, and newsworthy. Include quotations and statistics from experts, agencies, and/or industry organizations. Add testimonials if they contribute to the release's value.
- Concentrate on the news story, not advertising.
- Your headline should clearly state why this news is important to your readers.
- Contact the media persons who received the press releases—preferably not at their deadline times—to see if they received your news release. Ask if you can answer any additional questions or further explain the value of your story to your audience, and ask for their feedback.

The headline or lead will often be the determining factor whether or not your press release will be published or broadcast—it will have to "hook" the media contact and audience into

[Person that will be called for further information on the release:]
Contact: Sally Smith
(612) 555-0000

Release at Will:

ABC PARTY STORE OPENS BRAINSTORMING CENTER

YOUR TOWN, STATE: ABC Party Store announces the opening of its Brainstorming Center, a free service for persons planning: a) wedding celebrations b) celebrations of any kind. The innovative concept in customer service offers books, videos, software programs, idea files, and catalogs of unique products to be used for planning inspiration. Customers are invited to use the reference materials at their leisure, either on-site or (optional) on a lending basis. Users of ABC's Brainstorming Center can sit comfortably at a conference table to peruse a wide variety of materials, take notes, and confer with associates.

[Always include a quote from owner] "Our customers are always looking for new ideas and guidance in their planning" states Jane Doe, ABC Party Store owner. She continued, "We are excited to not only provide so many planning aids, but also thousands of additional celebration items in our catalog collection."

A) On Tuesday, June 12, from 5–8 P.M., you can help celebrate the opening of the Brainstorming Center. There will be music by Elite Entertainment, refreshments by Castle Catering, prizes, and favors for everyone. Barbara Jones, owner of Elegant Events, will be on hand to answer your planning questions.

B) The grand opening week is June 10–15. During the week you can receive a 10% discount on all party purchases.

C) During the grand opening week, June 10–15, you will receive 5% discount on all purchases and 5% will be donated to_____.

ABC Party Store is located at 1020 Main Street and is open Monday-Saturday, 9–5.

For information, or to reserve space, call: [This name will be published] Sally Smith, (612) 555-0000.

-End-

(Anything below the "end" sign is a message to the editor and will not be published.) Your invitation to the open house will be sent separately.

Figure 8.1 Sample of Y2K Party Event Press Release by Patty Sachs, author of *52 Totally Unique Theme Parties* (MN: Celebration Creations, 1993).

paying attention to it. Wait until you have finished writing the release, then jot down several headlines until you believe you have the one that best captures your press release's slant and purpose.

You will know your release was well written not only if it is chosen, but when your phone begins to ring with potential customers and publicity far beyond your expectations.

For More Information
Books

Handbook for Public Relations Writing, 3rd ed., by Thomas Bians (Lincolnwood, IL: NTC Business, 1996).

Six Steps to Free Publicity: And Dozens of Other Ways to Win Free Media Attention for You or Your Business by Marcia Yudkin (New York, NY: Plume, 1994). Press release tips.

Internet Sites

< www.netrageousresults.com/pr/ > NETrageous, Inc. Free zine: Paul's Publicity Pointers.

< www.publicityhound.com > *The Publicity Hound*. An 8-page, bimonthly subscription newsletter featuring "tips, tricks, and tools for free (or really cheap) publicity," and published by Joan Stewart, a media relations speaker and consultant. To order a sample copy or back issues, or to subscribe, visit the Web site or write to Joan Stewart, The Publicity Hound, 3930 Highway O, Saukville, WI 53080.

Community Involvement
If your target market is local, here are some ways to get your business "noticed" in your community:

❖ Have a "happening"—contest, party, picnic, celebrity appearance—for your customers.

❖ Give product or service donations to a charity auction.

❖ Give free talks to community groups.

❖ Host booths at local fairs.

❖ Attend local business group meetings and business card exchanges.

❖ Patronize other home-based and small businesses. Participate in cooperative advertising for special newspaper business supplements.

❖ Post your business flyers, cards, brochures, etc., on community bulletin boards.

For More Information
Books
Light One Candle: A Handbook for Bootstrapping Entrepreneurs by Michael Richards (Iowa City, IA: Innovation Press, 1998).

Newsletter and Tips
A newsletter is a great way to keep in touch with your customers. It can consist of a number of pages or be just one standard $8\frac{1}{2}$-inch by $11\frac{1}{2}$-inch sheet folded over. Sally Silagy, who started her own home-based greeting card business, expanded to start a newsletter, *Creative Expressions*, for those who wish to either publish their own greeting cards or to write and illustrate for the industry.

For More Information
Books
Home-Based Newsletter Publishing by William J. Bond (New York, NY: McGraw-Hill, 1997).

Newsletters
Henry Ruddle's company, Ruddle Creative, publishes a excellent newsletter, *Newsletter Nameplate*, about producing/writing newsletters < www.ruddle.com >. For more information write: Ruddle Creative, 111 N. Market St., Suite 715, San Jose, CA 95113.

Guest Columnist

If you have the knowledge and expertise of your subject—especially how-to—you may want to submit a guest column to local newspapers or industry publications. Your columns cannot be promotional pieces for your business—but rather should contain information that will be of benefit to your reader. Your "advertising" comes in your tagline (has to be brief in most cases) at the end of the article. It will establish you, your business ownership, and contact information.

If you are interested in this type of promotion for magazines, write for a copy of their writer's guidelines and follow the publication's submissions procedure. For newspapers (some may ask you to pay if you want to put in a regular column), write around ten sample columns then make an appointment to see the editor. Study the publications and papers for whom you write to make sure:

❖ The readership will be interested in patronizing your business.
❖ The readers will be interested in knowing more about your subject.
❖ Your style and the paper's style of writing are compatible.

Look for business supplements published annually in newspapers on topics such as gardening, bridal information, or travel. These may offer opportunities for you to submit how-to articles on these topics—another opportunity to establish you as an expert and interest potential customers in your business.

For More Information
Books
You Can Be a Columnist by Charlotte Digregorio (Portland, OR: Civetta Press, 1993).

Television
One woman who grows herbs as a business approached her local Central Pennsylvanian cable television company to ask if she could

host a program on herbs. The company received such a good response to her show that it now has a regular weekly spot. If your business involves something your target customer can view on television, you may want to consider this promotional avenue.

Advertising on local cable television can be very affordable. Before considering this advertising avenue, request a demographic breakdown of the audience, along with a listing of available commercial times. Then decide whether your product and service will be of interest to this audience. Look for ad agencies or freelance TV commercial scriptwriters who can assist you in writing the script for your commercial.

Shopping Channels

Shopping and distribution channels are becoming a good outlet for many home businesses that have products to sell. These range from new inventions to specialty foods. Besides the large shopping channels, QVC and the Home Shopping Network, there are local shopping channels. If you are considering selling your items, you should be aware that these channels might require a 45 to 60 percent discount off the intended price for the network. You will also have to be able to supply the demand of orders that (hopefully) may come your way. Here are some guidelines if you are considering selling on a shopping channel:

❖ Call or write to the shopping network for a product application (see Resources on page 398 for addresses of QVC and The Shopping Network).

❖ Your product should have universal appeal, and not be generally available in stores.

❖ It should be in the price range of approximately $12 to $45.

❖ Your product should be a good one for on-show demonstrations and in videos.

❖ Your product should meet the needs of the targeted customer and fit the requirements of the products sold on the shopping channels.

Take your time to evaluate what the channels are selling—the prices, the products, the sales techniques—and then decide whether you could supply a demand at a price suitable for the shopping channels, the customers, and yourself (can you make a profit?).

Making a Video

With a product or a service, you can often make sideline profits if you have an instructional or demonstrative video made. If you think you can parlay your experience and knowledge into an instructional video, you might want to get some estimates from video producers in your area*. If your business budget is under constraint, you might want to contact a local high school or college to see if they would be willing to do an instructional video as a project for you.

For More Information
Miscellaneous Sources

David Cotriss, a freelance TV commercial scriptwriter, offers information through direct mail, books, and courses. For information, write to him at 3653 Slopeview Dr., San Jose, CA 95148-2828.

Staging an Event

A local hardware store often has two-hour workshops on Saturday mornings on do-it-yourself repairs or decorating techniques for home owners. If you want to highlight a new product or your business, you can invite a personality or expert to talk at a community meeting room in behalf of your business.

A woman who bought a toy store had a kite contest to announce the opening. If you can think of some fun event connected with your business, you can get free publicity and also spread some "good will" in your community.

---

*See my book titled *101 Best Home-Based Businesses for Women*, Revised 2nd Ed., 1998 for video university web sites.

Teaching at an Adult Evening School

Here are just a few classes taught through an adult evening school program by local home-based entrepreneurs:

* Entrepreneur—Herb Grower, Course: "Growing and Using Herbs in Your Kitchen"
* Entrepreneur—Dried Flowers & Supplies, Course: "Create a Eucalyptus Wall Fan"
* Entrepreneur—Ceramic Shop, Course: "How to Get Started in Ceramics"
* Entrepreneur—Financial Planner, Course: "Financial Strategies for Successful Retirement"
* Entrepreneur—Computer Trainer, Course: "Introduction to Word Processing"
* Entrepreneur—Yoga Professional, Course: "Yoga for Beginners"
* Entrepreneur—Image Consultant, Course: "A New You"
* Entrepreneur—Furniture-maker, Course: "Introduction to Woodworking"
* Entrepreneur—Professional Genealogist, Course: "Tracing Your Roots"
* Entrepreneur—Landscaper (Natural), Course: "How to Set Up a Backyard Habitat"

Courses like these are being held around the country in high schools, vocational and technical schools, community and four-year colleges, because there is a big market of adults who want to learn all kinds of new skills for their own satisfaction. Recently, learning centers have started in many towns, and most need instructors of various subjects.

If this interests you, contact the school and the person in charge of scheduling. Rates vary between $18 to $30 per hour, depending on the pay scale, but remember that everything is open to negotiation—especially if your course topic is in demand. Most courses run four to six weeks, but if you are reluctant to commit yourself for such a long period, offer the school several one-night courses. These are popular because many people cannot attend every session in a longer course, and therefore like "condensed" versions of particular courses.

In most cases, you will have to submit a course synopsis and outline, as well as a materials list of items your students may need to purchase for the course. If you include everything in one price, you will not have to deal with handling the money from all the attendees.

Teaching courses like these gives you wide exposure in your community. Just as in seminars, avoid pushing your business products or services in a hard sell. You can have extra materials for sale, but generally people appreciate you more when you genuinely want to teach them something. Have business cards available for those who ask for them. (For more tips, see # 50: "Make the most of publicity opportunities.")

Certificates and Coupons

Almost every home business can use coupons and gift certificates as a low-cost method to boost their sales. Here are some tips if you choose this advertising tactic:

✤ Use them in a drawing at a local event.
✤ Use them as prizes in a contest.
✤ Offer gift certificates at a charity auction.
✤ Team up with another home-business owner to have a display ad in a local paper's business supplement and include discount coupons for new customers.
✤ Advertise gift certificates in your regular advertising as gift suggestions for certain holiday gift ideas.

For More Information

Office supply stores have gift certificate books.

Check your office supply mail-order catalogs (such as Viking), which offer low-cost, custom-printed gift certificates.

Books

Big Ideas for Small Service Businesses: How to Successfully Advertise, Publicize, and Maximize Your Business or Professional Practice, Revised 2nd Ed. by Marilyn and Tom Ross (Buena Vista, CO: Communication Creativity, 1994).

Getting Business to Come to You by Paul and Sarah Edwards (New York: Jeremy P. Tarcher/Putnam Publishing Group, 1997).

Growing Your Home-Based Business: A Complete Guide to Proven Sales and Marketing Strategies by Kim T. Gordon (Upper Saddle River, NJ: Prentice Hall, 1996).

Starting from No: Ten Strategies to Overcome Your Fear of Rejection and Succeed in Business by Azriela Jaffe (Dover, NH: Upstart Publishing, 1999).

Surefire Strategies for Growing Your Home-Based Business by David Schaefer (Chicago, IL: Dearborn Trade, 1997).

• SUCCESS SECRET 49 •

Know how to make the most of trade shows and conventions.

Many associations have trade shows. You can find a listing of associations (including professional, club, and hobbyists) in the reference section of your public library in the current edition of *Encyclopedia of Associations* (Gale Research, Inc. < www.gale. com >). Trade shows offer opportunities for small-business owners to exhibit new products, reach new customers, and network information with others in their industry.

Tips for Success

If you have a product or service that you are ready to sell to an expanded market, you may want to try exhibiting at a trade show. There are four basic types of trade shows:

❖ **Local**—often sponsored by your local business associations or a specific industry and usually located in or near your community.

❖ **Regional**—cover a certain section in the country.

❖ **National**—exhibitors usually include a particular industry whose attendees can come from a several hundred mile radius.

Customer Considerations

It costs less to keep a customer than to get a new one, and *word-of-mouth* referrals are one of the best advertising avenues. Here are some ways you can let your customers know you appreciate them:

✤ Send thank-you, birthday, and seasonal cards.
✤ Offer special sales for loyal customers.
✤ Handle customer complaints quickly and to their satisfaction.
✤ Always do a little extra for your customers.
✤ Be professional and respectful to all customers.

Remember: customer satisfaction is the best (and lowest-cost) advertising avenue of all. Put customers first, and your product and/or service will practically sell itself.

✤ **International**—attract worldwide exhibitors and attendees and usually are a showcase for new products and network industry information via workshops, seminars, etc.

To find a trade show that may be suitable for your business, check with local business associations and those in your industry to see if they sponsor any suitable shows for your business. Talk to other business owners in your industry for leads. Before you make arrangements to exhibit, make sure you visit the show to get an idea of how booths, etc. are set up.

Bert exhibits every year at three-day regional home show at a convention center outside of Philadelphia and at the Allentown State Fair, which features businesses from the surrounding areas. She is amazed how many new customers she picks up from her own hometown who were not aware that she carried certain curtains.

Iris Kapustein runs a home-based trade show consulting business. She offers this advice to trade show exhibitors: "How to Make Yourself Stand Out as a 900-Pound Gorilla at Trade Shows: Guerrilla Tactics That Can Set You Apart From and Above Large Competitors."

❖ Do not bother your budget by assuming you "must impress" prospects. Rather, be sure you communicate effectively the second a great prospect spies your booth. Studies prove that signage is not what draws a prospect; product is.

❖ Make your graphics BIG, **BOLD**, & SIMPLE. It's cost-effective—and more importantly, it works!

❖ Do not have costly giveaways—instead use cost-effective but creative premiums.

❖ Send customer-driven materials to qualified buyers within two days.

❖ Research by Trade Show Xpress finds attendees initially visit your booth to play the "rating game." Yes, they will be back if you satisfy their initial informational needs. In order to survive the cut, remember these six words: Communicate, Communicate, Communicate = Listen, Listen, Listen.

❖ Are there off-hours when you can afford to relax? Trade Show Xpress finds that serious buyers use less crowded hours to truly cut major deals. So be ready early morning and late afternoons—even when the pace seems slow.

❖ Major buyers are often members of teams, especially in high-ticket buys. So you must find out what other key decision makers they have at the show—and who must be contacted back at the corporate office.

❖ Plan to devote time to see and hear all you can at competing booths. Evaluate your competitors and have your staff do the same.

❖ The secret to appropriate trade-show attire is to take your cue from clients and prospects. While the overall trend is for casual dress, exhibitors in dressier attire than show attendees will still be approachable but look professional.

For More Information
Consultants
Trade Show Xpress, 6992 Lismore Ave., Boynton Beach, FL 33437. The "How-To" specialists of successful trade show exhibiting offer comprehensive "how-to" training programs—as well as a

self-study audio training program, consulting services, and out-sourcing services. Also advertising specialties for business promotions, <www. premierpromos.com> for more information.

Internet Sites
<www.tscentral.com> An Internet-based provider of information, products, and services for the worldwide events industries.

———

• SUCCESS SECRET 50 •

Make the most of publicity opportunities.

Purpose
Understand the power of publicity. You know your business best and know you offer quality work and service, but promoting it is often hard for us—women especially (though we're getting better at it!) because we are taught we should not be too boastful or proud. Well, modesty may have worked for your mother's generation, but not so for you as an entrepreneur! If you do not get publicity, your customers will never know you exist. There are ways to use publicity that make it seem as though others have discovered you. Here are some suggestions:

❖ If you will be exhibiting at an out-of-town show, contact the media that will be covering the event to get the name of the editor or writer responsible for reporting it. Send them a brochure and some information about yourself to give them a "friendly" contact to interview and get yourself free publicity.

❖ Do *regular* mailings of *newsworthy* information about your business (awards, new product, a different slant on a story, some way your business relates to a "hot" news story or event) to publications in your industry or small business publications looking to profile up-and-coming entrepreneurs.

❖ If you have been interviewed by a television or radio personality, send them regular mailings; plus let them know you are available for last-minute interviews should someone have a cancellation.

✤ Include photos of yourself and, if applicable, your product.

✤ Include contact information on your letters and queries and have everything double-spaced and typed.

✤ Write instead of calling the contact person—and make sure you have his or her name spelled correctly.

Learn the "rules" of generating publicity for your business and help the media with leads for future stories (on other entrepreneurs, for example) and they will respond in kind with good coverage for you and your venture.

Getting Clients to Refer You

Watch how many commercials on television feature testimonials and endorsements of products and services. Of course, those infomercials are not particularly believable (do you ever wonder where they get those "clapping" audiences?), the endorsers often lack sincerity, and the advertisers must list that this is a paid advertisement. Here is how you can get your clients to endorse your business:

✤ Ask customers to write or e-mail spontaneous comments and ask whether you can use their endorsement in future ads. Send them an edited version (if theirs is too long) for them to okay and sign.

✤ Send response postcards with short survey questions (with return postage).

✤ Make sure they know how and where you will use their endorsements and what information they prefer you not print.

✤ Offer in your general mailings to give customers a discount for every paying customer they refer to you.

✤ Use statements that highlight specific advantages that your business brought the customer.

✤ If it is another business associate, offer to return the favor if you used their business product or services.

Keep these endorsements and referrals in a file should you ever need to substantiate them, and do not forget to thank them for the nice comments. Word-of-mouth can be the most valuable of all advertising methods for a home business. Encourage it through good customer relations, services, and products.

_____

For More Information
Books
Don't Take Our Word for It by Godfrey Harris (Los Angeles: Americas Group, 1998).

Internet Site
< www.americasgroup.com > Web site for *Don't Take Our Word for It* (above).

_____

Overcoming Shyness
One reason you may have been attracted to having a home business was that you could be in your own little world and not have much interaction with others—especially if you are shy. Realistically, there are few businesses in which you won't have to talk to others. Customers, other businesspeople, suppliers, salespeople, and so on are just some of those you'll need to communicate with if your business is going to thrive. It will be even worse for you if you have to do "cold-calling" or public speaking. Here are some tips for you to overcome your shyness:

* Talk to other women business owners about how they handled situations they wanted to avoid.
* Set objectives for your business and force yourself to take a few steps each day toward achieving those goals. Handle the things you hate first in the day so you will not dread it all day long.
* Write your "script" or sentences beforehand so you will know what you are going to say on the phone, to a banker, or to a group. More times than not, you won't even use your script, but you'll have the assurance that you can look at it should you have a temporary mental lapse.
* Arrive early at gatherings so you can assimilate your surroundings and all "eyes" will not be focused on you should you arrive late.

❖ Encourage others to talk about their experiences or their businesses. It makes for a much more interesting conversation, and
people will be grateful that you listened to them rather than constantly talked about yourself.

❖ Push your "envelope." Accept that you are going to be nervous—
whether you're meeting new customers, making sales calls, or
speaking in front of a group—then focus on what you are going
to say. After all, if it is your business, you will know what you are
talking about. *You* are the expert.

Just do not let your shyness and fears prevent you from achieving all you can do with your business.

• SUCCESS SECRET 51 •

Promote your business through public speaking engagements or seminars.

You may have hated giving book reports in school, or quake at the
thought of having to stand up in front of more than five people. Now
as a business owner, you may be asked to talk at a local business
group or civic organization. Your first impulse to such a request may
be to respond with a resounding "No!" Before you do, realize that
you may be turning down a free and effective method of promoting
your business and establishing yourself as an expert in your field.

Many home-business owners find that they receive so many requests that speaking and conducting workshops can be a lucrative
sideline. Patricia C. Gallagher is often asked to speak at parents
groups because of her parenting books. Her audiences relate very
well to the escapades of her four children. Another woman who has
a thriving tutoring business is often asked to speak at teacher-parent
groups, giving tips for helping children succeed in school.

Here are some tips that other women business owners have
given on public speaking and/or leading workshops and seminars.

❖ Try to get some payment. Although you may want to give one
or two talks free (for the experience), you will want to get paid
if you choose to actively seek speaking or seminar engagements.

- ❖ Take some public speaking courses at local community colleges or enroll in such courses as those offered by Dale Carnegie.
- ❖ Find out the make-up of the audience with whom you will be talking—age, occupation, income-level.
- ❖ Make up an intriguing title to attract those attending and provide information that will benefit them so they feel their attendance is worthwhile.
- ❖ Practice your talk. If possible, have someone make a videotape of it so you can correct distracting mannerisms or determine whether you are speaking loud enough.
- ❖ Try to visit the room in which you will be talking beforehand to get some idea of the layout and facilities.
- ❖ Get someone to take a couple of good photos of you talking that you can use in future brochures or promotions.
- ❖ Get someone to critique your talk so you can improve your presentation.
- ❖ Give illustrations of real people in real circumstances to illustrate your statements. It will make your talk more memorable.
- ❖ Establish the time you are supposed to talk. Do not go over the set time, and do not be afraid of stopping a few minutes early (very few complain that a speech or talk was *too short!*). If you are teaching a class or seminar, give periodic breaks. This will also be the time when those who were hesitant to ask questions will most likely come up to speak to you one-to-one.

For More Information
Books
Speak and Grow Rich by Dottie Walters (Englewood Cliffs, NJ: Prentice Hall, 1996).

Internet Site
< www.walters-intl.com > Web site for *Speak and Grow Rich* (above).

Start-Up Guide
"Seminar Promoting," Entrepreneur's Business Start-Up Guides," $59 + shipping and handling. Call (800) 421-2300.

Successful advertising is that which effectively communicates to both your steady and potential customers that your product and service is durable, reliable, and can fulfill their needs and be beneficial to their personal or business lives. One more note: In your ads, make sure you include when, where, and how your customers can contact you (phone? business card? e-mail? visit?) and make it *convenient* for them (toll-free number? reply envelope with postage? coupon?). Do whatever your particular advertising avenue (and your budget) permits.

9

Resources for
All Entrepreneurs

If women's businesses keep growing as they have been, we can imagine owning half the assets in the world.

—Rona Feit

• SUCCESS SECRET 52 •

Choose the best experts to help
you with your business concerns.

Part of the challenge of being an entrepreneur is having to handle the tasks for which other companies have specialized employees—accounting and bookkeeping, publicity, marketing and advertising, for example. You may be able to do some of these tasks well, but you will probably not be able to take care of *all* of them competently, especially if your business takes off. What should you do? Know what you do well and can handle, and outsource the rest to others and consult with your experts in your business. If you do a poor job because of your lack of experience or knowledge, it can hurt the credibility and profits of your business.

When Chrissy Carroll was asked how she was able to manage everything from home—opening a second comedy club, managing her comedian husband, and being mother to two little girls, she said: "I hire the right people." Pam, who started her home business re-manufacturing toner cartridges six years ago and has since expanded to include eight employees, advises new entrepreneurs: "Surround yourself with talented people. I started my business with absolutely no experience, [but] found a good accountant, great vendors, and leaders in my industry."

Tips on How to Find Experts

What kind of experts do you need? Depending on your business, they can include the following:

✤ **Professionals**—Accountants, lawyers, insurance brokers, tax specialists, financial planners, bankers, business coaches, bookkeepers, home-office designers.

✤ **Specialists**—Computer consultants; professional organizers; virtual assistants; graphic designers; professional business planners; information brokers; advertising, marketing, and printing specialists.

✤ **Technologists**—Computer maintenance and repair, desktop publishing, Web site design and maintenance.

✤ **Other**—You can also hire other independent contractors or home-business owners to clean, shop, and run errands for you if you do not like or have time to do routine chores.

Because each business is different, you're likely to modify this list slightly. To find the experts you need:

✤ Check with trade associations like the Independent Computer Consultant's Association (ICCA) < www.icca.org > (314) 892-1675; or the American Woman's Society of Certified Public Accountants < www.awscpa.org > (800) AWSCPA-1; (800) 297-2721, for members in your area.

✤ Talk to other women business owners for referrals and recommendations.

✤ Check with local business organizations and chapters like the Chambers of Commerce, National Association of Women Business Owners (NAWBO).

Be Ready for Computer Troubles

Whether you are experienced with or new to computers, you will inevitably encounter computer problems—either with mechanical operations or with software. Here are some suggestions to help you deal with techno-breakdowns:

❖ Check your manuals and "Help" functions that come with computer and software. Should your file "crash" as you're working with it, try the "Help" menu for programs that can often "repair" the disk and save your file.

❖ *Before* you purchase any hardware or software, research what each manufacturer offers in terms of warranties, tech support, and so on. Dependability, fast repair service, on-line support, and home-office visits are all important to prevent delays in your business output due to malfunctioning equipment or software.

❖ Interview computer consultants in your community *before* you have problems so you know who to contact quickly and can get back to work with minimal disruption.

❖ If you buy a new computer system, keep your old one. Although it may be slower and lack the latest features, you can use it while the other is being serviced.

❖ Look in telephone directories like the *Yellow Pages* or in special directories like the *Women's Yellow Pages*.

❖ Look on the Internet at women's sites, such as "Field of Dreams," < www.fodreams.com >, and "Mom's Network Exchange," < www.momsnetworkexchange >, where women can list their businesses.

❖ See if a local school or college with business majors would be willing to help you with certain aspects of your business as one of their projects.

Trying to balance the demands of managing the business and being responsible for the service or production can be a drain on you both physically and mentally. By using experts and outsourcing the duties that do not impact directly on your bottom line, you can better focus your energies on fulfilling the needs of your customers and turning your business into a success.

Selecting a Lawyer

A lawyer familiar with home and small businesses is an expert who can help prevent you from making mistakes for which you could be liable in a lawsuit. Here are some reasons your home business might need to consult with a lawyer. Of course, lawyers have different areas of specialization, so you may be consulting with more than one in your course of doing business.

✤ To help you register a name for your business and set up the legal structure of your business, such as a partnership agreement or some form of corporation.

✤ To help you look over contracts with independent contractors, other businesses, etc.

✤ To assist you in writing waiver forms that you may ask your clients to sign.

✤ To help you in wording your advertisements so they comply with FTC (Federal Trade Commission) laws.

✤ To prepare for future growth, sale, or the bequeathing of your business to heirs or partners.

✤ To help you apply for a patent.

Tips for Lowering Legal Fees

It does not take much to have legal fees quickly mount up. Here are some tips to keep your legal fees affordable:

✤ Ask! So many of us do not ask doctors, lawyers, or other professionals about their fees. Unless they are working for a firm, many of these experts are running a business just as you are, so ask for their rates, just as they would request yours.

Make sure you inquire about additional billings—photocopying, research, assistants' fees.

If you know you will not be able to afford these services, get referrals from other small business owners to find a small business lawyer that can "fit" your business's budget.

✤ **Ask your lawyer** if she is familiar with the type of legal help you need. If she is not, you may want to go to one who is already versed in the area you seek information and will not have to do extra (expensive) law research.

✤ **Be specific** about what you want drawn up, reviewed, etc., relating to your business. Type up and organize your own version so your lawyer will be able to include all the specifics you have indicated.

✤ **Do preliminary research** that you can do yourself or have an independent paralegal or legal secretary (who charges lower fees) assist you. Many county seat courthouses have legal libraries in which you can do research.

✤ **Outline your meeting** with your lawyer on paper so you will go directly from one point to another without wasting time getting off track or trying to remember what it was you wanted to accomplish.

If you are in business, sometime or other you will likely need a lawyer. Choosing one who is fair and trustworthy can give you the peace of mind that someone dependable will be available to help with any legal concerns that might involve you and/or your business.

For More Information
Books
Legal Expense Defense by Dennis M. Powers (Grants Pass, OR: The Oasis Press, 1995).

Legal Guide for Starting and Running a Small Business, 4th ed., Vol. 1 by Fred S. Steingold (Berkeley, CA: Nolo Press, 1998).

Internet Sites
< www.abanet.org > American Bar Association; (312) 988-5000.

< www.courttv.com/legalhelp/business/ > —CourtTV Legal Help's Small Business Law Center; tips on locating a lawyer, composing business documents.

< www.nolo.com > Nolo Press—specializes in legal books, many dealing with small business issues.

Selecting a Small Business Accountant

When Sandy and Charlene, who operated a home-party crafts business, hired an accountant to help with their accounting, they said it was one of the best business decisions they made. "He showed us how to set up our bookkeeping system and then reviewed our accounts with us monthly, to make sure we were charging enough to even *be* in business."

Here is how you can determine whether an accountant is the right one for your business:

* Choose one familiar with home business financial concerns and taxes. Do not be afraid to ask for names of other clients who are home-business owners and contact some of them for their opinions.
* Ask about rates. You want to know early whether you can afford the services.
* Choose one that is licensed to practice in your state. Whether you want an accountant who is also a certified public accountant (CPA) is your decision (not all accountants are CPAs). The advantage of doing business with a CPA is that CPAs are certified to handle certain business matters that an accountant cannot—such as certifying financial statements and conducting audits.
* Choose one according to your accessibility needs—either one who works restricted business hours or one who is also "on-call," available for questions at other hours (though probably not at 2 A.M.!).

In choosing the best accountant for you, write down the needs for your business: What can your business budget afford? Ask for referrals from other home-business owners, then personally interview several accountants until you are satisfied that the one you have chosen will help you keep your business financially "fit" and stable.

Tips for Working with Your Accountant

The process of working with any of your experts is not just a one-way street. Sure, you are paying them for their expertise, but you will want to "help" your expert by learning methods of preparation you can do to make their job of helping you a little easier. This will foster a good working relationship (and save you both time and money). Cheri Hutchinson-Freeh, CPA, advises women in working with their accountants "to be as organized with your records as possible." She recommends you use software accounting programs like *QuickBooks* to help. Hutchinson-Freeh says: "The better organized my clients are, the less time I have to spend on preparing their accounts, and the less money I have to charge them."

For More Information
Associations
American Institute of Certified Public Accountants (212) 596-6200 < www.aicpa.org > .
American Woman's Society of Certified Public Accountants (800) AWSCPA-1.

Determining Whether or Not You Need a Consultant
Consultants are specialists in their industry or in aspects of business—start-up, marketing, business plans, or advertising, for example. How do you know when to hire one for your business?

✤ When you are overwhelmed with information on a particular topic and are unable to decide which information will have the biggest impact on the success of your business.

✤ When you are planning to expand your business and hire employees.

✤ When there is a problem with your business, but you don't know its cause or how to remedy it.

✤ When you're just starting your business (this is a good time to select the consultants to whom you'll refer repeatedly for expertise).

✤ If you have hit a slump in your enthusiasm (or in your business finances after working several years) and feel you've run out of ideas to make your business more profitable.

One woman entrepreneur whose home business is located in a commercial district hired a marketing consultant she met through her home-business association. She says: "He gave me marketing strategies that had never occurred to me, even though I have been in business over fifteen years. For example, simply adding a banner outside my home-based shop that said what items my business sells. Since I have put it up, I have had a number of customers stop in and tell me they did not realize I had the products they wanted."

Tips for Choosing a Consultant

✤ Get names from other home-business owners, business organizations, or trade publications articles and ads. Ask those who refer you how their businesses benefited from the consultants' services and what they did and did not like about these experts.
✤ Make a list of as many names as you can and meet with each of them so you can see whether they understand what your business goals are and in what directions you would like to head.
✤ Choose a consultant that specializes in the problem with which you need assistance.

Questions to Ask a Prospective Consultant

Here are some questions to help you select your consultant, but do not be afraid to ask as many questions as you need to help you make your decision.

✤ What is your area of expertise? Background? Experience? Training? Education? Certification? Is it related to my business?
✤ What are your rate terms? Free consultation? Rates per hour or by the project? Ongoing or sliding scale?
✤ Who are some other home business owners you have helped?
✤ Are you a member of any trade associations or business organizations?
✤ If I do not feel we can work together, can I expect to have all or part of the fees refunded?

Once you have selected a consultant, you will want to be open to his or her suggestions. After all, you have hired this person to help improve your business. If you are not ready to implement his or her suggestions, then you should end the working relationship and save both of you time and money. On the other hand, if you are not receptive to new ideas for your business, you risk stagnating as new trends and advancements take place. Your competitors will not ignore these ideas in their quest to attract new customers—possibly yours!

———

For More Information
Publications
Consultants & Consulting Organizations Directory (Detroit, MI: Gale Research, 1998) is a large two-volume reference, most likely found in larger public or college libraries. More than 400 consulting specialties are featured.

———

• SUCCESS SECRET 53 •

Take advantage of additional resources available to help entrepreneurs.

Community Resources
As was discussed in previous chapters, the resources available in your region will be a unique combination of local, state, and federal agencies; associations; and educational institutions. Check with your local government's office for their manual on requirements such as zoning or permits you'll need to conduct business in your community.

Libraries
One of the best places (and it's free!) is your local public library. If you have not been in a library since you were in school, it's worth your time to visit and take a tour. If you visit when it isn't busy, you can ask one of the librarians or assistants to give you a quick tour—depending on the size.

Libraries are supported by public or private funding. Now many public libraries are connected to one another in a countywide or citywide (or even statewide) computer system, enabling you to request a book from another library via inter-library loan. A community college in your county, for example, may be encompassed in such a system. If there are four-year colleges or universities in your area, you can do research there and may also be able to check out books.

First, learn how to operate the online catalog, which can locate books, periodicals, and other resources, depending on the systems available. Here are just a few of the business resources you can find in a public library (depending on its size and budget):

❖ **Publications and Periodicals**—consumer and business magazines (home, small, and large business) and local and national newspapers, such as the *Wall Street Journal* and *The New York Times*.

❖ **Books**—business books are usually found in the 300 and 600 sections (according to the Dewey Decimal System). Books on specific businesses may be listed by their subject matter. Also check to see whether your library system has the *Books in Print* database, with which you can look up almost any book on any subject that is in print.

❖ **Reference**—Larger libraries have specialized reference librarians who will help you answer questions, and some even have special reference sections for business.

Here are just a few of the many, many sources available to help you find business information:

❖ **Community**—telephone directories, local business listings, local ordinance books, etc.

❖ **State**—directories of state offices, colleges, grants, etc.

❖ **Federal**—references containing government agency offices and contact information, etc.

❖ **Business Reference Annuals:**
  • *Business Information Desk Reference: Where to Find Answers to Business Questions* (Macmillan, New York).
  • Gale Reference Books (Detroit, MI; Gale Research, annual). May be available in larger libraries or through their Web site: < www.gale.com/gale.html > .
  • *Business Plans Handbook*
  • *Encyclopedia of Associations*
  • *Encyclopedia of Business Information Sources*

- *Gale Directory of Publications and Broadcasting Media*
- *Industry Surveys* (Standard & Poor's). Details U.S. industries and trends.
- *National Directory of Women-Owned Firms*
- *The Small Business Sourcebook*
- *Thomas Register of American Manufacturers* (Thomas Register < www/thomasregister.com >)
- *Word's Business Directory of U.S. Private and Public Companies*
❖ **Special Sections**—Libraries often include designated sections, in which you can:
  - Read documents on microfilm, microfiche, or locate articles in the library via another computer system.
  - Access vertical files—such as collections of pamphlets or articles on certain subjects.
  - Get free booklets and pamphlets, such as tax booklets, forms, community organization brochures, college and high school adult evening course schedules, and (if the library is designated a depository for SBA documents) pamphlets detailing governmental programs and information for start-up businesses and loans.
❖ **Programs**—Many libraries have community rooms where various speakers and organizations conduct presentations and meetings. Get a copy of the library's schedule because you never know what expert or group you might encounter that could be of assistance to your business. It might be an opportunity for you to give a talk on your expertise and promote good public relations for your business at the same time.
❖ **Online Resources:**
  - **Internet Access.** If you do not have access to the Internet from your home, many libraries offer access, but you will probably have to sign up in advance to use it because of the demand.
  - **Commercial Online Databases.** These can include the following: *American Business Disc* has the addresses, telephone numbers, and contact names of thousands of U.S. businesses.
  Commerce Business Daily lists the procurement needs of U.S. government agencies.
  National Trade Data Bank lists of U.S. government databases on U.S. domestic and international trade and exporting.

Lexis/Nexus < www.lexis-nexis.com > The Lexis part pertains to law and court cases; the Nexus part contains business articles and reports.

✤ **Other:**
- Library Spot < www.libraryspot.com > Extensive Web site of research and business resources.
- Internet Public Library < www.ipl.org > University of Michigan's Web site of business information.

State Resources
State Chamber of Commerce
Chambers of commerce provide start-up kits, information about state legislation affecting small businesses, and numerous publications for entrepreneurs.

Check with the local office of your state representative and/or senator for free information on state agencies that help promote women's and small businesses within the state. Most states have free (or low-cost) manuals of business start-up information—concerning taxes, licensing, registrations, and so forth. Or you can check in your local library or bookstore for the latest edition of *Starting and Operating a Business in . . .* (there is one for each state) by Michael D. Jenkins (Grants Pass, OR: The Oasis Press).

You can also inquire about which state office can provide you with information on selling your products and/or services to your state government. Also see *Bootstrapper's Success Secrets* by Kimberly Stanséll (Franklin Lakes, NJ: Career Press, 1997), which lists a "Directory of Small Businesses" in the appendix.

States' Web Sites
Begin by using this address: < www.yahoo.com/r/us/ > .

Federal Government
(See also "Government" under "Resources" in the appendix.)

U.S. Small Business Administration
Offices sponsored by the U.S. SBA are located in many communities. They work in conjunction with state offices and some educa-

tional institutions to provide services to women and men wishing to start or grow their small businesses. Start with the SBA Answer Desk to help you find the information (offices listed below) for which you are looking as well as offices listed in your local telephone directory under U.S. Government.

* Business Information Centers—technology, on-site business counseling.
* Office of Small Disadvantaged Business Certification and Eligibility—(800) 558-0884. Call for information to see if your business qualifies.
* Office of Women's Business Ownership—(202) 205-6673 < www.sba.gov/womeninbusiness/ >.
* SBA Answer Desk: (800) 827-5722 [800-U-ASK-SBA]; (202) 205-7064, fax; (202) 205-7333, TDD for the hearing impaired.
* SCORE offices—retired businesspersons who volunteer their time for business counseling, (800) 634-0245. < www.score.org >.
* Small Business Development Centers (SBDCs)—work in conjunction with universities to provide business counseling and services. They are located in over forty-six states, the District of Columbia, Puerto Rico, and the Virgin Islands. Look in your telephone directory (white pages) under "Small Business Development Center."
* U.S. Small Business Administration (SBA). (See "Resources" in appendix for address.) At their Web site (< www.sba.gov/ >), look for the "Counseling and Resources" button and click it to go to the SBA Resource Directory for Small Business Management. Here you'll find low-cost brochures as well as videos for sale.
* Women's Business Centers—new federally funded women's business centers that offer various start-up business programs and guidance. Call or visit their online site to find the center nearest you. (202) 205-6673; < www.onlinewbc.org >.

Government Online
Here are some additional Web sites for U.S. government offices:

* Internal Revenue Service, Help for Small Businesses (800) 829-3676 < www.irs.ustreas.gov >.
* Minority Business Development Agency, 14th & Constitution Ave., NW, Room 5055, Washington, D.C. 20230, < www.mbda.gov >.

❖ The Small Business Innovation Research program gives small-business firms the opportunity to compete for financial awards to conduct research and development. < www.sba.gov/sbir/ >.

❖ The U.S. Business Advisor < www.business.gov >.

❖ U.S. Equal Employment Opportunity Commission, (800) 669-4000 < www.eeoc.gov >.

❖ U.S. Patent and Trademark Office, (703) 305-8600 < www.uspto. gov >.

❖ Welfare to Work (provides information about hiring welfare recipients and the related tax credits). < www.sba.gov/welfare >.

Other
Cooperative Extension Services
Every county in the U.S. has a cooperative extension office sponsored by the U.S. Department of Agriculture (USDA). These offices work in affiliation with state universities, and in some states, they sponsor courses and programs for home-business owners. Contact your local office (in the white or blue pages of your telephone directory), or visit the USDA Web site (< www.reeusda.gov >), which provides links to cooperative extensions.

Business Incubators
If your home business is ready to grow or expand out of your home, or running the business you want from your house or property is just not feasible, you might want to investigate the possibility of applying to a business incubator. Business incubators consist of two types: "mixed-use" (those serving a diversity of businesses) and "niche" incubators (concentrating on just one kind of business, often associated with nonprofit organizations or universities).

Incubators in general are supported partly by government or grant funding and often are housed in remodeled vacant buildings (factories, warehouses) that may or may not be in disadvantaged areas.

The purpose of incubators is to encourage the growth of new ventures, which will help provide economic opportunities and new jobs in that community. The financial support allows rents to be offered at a lower rate to these growing businesses with the added benefit of business management and support services, shared office support staff, and conference and meeting rooms.

To qualify to be included in a business incubator, you must fill out an application, submit a business plan, and fulfill other requirements. The usual term of involvement for a business is around three years, then you will be expected to move on.

Business incubators work better for some types of businesses than others. To find an incubator near you, contact the National Business Incubation Association listed below. The association will provide entrepreneurs with a state incubator listing upon receipt of an e-mail message or a self-addressed, stamped envelope. Their Web site includes additional information as well as business books. National Business Incubation Association, 20 E. Circle Drive, Suite 190, Athens, OH 45701, (740) 593-4331 (phone), e-mail: info@ nbia.org, Web site: < www.nbia.org >.

Networking

At least once a month, Doree Romett, owner of Presentasia < www. presentasia.com >, a home-based gift basket Business, meets with a women's business ownership group for lunch at a local college town's restaurant. Romett says: "The benefits of networking have been so incredible for me, both personally and professionally, that I do not know where to begin to explain the value."

She continues: "Networking allows others to get to know you as a person and a professional, which builds customer confidence and friendships. People like to do business with those they consider to be their friends and those people who are confident regarding their product/service. Once you join a networking group, organization, chamber of commerce, etc., get involved and volunteer for committees. Don't just walk around throwing out your card and think that because your cards are gone, you've had a successful networking experience."

Romett continues: "Build three or four good relationships, and that is a successful networking experience. Also, the contacts for advice and support that I have made networking are so important to me. Especially when we are in a home-based working situation, we lack a support system and networking allows us to meet others to share experiences, opinions, resources, etc."

A person who is the ideal networker demonstrates the following characteristics: professionalism, perseverance, tolerance, and constancy. Professionalism means that a networker does not take the other for granted. The perseverance, tolerance, and constancy mean that you work to help your other networking partners and follow through with the information you promise to give them.

Networking is a marketing tool that takes some time to develop, but the benefits it brings you and your business are well worth the efforts.

Finding a Mentor

One of the best resources to help guide and encourage you in your business start-up and beyond is a mentor. A mentor is usually a person who has already been through an experience—in this case, a successful home-business owner—and can help give you suggestions and feedback as you develop as an entrepreneur.

Where can you find a mentor? Attend meetings of business organizations, women's business conferences, and seminars held by Women's Business Centers, or read local publications to find other women business owners in your area. Write or approach them with the attitude that you can both benefit from the networking of information. You can have more than one mentor, and you can have mentors via the Internet and e-mail.

A mentor relationship is one that "works" for both of you—even if you have just begun. It requires honesty, a willingness to listen, and an investment of each other's time to help one another. Madelyn Weil,* whose home business, Small Business Solutions, specializes in the writing of marketing materials for small businesses, says: "When I opened my business back in 1988, my husband, Michael, served as my mentor. He still does and is my greatest source of inspiration. He is an accountant with a great business sense . . . and keeps me on track!"

Here are some other attributes of a good mentor:

❖ Will have expertise, experience, and success in your industry or in business in general.

---

*Madelyn Weil, an active member of NAWBO, can be reached at Small Business Solutions, 2244 N.W. 37 Ave., Coconut Creek, FL 33066 or via e-mail < MLWEIL@aol.com >.

❖ Is forthright but patient and willing to take the time to answer your questions.

❖ Has the ability to analyze your business problems and give you specific suggestions to help you solve them.

❖ Has a network of business associates to whom she can refer you if you need expert help.

It will be up to you to try the suggestions of your mentor to help your business. Then, when your business is a success, you can in turn be a mentor to other women business owners just starting out.

For More Information
Books
Mentoring: A Success Guide for Mentors and Protégés by Terri Sjodin and Floyd Wickman (New York: Irwin/McGraw-Hill, 1998).

Mentoring Program
Women's Network for Entrepreneurial Training Mentoring Program. Program for helping established women business owners to mentor to new women entrepreneurs; (800) 827-5722; < www.sba.gov/womeninbusiness > .

• SUCCESS SECRET 54 •

Be aware of the entrepreneurial sources for the differently abled.

A woman who had severe disabilities from multiple sclerosis once said: "I call people who have no physical disabilities 'TABs' or 'temporarily abled' because at any time a person can become physically disabled due to an unfortunate accident, disease, stroke, or some other unforeseen circumstance." While this is a depressing thought, the fact is that currently many people are differently abled, yet need to earn money to support themselves and/or their families.

Additional Internet Sites for Accessible Technology

www.smalloffice.com > —*HomeOffice Computing (HOC)* magazine's online site. This site regularly reviews and recommends home office technology, including products that are ergonomically and/or disability-friendly. In a June 1999 article, "Bringing the Disabled Online" (p. 20), *HOC* listed these additional Internet sites for persons with disabilities:

❖ www.microsoft.com/enable—Accessibility site of Microsoft

❖ www.adaptive.org—Site of Adaptive Computer Empowerment Services

❖ www.assis-tech.com—Site of Assis-Tech Inc.

❖ www.keytools.com—Site of KCS Tools for the Computer-Enabled

ADA

Fortunately, with the technology today and laws such as the 1990 American Disabilities Act (ADA), more people with physical and cognitive disabilities are starting and running successful businesses. Some of these home businesses include desktop publishing, freelance writing, virtual assistant office support, paralegal assistance, and referral companies, to name just a few. These entrepreneurs are no different than any other entrepreneur—they come up with a business idea they are interested in and can do, then they do market research and business start-up steps just as any other person would to start a home business. They start a venture because their business plan tells them the market exists for it—for the products and services that fulfill the needs of their customers.

The 1990 American Disabilities Act (ADA) has created products and consulting opportunities for persons with disabilities to earn money and become independent, whether as employee or entrepreneur. If you have a product for persons who are differently abled, you may want to market it at expos and trade shows to help others. Other disabilities can include brain damage from strokes, medical syndromes, or those that are inherited or result from unknown causes.

Such was the case of Terri Bowersock, who overcame dyslexia, a learning disability that makes it difficult to learn to read. When she left high school, she read at a third-grade level. In 1979, with a $2,000 loan from her grandmother and furniture from her mother's and her own houses, Bowersock launched Terri's Consignment World. Today she oversees a thriving furniture consignment conglomerate of retail and franchise stores with annual sales of $15 million.

Bowersock credits the disability with giving her the drive to succeed. "Because I have dyslexia, I have more determination than most," she explains. "That determination made me what I am today."

Here are some resources to help you find information on technology and self-employment for you or a loved one who has a disability:

For More Information
Books
Accessible Gardening for People with Physical Disabilities: A Guide to Methods, Tools, and Plants (Bethesda, MD: Woodbine House, 1994).

Publications
Enable Magazine, Suite 120, 3657 Cortez Rd. West, Bradenton, FL 34210-9878 "Written *by* people with disabilities *for* people with disabilities."

New Mobility, P.O. Box 220, Horsham, PA 19044-0220 "America's leading magazine of disability culture and lifestyle."

Associations
Alliance for Technology Access, 2175 E. Francisco Blvd., Suite L, San Rafael, CA 94936, (415) 455-4575, <e-mail: ATAinfo@ ATAccess. org>. A nonprofit organization that refers people to

local centers offering technological resources for persons with disabilities. *Does not* have information on self-employment. Call for the location of a center near you, or access its Web site: < ataccess.org >.

Disabled Business Persons Association™, 9625 Black Mountain Rd., Suite 207, San Diego, CA 92126-4564. National nonprofit organization that is "Nationally recognized as the leading authority on the self-employment of individuals with disabilities."

Job Accommodation Network (JAN) — The President's Committee on Employment of People with Disabilities, 918 Chestnut Ridge Rd., Ste. 1, P.O. Box 6080, Morgantown, WV 26506-6080, (800) 526-7234 U.S., (800) 526-2262 Canada. Tells persons with disabilities their rights according to ADA regulations and how they can be accommodated on the job.

National Organization on Disability, 910 16th St. NW, Suite 600, Washington, DC 20006.

The Disability Resource, 12200 Academy Rd. NE, Suite 1212, Albuquerque, NM 87111-9915. Carries such books as *The Complete Directory for People with Disabilities, Resources for People with Disabilities, Women with Physical Disabilities,* and others. Write for current listing.

Expos

Abilities EXPO, < www.abilitiesexpo.com >. Sponsors expos in New Jersey, California, Illinois, and Virginia featuring assisted living products and services.

Living Better Expo Tour, RDP Group, 30 Tower Ln., Avon, CT 06001, < www.rdpgroup.com >. Expos in Florida; New York City; and Pasadena, California.

Internet Sources

< www.blvd.com > The Boulevard is a Web site containing information on products, resources, publications, employment opportunities for the disabled, and more.

< www.access-by-design.com/ > Contains information about the American Disabilities Act (ADA).

Products & Technology

The Complete Product Guide (for people with disabilities), P.O. Box 220, Horsham, PA 19044.

ABLEDATA, (800) 227-0216, < www.abledata.com >. Sponsored by the National Institute on Disability & Rehabilitation Research, which has a comprehensive listing of assistive technology products and their manufacturers and distributors.

SAFE COMPUTING, 2059 Camden Ave., Suite 285, San Jose, CA 95124. "Ergonomic Products for Computer Users," including voice recognition products. < www.safecomputing.com >.

• SUCCESS SECRET 55 •

Know the resources to help foster entrepreneurship for teens and children.

Even in good economic times, the days of job security are gone. Companies are regularly bought and sold, downsized, and "reorganized," all laying off workers in a day's notice. Add to that fact that the U.S. Department of Labor said nearly seven out of ten women earned less than $25,000 in 1995. The Department also predicts that six of the ten occupations that will provide the largest number of jobs for women into the early part of the twenty-first century—cashier, janitor or cleaner, sales clerk, waitress, food-server, and home health aide—will pay annual wages that would classify a family of four at the poverty threshold.

With statistics like these, it is important that we encourage entrepreneurial education for young people to give them the business skills needed in the future job market—or in the event they are forced to, or choose to, start home or small businesses. One young girl who lived in the county seat of a Southeastern Pennsylvania town decided to sell homemade muffins in the local courthouse lobby to help earn money. She was so successful that the muffin business became a family project and she eventually opened a small soup and sandwich shop, selling her famous muffins for dessert.

One home-business owner took her two nieces (her sons were out of school and she had no daughters) out of school on the Take Your Daughter to Work Day™. She says: "I introduced them to a number of women home and small business owners, plus professional women with home offices, because I wanted them to see the various options—including being a business owner—they had open to them."

As mentioned previously, entrepreneurs "beget" entrepreneurs. It will continue to be a challenge for women and men to try to earn a decent living while trying to support themselves and a family. For that reason, it's important that you be an advocate for entrepreneurial education in the schools and colleges in which you have an interest in order to train our young persons in these business skills.

Home businesses can be an option for young adults who seek unlimited earning potential as well as control of how they spend their time. Even those who'd rather be employees will find that entrepreneurial skills such as those listed in the sidebar above will help them contribute to the success of the companies for which they work.

Entrepreneurial Skills Recommended for High School Graduates

❖ Know how to assess your skills and strengths in order to use them in an entrepreneurial venture.
❖ Know how to choose a business idea based on market research and demand.
❖ Know the components of a business plan and how to write one.
❖ Understand business management principles through small entrepreneurial projects and experiences.
❖ Know the resources available to an entrepreneur in her community, in her state, and offered by the federal government.

For More Information

Books

Girls and Young Women Entrepreneurs: True Stories About Starting and Running a Business Plus How You Can Do It Yourself by Frances A. Karnes, Ph.D., Suzanne M. Bean, Ph.D, and Elizabeth Verdick (Minneapolis, MN: Free Spirit Publishing, Inc., 1997).

Education

Association of Collegiate Entrepreneurs (ACE) Young Entrepreneurs Organization, 1321 Duke St., Suite 300, Alexandria, VA 22314. An association helping student entrepreneurs and those under the age of 30. Check to see if a chapter exists at your local college or university, or type in the name in popular search engines on the Internet.

Center for Entrepreneurial Leadership, Inc., Ewing Marion Kauffman Foundation, 4801 Rockhill Rd., Kansas City, MO 64110-2046, < www.emkf.org >. Nonprofit organization dedicated to encouraging entrepreneurs, including youth and children in elementary school grades. Write for details of programs available in your area or visit their Web site.

The Entrepreneurship Academy Center on Education and Training for Employment, The Ohio State Universtity, 1900 Kenny Rd, Columbus, OH 43210-1090, < www.entre-ed.org >. Promotes entrepreneurial education in high schools and vocational/technical schools, colleges and adult education programs.

Internet Sites

< www.anincomeofherown.com > Independent Means (formerly An Income of Her Own) is an entrepreneurship "place for women under-twenty (and their over-twenty mentors) to find *an income of her own.*"

10

Pricing and Profits

There's no such thing as a free lunch.

—Milton Friedman

• SUCCESS SECRET 56 •

Learn how to cope with the problems of cash flow.

Pricing can be one of the biggest dilemmas you will face in operating your business, especially if you're the sole owner and operator. By better understanding the cash flow component, you will be better able to arrive at a price that makes a profit for you while it satisfies your customers' needs or wants.

Know Your Cash Flow

You will need to estimate your average monthly net income (after taxes) and then project it over the next 12 months so you can better picture what you earn. This is especially important if you have a seasonal business, or if your earnings fluctuate. In your first months of your business start-up, you will have to keep good records of the following:

❖ **Prices.** This chapter will help you determine the best prices for your business, but you will have to start with prices suggested by

252

your profession and industry then "test" them on your market for a response. Pricing will be an ongoing process—something you and your accountant can monitor to ensure you are making a profit.

❖ **Costs.** You will have to see what start-up costs and ongoing expenses average per month.

❖ **Customers.** As your business operates, you will be able to get an average number of clients you can handle or the number of items you can produce. Of course, you will want to allow for continued growth.

❖ **Incoming earnings.** You will need to know the average time it takes your clients or customers to pay for your services or products.

Your cash flow statement will show how money flows into and out of your business. This important assessment will tell you how much money you will need, from where it will come, and when you will need it. It is a monetary guide to your business's financial position that can make you aware of when you will need to budget for potential cash flow shortages. It is the indicator to help you control your business's expenditures and pricing to ensure you will have a successful (and profitable) business.

Managing Your Cash Flow

As you operate your home business, you will want to manage your cash flow to ensure your business will continue to thrive. That means also coping with erratic monies and expenditures and the ups and downs of business cycles. If you should have a bigger demand for your business products and services than you can handle, you may want to raise your profits. One woman who has a home-based medical transcriptionist business has been working 18-hour days for two years, even with three employees. She must decide whether to raise her prices, let some of her clients go, or expand her business with her role being a supervisory one.

Here are some suggestions to help you keep your cash flow moving:

❖ If your business makes a product, cut back on some of your production to reduce inventory—unless you need to get ready for a traditional strong buying period like the holidays.

❖ See what overhead expenses you can reduce—for example, conserving on heating or cooling of your home office or making long-distance calls from the East to the West Coast after 5 P.M. (or getting up earlier to call the East from the West Coast).

❖ Track your advertising to see which ads are bringing in the most new customers. Try a new promotion that is more creative than costly.

❖ Decide which association memberships, professional business publications, online services, and other affiliations are the most beneficial to you and your business in terms of leads, networking, and participation. Drop organizations whose meetings you have not attended in a year or magazines you have not read in three months.

❖ Set limits for customer payments. State the terms by which you expect payment and clarify any penalties you will impose if you're not paid in that time period (a surcharge, only CODs accepted in the future, etc.)

❖ Reuse and recycle. See whether you can get your printer and copier cartridges refilled instead of replacing them; use flyers and unrelated correspondence that are printed on only one side for scrap paper or to photocopy information for your own files.

❖ Pay down debts—both personal and business. Try to pay off some small credit card balances to save money on interest or shop around for ones with lower interest.

❖ Sell seldom-used equipment or other assets that are just "taking up space."

These are just a few of the methods you can use to keep your expenditures low and extend your business cash flow to keep it operating. Using methods like this may help you to keep your prices more competitive because you will not need to increase them.

———

For More Information
Books/Software

Up Your Cash Flow by Harvey A. Goldstein; book and software (Granville Publications Software). To order, call (800) 873-7789 or visit < www.cashplan.com > .

Internet Sites

< www.bizproweb.com > General information for home-based and
small businesses and professionals. It has 675 pages of links to
other sites and resources.

< www.cardtrak.com > CardTrak lists the credit cards with the low-
est interest rates in the country.

• SUCCESS SECRET 57 •

Learn how to do a break-even analysis.

The point at which your business can begin to make profit is called
the break-even point—when your projected income just covers your
costs. At this point, you do not make or lose any money. Once you
know this point, then you can begin to set a price for your services, know that you must charge at least the amount to reach this
point. Keeping in consideration the three main components of pricing—materials, labor, and overhead costs—you need to do a complete cost analysis and set a price that coincides with your
marketing strategy.

In almost every home and small business book, you will come
across "formulas" for determining a break-even analysis as well
as those for determining formulas. Study several of these then discuss with your accountant the best ones for determining your business's rates.

The SBAs pamphlet, *Business Plan for Small Service Firms*, gives
this formula to find the break-even point:

Total fixed costs

$$\frac{1 - Total\ variable\ costs}{Break\text{-}even\ point\ (in\ sales\ dollars)} = Corresponding\ sales\ volume$$

With the break-even point, you can determine a service price for
each job by using a formula like:

Material/supply costs

+ labor (your time) + overhead
= Your price
+ the percentage of profit you want to make

Overhead costs include all expenses other than materials used and your labor. If your business is your sole income, do not forget to include costs such as health insurance, Social Security, taxes, loan payments, and so forth in your overhead calculations. Also do not forget to charge for your time and/or labor.

Determining Your Take-Home (Profit) Pay

Take-home pay is your profit, the money you can spend without needing to borrow or withdraw from your savings. You will want to determine this sum so you know how much you can spend each week without bankrupting your business or yourself. Here are some tips to keep your take-home pay manageable:

✤ Work with your accountant in determining your net business income minus taxes, but take into consideration your business's tax deductions. You may want to have a separate savings account for taxes.

✤ Make an annual spending plan and figure your annual spendable cash flow.

✤ Keep your personal and business accounts separate.

✤ As was mentioned previously, if you're planning a full-time business and have no other income, business experts recommend you save at least six months to two years of living expenses to help support you until your business brings in sufficient take-home pay.

✤ After figuring out how much take-home pay you need, keep to your spending limit.

✤ Monitor your financial plan periodically to stay ahead of expenses and expenditures.

Dangerous Spending Hazards

Here are several spending hazards that can jeopardize your business:

Being *Too* Frugal in Your Business Start-Up

When a woman first starts a business, naturally she wants to spend her money carefully (which is wise), but business experts say not to be miserly when it comes to spending on items that are important for your business. Amateur-looking promotional materials, a poor answering system, cheap equipment, little or no spending on advertising and marketing will make your customers and business associates think that you are not serious about your business's outcome and growth.

Not Reviewing Your Pricing Strategies
Your clients or customers may not respond well to the way you approach them about your rates or prices. They may fear you will charge them for services they do not need or that they will be unable to afford your service or products. Pam, who had a successful bookkeeping business, charged new clients a flat rate for an initial consultation then gave them a rate sheet to review so they'd know the rates for each bookkeeping and office support service she provides.

Having Different Spending Beliefs than Your Partner
It's all right for partners to have differences in how the business's money should be spent, but if one another's attitudes undermine the business's future financial goals, then it's time to have a truthful meeting and compromise or dissolve the partnership.

Having an Employee Rather than an Entrepreneurial Mindset
As an employee, you might have had a business spending allowance for your department or project; but as an entrepreneur, you have the fiscal responsibility of not just one area but of your entire business. Every dollar must be spent as an investment to further your business.

• SUCCESS SECRET 58 •

Put your business on a budget.

Corrina had a successful home-party craft business when a recently remodeled stone building became available for rent. It had been an old country store, and Corrina planned to open her own version of a country store, with crafts and homemade breads and hand-dipped ice cream. She was able to get a bank loan to purchase inventory and other stock, but found she was spending the loan money at an alarming rate and feared she would not have enough left to continue her business.

Another home-business owner who had a working business budget gave Corrina some tips for drawing up a budget for her country store. Corrina also consulted with her accountant and, as a result, planned a budget that allowed her to open up and successfully manage her store. Here are some tips for improving your business's budget:

❖ Review your expenses and cash flow so you know approximately how much money comes in and goes out.
❖ Create realistic financial-spending goals based on your sales and future business trends.
❖ Put your budget to work and then analyze it at the end of the month to see if you spent more than your business's profits or had a surplus. Make any adjustments necessary to keep a positive cash flow.
❖ Keep your budget current and adjust it accordingly, allowing for seasonal fluctuations.

By staying on a business budget, you will actually have more control of your business's finances and its future success.

• SUCCESS SECRET 59 •

Use a pricing worksheet to assist you.

When Judy started her balloon-decorating business, she purchased several videos from a party-supplies magazine. The video provided pricing recommendations for particular structures, types of parties, and other examples of commonly used balloon arrangements that gave Judy an idea of what to charge her customers. She also factored in her expenses, which included paying two assistants, to ensure she made a profit.

Judy determined her prices by using several planning and worksheets:

Client Planning Sheet
❖ Client's name, address, telephone, fax number.
❖ The address of the place of the event, the reserved room/space, time/availability of room/space.

Add "Back-Up Value" to Your Prices

Customers will often pay more for your products or services if they know you will give them a money-back guarantee or extend your repair warranty or return policy period beyond the manufacturer's offer. You will gain the reputation of standing behind your operations and policies, thus increasing the value of your business.

❖ Contact person's name (in charge of the facility) and telephone number, key pickup time and location.

Schedule Event Sheet
❖ Title/theme, day/time.
❖ Event colors, structures (arches, trellis), estimated decoration time, miscellaneous information.
❖ Room sketch with dimensions, ceiling height, location of doors, windows, light fixtures, electrical outlets, switches, table placements, honored guests' seating.
❖ Equipment available (lifts, ladders, hand trucks).

Event Estimation & Planning Sheet
❖ Client's name and address, telephone, fax.
❖ Structures (yes or no).
❖ Balloon sizes, colors, additional decorations (centerpieces, bouquets, corsages, etc.)

Estimated hours: Judy's time of
assembly and installation, travel time   = TOTAL COST
  + cost of balloons and supplies
     (ribbon, helium tanks, etc.)

Terms: $___ Deposit required for reservation (non-refundable) and Balance Due _____.

Judy would meet with her client and fill out the sheets to give a rough estimate of the costs. If she received the booking, she would go to the event site to take measurements to create a more detailed plan with her client based on what supplies and decorations would be needed. She then asked for a nonrefundable deposit to purchase the supplies she needed, with another part of her price due 60 to 90 days before the actual date. Judy requested that the balance be paid the week before the event.

She also had fixed prices for certain events and an *a la carte* price list of extras, such as her table centerpieces or the decorative arches her husband had designed and built for her.

This example shows how just one woman arrived at her prices using work and estimate sheets. Linda C. Wisniewski, an information broker, says: "I charge for my time in quarter-hour increments, and for my expenses, which would include online databases, postage, long distance calls, and shipping charges."

You can devise your own or look for suggested price sheets in start-up business books about your specific business, in any industry how-to manuals, or by using industry and/or accounting software. The more you are in your business, the better you will be able to set your prices—from your customers' responses and monitoring your business's outlay and income.

• SUCCESS SECRET 60 •

Determine the price of your product or services to cover all costs and return a profit.

If you offer a product, your work and materials will impact your price. However, if your business provides a service, your prices will be influenced by the costs of your equipment and time. Consultants and other professionals who provide their advice and expertise will base their prices on their billable hours and expenses. The amount you charge for a product must cover all costs and return a profit. Many home and small business owners forget to consider all the inconsistencies of producing their products or offering their services. This leads to either failing to generate a profit or charging more than the market will bear.

Pricing Guidelines

Here are some guidelines to help you in pricing considerations:

✤ Write a business plan to determine your operating expenses (overhead, labor, and materials' costs); taxes and insurance costs (including health insurance, if not covered); your time spent for management, marketing, and production; and the percentage you want to save for retirement savings. Keep accurate records to better analyze your time and expenses.

✤ Use your business plan to determine a break-even point—when projected income equals costs. This figure will help you set your prices knowing that you must *at least* charge a certain amount to reach this point—and *more* than this to make a profit. Use accounting software specific to your industry or for businesses in general to assist you.

✤ Ask yourself whether your service or product will be sold to an exclusive market, be offered to many customers, or mass-produced. Know what your customers are willing to pay and the value your customers place on your service or product, and if it is in high or low demand.

✤ If your business is so busy that you cannot schedule any more work hours, it is time to raise your prices. Two women with a clowning business were overwhelmed with requests for their entertainment services, so they raised their rates. "We had fewer parties, but made the same profits, plus we had more time for planning and to be with our families," they said.

✤ Decide an annual income goal but do not forget to factor in and add your taxes, overhead costs, your profit margin, etc.*

✤ See if your industry has pricing guidelines. Some trade associations publish and sell rate guides.

✤ Research and compare your prices to your competitors' and set them accordingly—though this does not mean you have to offer lower prices. Customers may be willing to pay more for

---

*If you're running a one-person business, it is impossible for you to work 2,000 "billable" hours per year (based on a 40-hour workweek, 50 weeks per year, with two for vacation). You will be involved in marketing and other business operations so will only be able to "bill" approximately 1,000 hours a year.

personal attention, better quality, or for your special "niche."
Pricing is actually concerned more with marketing, not what
your service/product costs.

❖ Analyze your competitors' services to see what they *do not offer*,
and offer that as part of your business (for example: free delivery
and pick-up, estimates, discounts for referrals to other customers).

❖ Be flexible in pricing. Just as you "test market" your product or
service, you will have to test your prices, which will vary as your
business grows or your market changes.

❖ Have different prices and packages from which your customers
can choose. Sometimes it is how you present your prices that in-
fluences sales. If you, for example, state your rate at $100 an
hour, clients may hesitate to do business with you if they do not
know how many hours will be involved. Instead present a total
dollar amount for the entire project (based on your hourly rate).

❖ For products, be aware of the psychology of pricing (for example,
$3.99 sells better than $4.00).

With a service business, factor into your estimates some room
for extras that customers might request. Have a signed contract listing additional charges for options in the event a project is more
complex than anticipated.

Pricing is based on an ongoing evaluation of the cost and time
involved in running your business and meeting your customers'
expectations. Look for ways to increase your profits by lowering
your operating costs, but not at the expense of the quality your customers expect. Your prices signify the value of your product/service
to your customer.

Meeting with your accountant each quarter—especially in your
home business's start-up years—is one of the wisest investments
you can make. She can help you set realistic financial goals and ensure that your business will continue to be a profit-making venture.

Here are some additional topics that will help you to better understand what is involved with pricing:

Lowering and Raising Prices

You may have worked out the price you must charge for your product or service in order to realize a profit, but you also need to know

customers' responses to that price. Start out with a price and "test" it by exhibiting and getting feedback at trade shows, through customer questionnaires and surveys, and by comparing your product or services to those of similar businesses. Sharon, who has a thriving wholesale crafts business, tests new craft items by exhibiting at retail craft shows to see what the public is buying (and paying) as well as to test-market new product ideas.

If clients or customers balk at your prices, you either need to lower them and search for ways to lower your costs, or find ways to add desirability to your product or service that will justify your higher price to potential customers. Lowering prices does not necessarily mean you will automatically get more customers since lower prices are often equated with cheapness and poor quality or service. Most business experts recommend adding value instead, or offering a discount for new customers, referrals to other customers, or some other benefit.

Pricing: Cost-Based

With this type of pricing, you take the break-even point at which you established the "floor" for your price and set your prices based on financial goals. These include the following:

❖ Adding a determined percentage profit (such as adding 100 percent to a wholesale price) to get your retail price or vice versa.

❖ Starting with a high price for a new product to recoup your investment.

❖ Setting prices to meet a desired profit goal by adding on a percentage to your service per hour or per unit of a product (after including your fixed and variable costs).

❖ Selling one item or specific service at a lower price as a special offer to new customers with the hope they will pay for your higher-priced items or services. Be sure you provide this advertised item or service to the customers who are attracted to it—and without high pressure to purchase the other more expensive items or services— or you can be accused of "bait and switch" (advertising an item at a low price to get customers' interests, then telling them that item is no longer available and trying to sell them a higher-priced item) and misleading advertising!

Cost-based pricing is the most popular form of determining charges, but is less flexible in reacting to changes in demand or competition.

Pricing: Competition-Based

With this type of pricing, you compare your products and services with prices of competitors and either raise or lower them in comparison. You (or some other designated person) can pose as a potential customer to find out your competitors' rates. You do not have to undercut them, though, to get new customers. You can poll some of your competitors' customers to learn what they do or do not like about their products and services, and then offer an improved product or service—emphasizing this unique business benefit for which you can charge more.

Pricing: Value-Based

Entrepreneurs commonly underestimate the *value* of a service or product to customers and tend to undercharge, thinking that if they price too high, they will not have any customers. Business experts suggest they should think, instead, about how their product or service will fulfill their customers' needs or desires.

Because her service was in such demand, the woman working eighteen-hour days with her medical transcription service could have raised her prices and had more "normal" working hours.

You can increase the perceived value of your product in the following ways:

* Offer a service or product or serve a "niche" market that is unique to your business.
* Promote your special customer service or welcoming of special custom orders.
* Promote the image that you serve more affluent clientele.
* Provide customers with a product or service that will help them get ahead in their personal or business goals.
* Advertise that your products will help your customers save time or money.
* State that your product or service is exclusive and one of a kind.

Your value can be enhanced by the reputation of the quality of your goods and services—to a point. You can price yourself right out of the market, so will have to be alert as to customers' perceptions and opinions.

Pricing Your Service

This can be more difficult to determine, because *you* are the business—your activities and performance, knowledge, and expertise—and because you will also be involved in the other operations of a business (especially if you are a sole proprietor) such as marketing, writing ad copy, and billing.

Next, you want to add up your projected yearly expenses: your salary goal (an average salary that you would be paid by an employer); your overhead and the percentage of the cost benefits you now have to pay because you are self-employed; plus add your profit margin.

Divide that total by your approximately 1,000 billable hours, and you will come up with an *hourly billing rate.* Hourly billable rates can range from recommended industry standards upwards depending on the demand of your services and how you compare with similar experts or businesses. With this hourly billing rate, you can charge per hour or per day, flat rates or per-project fees.

Remember: some customers will be afraid if you quote a $130/hour rate yet be receptive to standard fees for certain projects. Others may prefer to pay you by the hour. You will have to operate your business for a period of time, keeping a close record of your preparation and actual work time, incurred expenses, and business expenses to accurately determine the best prices for your services. If you have any questions, consult with your accountant in your start-up operations.

Madelyn Weil says she always charges by the product rather than the hour for her writing and marketing materials service. "However," she says, "I try to determine how much time it will take to complete the project and factor that into my quote, along with factoring in payment to outside contractors, overhead, and other expenses."

Pricing Your Product

If your business produces a product, you have to include the following costs in determining your price: production; shipping, a percentage of your overhead (fixed and variable operating expenses); plus your profit percentage. Lorain, who makes wood toys, says this about deciding how much to charge for her crafts: "I determine how much my materials cost. Then I double that amount and double it again; that's just where I start my pricing!" She also figures in her overhead costs, benefits, taxes, etc.

You can ask for higher prices compared to competitors' similar products by using distinctive presentation techniques—such as colorful wrapping and packaging, unique labels, or more expensive materials. Your markup has to cover your overhead costs plus your preferred profit. Lorain also timed herself to see how long it took her to make one of her wood toys and considered that in her pricing.

In your business, have a selection of low- and higher-priced items to attract all kinds of buyers until you see which are your best sellers.

Wholesaling

The wholesale price of an item is how much you would charge a retailer who typically will put a 100 percent markup on your wholesale price to sell to the public. Sharon, who sells her crafts mainly through wholesale craft shows, says: "I look at one of my items and ask myself, 'What would I pay for this?' Then I half that price because shops will usually add 100 percent onto the price, and see if I can make a profit at that wholesale price."

Business experts recommend a *minimum* wholesale price be the total of your fixed costs (percentage of your rent/mortgage, utilities, and your salary), your variable costs (the materials and your labor), and your profit percentage. You can then evaluate your customers' responses to your prices to see if they need to be raised or lowered (or production expenses lowered).

The right price is the one that makes you an equitable profit and is acceptable and fair to your customer. The suggestions that were presented here are only for information purposes. To determine the ideal prices for your service or products, you will have to consult with your financial and marketing experts, follow industry guidelines, and adjust according to your customers' responses.

———

For More Information
Books
The following contain chapters with pricing tips and "formulas."

Homemade Money, 5th ed., by Barbara Brabec (Cincinnati, OH: Betterway Books, 1997). Excellent information on determining pricing.

Working from Home by Paul and Sarah Edwards < www.paulandsarah.com >.

Entrepreneur Magazine's Starting a Home-Based Business by Entrepreneur Magazine Group (New York, NY: John Wiley & Sons, Inc., 1996).

Internet Sites
< www.onlinewbc,org > The SBAs Online Women's Business Center (Under "Marketing" has "Pricing: How to Understand Costs & Prices for Profit").

———

• SUCCESS SECRET 61 •

Know some tactics for getting the prices you want and need.

Conquering Price Objections
You may have completed all the financial figures, perhaps even consulted with a financial advisor to come up with what are fair prices for your customers, only to be challenged by customers' objections to your prices. It does not mean that either of you is wrong—so how do you handle these challenges? Here are some suggested tips:

❖ If your product is new or you have just started selling your services, allow your product or services more time in the market.

You might not have reached the customers who really want your product or service who would be perfectly happy to pay your prices.

❖ Analyze your prices—again. Review your research as to what other similar services are charging. Maybe yours is too high for your area, or maybe you have not thoroughly communicated to potential customers what sets your business apart from others, and what makes your business more valuable to them.

❖ Look at your advertising copy and see whether you have stressed the positive benefits to your customers of using your business.

❖ You may be perceived as "behind the times" with your product or service. Have you kept up with trends, technology, or updated your training and knowledge? If so, did you advertise this fact? Today's customers want more for their money than ever. Can you offer a coupon for a free consultation, evaluation, or sample for their just contacting you? Can you offer a faster turnaround time or free delivery?

❖ Be ready for any price objections by anticipating customers' arguments and counteracting them with good arguments of your own to stress the overall benefits of your service.

❖ Stand by your price as a demonstration of the quality you pledge to all your customers, and show them a few of your customers' complimentary letters (with those customers' permission!).

Sometimes, though, no matter what you do, all a person can see is the price. Then the best you can do is to thank them politely and move on to the next customers. Be professional in your acceptance, because they may change their minds and come back later to patronize your business.

Getting Clients to Pay You

To keep your cash flow coming in, you need to get your customers to pay you as soon as possible. Here are some tips to help you get them to send you those checks:

❖ Send a professional-looking invoice as soon as a service or product is sold. You can have them printed at your local printers, buy standard ones in office supply stores, order them through mail-order office supply companies (see Resources on page 398), or design them yourself using specialized software (see the next section).

❖ Make sure you know to whom the invoice is to be sent; include the person's name and/or the department or your invoice could get lost amid other mail received. If you will be regularly billing a client, talk to the bookkeeper or accountant and ask whether there are any particulars they would like you to include on your invoice as standard procedure.

❖ Set the payment terms as soon as you make a sale or are contracted for your services. Have all payment terms—including any late fees you may charge*—listed in your promotional literature and brochures. If you are contracted, make sure the payment terms are written and signed by both of you. If you are going to be investing a large amount of time and/or your money into a project, have a credit check performed.

❖ Ask for down payments and payments in stages. Judy, who had the balloon-decorating business, asked for a nonrefundable deposit to reserve her time. She used this money for the supplies. "At least I was covered if the event was canceled," she said. Judy also asked for a second payment a few weeks before the scheduled celebration, with the balance due the Wednesday before the actual event.

❖ For larger projects, estimate your costs and ask for a retainer fee; print out all extra costs, clarifying who is responsible for paying them; and be sure this contract is signed by both parties.

❖ Accept credit cards. Then you will be paid; and if the customer defaults, it is the credit card company's problem.

❖ Offer incentives and discounts for early payments.

❖ Designate your spouse or hire your teenager to make follow-up calls several days after you bill your client to make sure they received it and to ask if they have any questions.

It is not an easy role, being the bill collector for your business; but if you keep the cash flowing in, then some day your business will be profitable enough to hire a bookkeeper to do the billing for you.

---

*Late payment interests are regulated by each state, so check your state's regulations.

Invoices

As mentioned previously, you can buy generic invoices at office supply stores or have them printed with your business name and logo. Better yet, you can buy software that customizes and fits your billing needs. Before you buy any invoicing software, read your trade publications for their specific recommendations, ask other home-business owners the ones they prefer, and get demo copies of the ones that interest you so you can try them out.

Also list the invoicing features your particular business requires, and find out if these are available in the software you review. Here are just some of the many tasks invoicing software can perform:

❖ Print invoices
❖ Run accounts receivable
❖ Do open accounting invoicing (payments get matched to specific invoices)
❖ Customize invoices
❖ Run state tax reports
❖ Automatically calculate totals and taxes
❖ Include "mini-statements" at the bottom of invoices to remind customers the age of outstanding invoices

If customers pay sooner when they receive these software-generated invoices (as some of these companies claim), then you will recoup the money you pay for the software many times over. These are a few of the many software programs available. Check your favorite business supply or computer store for others.

❖ *Microsoft Publisher* by Microsoft, (800) 426-9400, < www. microsoft.com/publisher > .
❖ *MyInvoices* by MySoftware Company, (800) 325-3508, < www. mysoftware.com > .
❖ *Timeslips* by Sage U.S. Inc. (972) 818-3900, < www.timeslips. com > .
❖ *QuickBooks* by Intuit (800) 4-INTUIT (446-8848), < www. intuit.com > .

How Competitors Can Help You Make Money

Three antique shops in one small town, including one that was home based, all advertised in the county brochure the tourist commission distributed free to visitors. One owner, when asked why she would advertise with her competitors, said: "Because when people go for the day to shop for antiques, they like to visit more than one shop. Customers say they like coming to our area because we have so many antique and collectible establishments to visit. Besides, each one of our shops is distinctive in its own way so we really complement one another."

Working together with others in your industry is beneficial in the following ways:

✤ You can refer a customer to a competitor if they handle a specific service or product you do not choose to do or are not capable of and vice versa. One small women's home-business group includes three desktop publishers, each of whom sells services to a different customer and regularly refers one another's services.

✤ Do joint advertising or buying. Three women home-based business owners—two desktop publishers and a small book publisher—paid for a large display ad in their newspaper's annual business supplement, resulting in more business for all three.

✤ Go together to save printing costs. Sharon, who sells her woodcraft items, shared costs with another woodcrafter to produce professional photo/ordering sheets for their items (they needed these sheets for the wholesale shows they attended). Even though both made wood items, Sharon says their products sold to different types of shop owners.

✤ Network! As discussed previously, exchanging information within your industry can be as good, if not better, for getting leads and keeping up with trends as is placing ads in the latest trade journal.

You do not need to give away all your trade "secrets" to your competitors, but making a competitor your friend is to have one or more people understand exactly the business problems you are having. Make sure you congratulate them on any successes. Try not to have that professional jealousy "eat" at you—your turn at success will come if you persist and keep marketing!

———

For More Information
Books
Bootstrapper's Success Secrets: 151 Tactics for Building Your Business on a Shoestring Budget by Kimberly Stanséll (Franklin Lakes, NJ: Career Press, 1997).
Priced to Sell: The Complete Guide to More Profitable Pricing by Herman Holtz (Dover, NH: Upstart Publishing Company, 1996).
Surefire Solutions for Growing Your Home-Based Business: Win More Clients, Charge What You're Worth, Collect What You're Owed and Get the Money You Need by David Schaefer (Chicago: Dearborn, 1997).

———

• SUCCESS SECRET 62 •

Know how to determine an estimate and/or quote for your business's services or products.

When you start advertising your business and begin to get your first calls, you may feel panicky when customers ask you to give an estimate or bid on a project. Here are some suggestions to help you:

❖ Have some industry standard pricing books or manuals in your personal library. Check with your trade association to see if they have any pricing guides to help you in your estimation.

❖ Never give an immediate answer. Tell your client you will get back to them.

❖ Meet with your client to get as many specific details about what they do or don't want. Make careful notations and even tape your conversation (with their permission) to make sure you get all the details correct.

❖ Go home and figure out all the costs of supplies, materials, your time (and any assistants' hours) and any variables that may affect the time you will need to do this project. Always factor in some time for kids being sick and other daily "crises" that could occur.

✤ Write up your estimation and go over it with your client and/or customer. Here is where you negotiate who uses what equipment and who pays extra costs due to unexpected causes.

✤ If a contract is drawn up, ask your lawyer to look it over.

After each project or job is completed, write up an evaluation of it, including what you learned. This way you have a record of what you did, and what you can improve upon. If you are a decorator or create a one-of-a-kind product, take photos of your products or your work so you can show your next clients. One woman who painted signs and murals always took a photo of each sign and mural and included what she charged, how long it took her to do, and what supplies she used.

The more jobs and projects you do, the better you will become at estimating your time and the costs involved.

For More Information

Books

The Contract and Fee-Setting Guide for Consultants & Professionals by Howard L. Shenson (New York: John Wiley & Sons, 1989).

Software for Estimation

MyAdvanced Invoices & Estimates by MySoftware Company, (800) 325-3508. < www.mysoftware.com >.

• SUCCESS SECRET 63 •

Know how to obtain merchant status for your home business.

In years past, it was almost impossible to get merchant status for your home-based business in order to receive customers' credit

Cut 'Em Up to Save on Business Expenses

If you pay your business expenses using cash or check, you will reduce your impulse-buying and shop more wisely than if you use credit cards. Experts recommend you use just one credit card to pay for your business expenses and choose the card with the best interest rates. Cut up and throw away the rest of your cards, and over time you will "find" more money to invest in your business. Another alternative is to carry traveler's checks instead of a credit card for business expenditures.

cards. With the continued growth, however, of home businesses (including those that advertise on the Internet), more banks are granting credit card vendor status. A home business that has existed for several years and has a good sales and financial record is more likely to be granted vendor status.

Many customers prefer the convenience of paying by credit card. If you wish to get their business—especially if you have a mail-order company—you need to be able to accept credit card payments. If a bank accepts you, expect to pay a commission percentage for each transaction. You will probably be charged a monthly support or rental fees for equipment.

Ask other home-business owners who have vendor status with whom they have accounts. If you are turned down by one bank, try others. If none will accept you, ask your bank to recommend an independent service organization (ISO), that will match you with a bank that meets your needs. The disadvantage is that it may cost you much more go to through an ISO than to deal with your local bank. Check also with the bank and your local Better Business Bureau with whom the ISO claims to do business to make sure the ISO is legitimate!

In the magazine *Crafts Report*, < www.craftsreport.com > , one crafter wrote that she was able to get two banks to offer merchant services for her business so she could accept credit card payments at craft shows (she used a manual imprinter). Her bank required that she have a commercial account at their bank, pay a small set-up fee, fill out an application, provide her tax ID number, and allow them to visit her studio to establish she was a legitimate business. In addition to the almost 5 percent transaction fee she pays with each sale, she pays a monthly service charge of less than $10.

Despite these charges, she considers it worthwhile, especially for the sale of some of her higher-priced items. Her sales have increased since she's been able to accept credit cards. Bert says most out-of-state sales for her mail-order lace-curtain business are from customers using credit cards and her 800-ordering number.

Some industry and business associates work with major credit card processing service companies to provide their members with the benefit of having credit card vendor status. Check with the business associations to which you belong or with others in your industry that provide this benefit.

Advantages of a Credit Card for Your Business*

Business experts suggest some advantages to having a credit card for your business:

+ Enables you to purchase equipment and supplies that you need immediately to start your business.
+ Keeps your business and personal expenses separate.
+ Easier to track your business's expenses and records to help you monitor your expenditures and keep tax records.
+ Interest and annual fees are tax-deductible (check with your accountant before you make any large expenditures to be sure).

*Just as with personal credit cards, try to pay off the balance as soon as possible to avoid paying costly interest rates and incurring debt that could jeopardize your chances of getting future business loans.

For More Information

Associations

The following are among the associations that provide credit card vendor status for qualified members (see Resources on page 398 for addresses).

The National Association of Women Business Owners <www. nawbo.org>, NAWBO members who qualify can apply for the Platinum Plus Program.

The Small Office Home Office Association (SOHOA) <www. SOHOA.com>. Business Credit Card Program for its members through Bancard Systems, Inc.

Women Incorporated <www.womeninc.com>.

Also check with the associations in your industry to find out whether they offer merchant vendor status to their members.

Books/Publications

The Complete Guide to Getting and Keeping Visa/Master Card Status by Pearl Sax and Larry Schwartz. Fraud and Theft Information Bureau, or <www.fraudandtheftinfo.com> or <www.checks-byphone.com>, (561) 737-8700.

How to Get, Keep, and Use Visa, MasterCard and American Express Credit Card Merchant Status to Earn Millions: Even If You Work at Home, Operate a Mail-Order Business, or Are Just Starting a New Company (InterWorld Corporation, 1992).

Master Directory of Bank Credit Card Programs (Gordon Press, 1992); $225.95

Internet Sites

<www.charge.com/> Charge.Com Merchant Services is among the firms that specialize in small and home-based operations that do business online. (800) 70-MERCHANT (706-3724).

<www.echo-inc.com> Electronic Clearing House (800) 233-0406; 28001 Dorothy Dr., Agoura Hills, CA 91301.

< www.shopkeeper.net > Shoppers World acts as a storefront for Internet merchants. Contact for setup and monthly fees and other terms.

———

• SUCCESS SECRET 64 •

Learn other cost-saving tips for your business.

✤ Depending on the size of your mailing, send direct mail first-class to your valued customers. That way, undelivered mail will be returned to you, and you can keep your mailing list current.

✤ In estimating the cost for a project, do not forget to factor in travel time, working on holidays, and so on. If you finish a project substantially early, wait a few days before delivering it to your client; otherwise, they may think the project was too easy and that they overpaid you. Remember you are being paid for your information as well as your time.

✤ Charge by the project or job rather than by the hour (though you can state your hourly rate) so the customer will feel more comfortable with your pricing.

✤ If you have a customer who is never satisfied, try to refer that customer elsewhere because trying to please him or her will take up valuable work time—time you could be making money serving other, more pleasant clients.

✤ Network money-saving tips with other home-business owners. Learn from their experiences and legwork where to get the best prices and services for equipment and supplies.

11

Open for Business

Work expands to fill one's time.

—Author unknown

You may think the biggest challenge is getting your business up and running, but actually, that may be the easiest task. The biggest challenge is keeping a business open. Various business studies have shown that home businesses have a better chance of succeeding than traditional new small businesses, but it still takes good business management skills, lots of hard work, and persistence to prevent a new business from failing.

This chapter provides practical strategies and recommendations you can use in your everyday home-business operations to ensure a successful business and future growth.

• **SUCCESS SECRET 65** •

Learn the principles of time management to improve the efficiency of your business.

The "many hats" worn by you, the home-business owner, can make it extremely difficult to run a business efficiently; however, it can be done. You must plan ahead and create a schedule that allows

278

you to realistically "balance" your routine and creative business duties, while still allowing time for the other situations that occur
regularly in your life. Here are some time-management tips to help
you not only maintain your business, but improve it at the same
time.

Time-Management Principles

If you ask a woman you have not seen for a while how she is, she
will often answer, "Busy." That is because, like you, she is probably juggling a multitude of tasks—family and community activities,
a full- or part-time job, *and* (like you) may be trying to start or run
a home business. To attend to all this, you have no choice but to
be as organized as possible. Organizing *includes* scheduling some
"down" or free time for yourself and the people you care about
and pastimes you enjoy.

Working from home poses even more challenges for running a
business: doing laundry, answering impromptu telephone calls, getting visits from family members, and taking care of sick children. Yet
at the same time, being at home and having a more flexible working schedule are reasons many women start home businesses.

If you can master the principles of time management, you will
find yourself much more likely to achieve any business and personal
goals you have set for yourself. Here are some suggestions for helping you make the most of your time.

Assess Your Business Goals.

Along with having a business plan to help guide your developing
business, you will want to review any business and personal goals
you have made. Like a mountain climber who wants to reach the
mountaintop, you'll need to keep the peak in sight as you progress.
To do so you have to:

❖ Plan your path.
❖ Watch where you place your feet so you do not slip and fall.
❖ Take many steps to reach that peak.
❖ Keep climbing toward the peak, even if you sometimes have to go
   around an obstacle or find another path to reach the top.

Focusing on your goals will help you better organize your time so you can achieve them.

This translates to always keeping your long-range home business and personal goals in mind, but accomplishing the short-term goals and daily tasks to reach the long-term goals. Of course, you will have more than one goal (mountain to climb) and you alone will know which you want to reach first. As you plan each year, month, week, day, and hour, direct each component toward achieving your ultimate "peak."

Discipline yourself to "act" on your goals.

If you feel yourself going in too many directions with your business but not really accomplishing anything, keep a time diary for a week or two and note how long each activity—business and personal—takes to complete. Then ask yourself the following questions to help you evaluate how you used your time:

❖ How many times a week (or day) did you make telephone calls?
❖ How many business errands and trips did you take?
❖ What times of the day were the most productive for you?
❖ How much time did you spend on correspondence—letters, e-mails, faxes?
❖ How many hours did you spend on the actual production of your goods or services?
❖ How many times were you interrupted, and by whom or what?
❖ How much time was involved in organizing paper and computer files?
❖ What did you feel were "time-wasters" for your business?
❖ How much "fun" or relaxing time did you take for yourself?
❖ Did your family or acquaintances complain that they did not see enough of you?
❖ What time did you spend on "community" activities?

Now total the hours and minutes spent on each activity and see what kind of time patterns you have noticed.

Taking Control of Your Business Time

When you own your own business, it is hard to keep the line drawn between business and personal time. Following are some problems that may interfere with your business time and ways to avoid them:

Distractions   Family, friends, neighbors, and community acquain-tances will all demand your time—often unexpectedly due to mi-nor or major emergencies or perhaps because of commitments for which you have volunteered.

❖ *Control strategies:* One well-known woman business owner puts God, family, and business in that order of importance. Work out "ground rules" and schedules with your immediate family so you won't feel you're neglecting them and they won't be resentful of the time you work at your business. With extended family, neighbors, and community activities, learn to say "No" when you're asked to do something. *You* take control by suggesting the activity when you know you will have some free time. Use your business activity time to help with mentoring, or for supporting causes you feel strongly about.

Communications and Correspondence   Unexpected telephone calls, e-mails, deliveries, and letters to be answered can all disrupt your production and work time.

❖ *Control strategies:* Let voicemail take your incoming calls when you're working. Let your message encourage callers to leave their name, reason for calling, and best time to return their call. Do not answer your home phone line except when you are "out" of the office.

    Keep a record of outgoing calls. Include who you called, why you called, and what the discussion was about. Date correspon-dence that comes in and answer a few each day in the order in which you received them.

Paperwork   Clutter and misplaced papers can affect your efficiency.

❖ *Control strategies:* Take a few minutes at the end of your working day to straighten your office. Once a week do a better job, in-cluding going through one drawer or file a week to see what can be discarded. Cut down on papers filed by keeping information on electronic disk.

Finances   Avoid spending too much time on bookkeeping and on projects that do not pay well.

❖ *Control strategies:* Consult with your accountant and get book-keeping software to help you. Look at your goals to determine which projects are worth your time, and which best pay your bills; eliminate those you have outgrown.

Setting Up Your Work Schedule

Now that you have analyzed your log of activities, and have planned your control strategies, you can better plan your work schedule. Here are some suggestions:

❖ Sit down with your goals and business plan list at the beginning of each week; set up the week's steps that best direct your activities toward those goals.

❖ Prioritize the most important tasks to do first. Tommie M. Bryan, a professional organizer from Somerset, New Jersey, says:

> Divide your activities into must, should, could (or it would be nice to). Do as many "shoulds" as you can. They are often postponed because they aren't urgent. Next, plan before you start. One minute of planning frees five minutes for execution. Last, learn to estimate how long a task will take. Double (or even triple) your 'guesstimates' at first. You'll become more accurate with practice.

❖ Look at your non-business schedule of family activities and other commitments and estimate the time that each will involve.

❖ Make a "to-do" list each day.

❖ Block times to do those business maintenance duties such as billing and correspondence.

❖ Save the hours that you work best for production and creative time.

❖ Leave some "white space"—especially if you have an upcoming deadline—to allow for unexpected equipment breakdowns and other unforeseen circumstances.

❖ Be flexible. Recognize that some days you will accomplish much and other days little. Don't be too hard on yourself when you get sidetracked. Just get organized the next morning and go from there.

LaDonna D. Vick, founder and creator of Mommy's@Work, says:

> I found using a daily planner helps tremendously. When you work at home, your time can really get away from you. On Sunday, I plan the week ahead, and then the night before I check the next day's events.

I've found that if I write down in my planner everything I need to do that next day, it gets done. If you have little ones, make sure you write in time for them, too (for example: nap, lunch, playtime). Be realistic, though, because children don't always cooperate with time schedules. Once you get a routine going, they'll get used to it. They really start looking forward to their time.

Hire a Professional Organizer

If you start your organizing task and find it overwhelming, then call on a professional organizer. One professional organizer in Chicago has not only organized every office type imaginable, but has found money, an airline ticket, and many other items clients thought were "lost forever"!

Follow a Task "Recipe"

To tackle any job for yourself or a customer, the following "recipe" will help you plan and execute it.

TASK RECIPE

Task/Job (description)

_____

List "Ingredients" (what information and
    or materials you will need to do the task)

_____

- Where to get them:

_____

- How to get them:

_____

- Persons to contact:

_____

Gather "Ingredients" (get the materials
    and or research for the information)

Complete the Job—"Bake" (time involved)

_____

Evaluate Your Results

_____

Deliver and Bill or File

_____

For More Information
Books
Get Organized (book and CD-ROM) by Bobbi Linkemer, Colum McCann, and Rene Richards (New York: Amacom, 1998).
Home-Based Mom: A Practical Guide to Time Management and Organization for the Working Woman by Juli E. Shulem (Santa Barbara, CA: Newhoff Publishing, 1998).

Internet Sites
< www.everythingsorganized.com > Web site of Lisa Kanarek, organizing expert and author.
E-mail newsletter: LaDonna D. Vick's. To subscribe, send an e-mail to: < mommywork@smartbot.net > Web site: < www.momsnetwork.com/suites/momsatwork > .

Associations
National Association of Professional Organizers, 1033 La Pasda Dr. #220, Austin, TX 78752-3880. Write for a listing of members' names in your area.

• SUCCESS SECRET 66 •

Improve your organizational techniques with software.

Personal and Office Organization Software
Once you have some idea of how you want to be organized, consider using some of the software and organizers listed below (or others recommended by professional organizers and other home-business owners). They can help make your work life less difficult, save you time and money, and help you improve your overall service to your customers.

Contact Managers/Personal Information Managers
❖ *Act!* by Symantec Corp., (408) 253-9600.
❖ *Info Select* by Micro Logic, (201) 342-6518.

❖ *Lotus Organizer* by Lotus Development Corp., (617) 577-8500.
❖ *PackRat* by Polaris Software, < www.polarissoftware.com >.
❖ *Rex PC Companion* by Franklin Electronic Publishers, < www. franklin.com >.

Calendar/To-Do
❖ *Alarming Events* by CE Software, Inc., (515) 221-1801, < www. cesoft.com >.

Contact List Software/Electronic Card Files
❖ *Address Book Software* by SoftExeC Publishing Co., P.O. Box 1072, Hunt Valley, MD 21030, (410) 666-7594.

Handheld Organizers
❖ *Palm Computing® Connected Organizers* by Palm Computing, Inc. (408) 326-9000, < www.palmpilot.3com.com/ >.
❖ *Sharp Wizard* by Sharp Electronics, < www.sharp-usa.com >.

Organizing Your Computer Files
If you have been using the computer for your business for more than three years, chances are your hard disk is quite cluttered. You will want to first back up your entire disk drive (using tape, zip drives, or another method). Then organize your files by discarding unneeded files, rearranging others into new folders as needed, and archiving seldom-used ones. If you need help, call a computer-literate friend or a computer consultant who can teach you how to regularly organize your date files in a logical and consistent routine.

For More Information
Associations
Independent Computer Consultants' Association (ICCA), 11131 S. Towne Square, Suite 7, St. Louis, MO 63123, < www.icca.org >. Contact them for names of members in your area.

• SUCCESS SECRET 67 •

Set up a record-keeping and bookkeeping system that works for your business.

Many home-business owners are good at their business specialty, but avoid the bookkeeping and accounting. One woman who expanded from a home-party business to a country store was overwhelmed with her business's bookkeeping and paying of her crafters.

Finally, her accountant told her she had to start keeping better records. Luckily, her neighbor, who also had a craft business, showed and encouraged her to use an accounting program. She needed someone to show her how to set up her accounting system, but still likes figuring her accounts on paper sometimes.

Computerizing your business can help you save time and money. Again, talk with a professional bookkeeper and accountant for the best tips. If bookkeeping becomes too much for you to handle and you can afford help, you may want to consider hiring experts to do it for you.

One very important reason to keep good financial records is for tax-paying purposes. Being self-employed, you regularly pay estimated taxes to the IRS, state taxes, and of course, any local taxes that apply to your business. With tax changes and laws in constant flux, it's important that you're able to call financial experts whenever you have a business tax concern or questions about deductions; if you wait, you may be penalized for not paying a particular tax. Here are some tax deductions you'll want to discuss with your tax expert:

Business Tax-Saving Deductions
(Ask your accountant about these.)

❖ If you employ your children, you can deduct their wages and not have to pay Social Security or Federal Employment taxes.

❖ Educational expenses can be deducted if training and courses improve the skills you use in business.

❖ Deduct a percentage of the cost of home-cooked meals if you entertain clients at home.

❖ Certain deductions may apply if you incur expenses related to your charity work or work as a community volunteer.
❖ Deductions may apply for any casualty or damages that occurred to your home and business property due to earthquake, wind, fire, or theft.
❖ Deductions can be taken for health care or insurance. Check for the current level of deductibility.
❖ Home-office deductions may be applicable. See what home-business owners and self-employed people qualify for this.

Tax Mistakes
(These are often made by owners of newly started home businesses.)

❖ Poor record keeping. It is essential to the success of your business that you keep accurate records!
❖ Not paying the taxes required of a business, such as estimated taxes to the federal and state governments.
❖ Failure to keep business purchase receipts and records.
❖ Not keeping your personal banking accounts separate from your business accounts.

Even if you hire a financial expert to keep all your accounts, it is important that you have basic knowledge of the tax concerns and procedures of your business. Read books, IRS publications, and articles in home and small business publications, and take courses at local business schools and colleges offering business management courses.

End-of-the-Year Tax Tips
When the December holidays come around, usually the last thing on a person's mind is business taxes, but a couple of hours of consideration can save you some money in tax savings. Here are some ways you can prepare for tax time:

❖ Get your business records and receipts in order.
❖ Review personal telephone bills to find any overlooked long-distance business calls that you might deduct.
❖ Review your mileage to make sure you didn't miss the local miles that you ran business errands. Jan Zobel, tax expert, advises:

On December 31 or January 1, go out to your car and write down the odometer (mileage) reading. If you do that the same day each year, you'll always know how many total miles you've driven during the year. In the new year, use a trip meter to help with mileage totals. If you have not kept good track of business mileage, go over your year's appointment book and reconstruct the local trips you made to clients, business meetings, professional education, etc.

✤ Check to see whether you deducted any professional or trade publications used in your business.

✤ Review your retirement and savings plans in comparison with your year's earnings to decide how much to contribute to your plans.

✤ Decide whether it will benefit you to make any large purchases before the end of the year. Judith Dacey, CPA, advises: "But never, never, never buy something just to get the tax deduction. Only spend the money if the asset is a needed business acquisition. If a 25 percent price cut is expected within 90 days, wait."

Hobby or Business?

Many people turn their hobbies into profitable businesses. It may start out as something fun to do, then people offer to pay for your service or your products. Polly, who loves plants and herbs, used her knowledge to make money with homemade potpourri and then handmade herbal soaps. What designates the difference from a hobby and a business? Generally, financial experts say it is not the profit but the profit motive. If you keep accounting records, make a profit some years (the IRS realizes that you may show losses in the start-up years), and are able to demonstrate that you are trying to make a profit, you will probably be classified as a business.

The IRS considers a number of other points when judging the difference between a hobby and a business. To be sure, consult with your accountant and tax advisor.

For More Information
Books
Minding Her Own Business: The Self-Employed Woman's Guide to Taxes and Recordkeeping by Jan Zobel (Oakland, CA: East Hill Press, 1998).

Internet Sites

< www.accountingnet.com > "CPA" link. Information and directory of accountants and accounting firms in small business and specialized areas.

< www.easyas123.com > "Destination: Success, Inc."—"A support network dedicated to entrepreneurs." Visit for more information and articles by Judith Dacey, CPA, who gives talks and workshops on entrepreneurship.

< www.tax.org > Tax Analysts, a nonprofit organization providing the latest information on tax developments at the state, federal, and international level.

< www.taxweb.com > TaxWeb is "the Internet's first consumer-oriented source for federal, state, and local tax-related developments."

Accounting/Bookkeeping Software

< www.accpac.com > *Simply Accounting,* by ACCPAC International.

< www.intuit.com > *QuickBooks Pro 6.0* by Intuit.

< www.intuit.com > *TurboTax* by Intuit.

< www.microsoft.com/money > *Microsoft Money* by Microsoft.

< www.onewrite.com > *One-Write Plus* by ADP.

< www.peachtree.com > Peachtree Small-business accounting packages.

Audiocassettes

"Tax Strategies for the 1990's" by Sandy Botkin, c/o Tax Reduction Institute of Germantown Maryland, 13200 Executive Park Terrace, Germantown, MD 20874. Send a long, self-addressed, stamped envelope for prices and ordering information.

Billing

Timeslips by Sage U.S. Inc., (972) 818-3900; < www.timeslips. com > 17950 Preston Rd., Suite 800, Dallas, TX 75252. Customized invoicing and bill formatting.

Business Forms

FormTool Express by IMSI Corporation, (800) 833-8082; < www. imsisoft.com > Many ready-made forms; company produces several software form programs.

Forms Unlimited by Parsons Technology, (800) 973-5111; < www. parsonstech.com > Custom forms for business and home.

OmniForm by Caere, < www.caere.com > Form scanning and database capabilities.

Government Sources

Internal Revenue Service, (800) 829-1040 < www.irs.ustreas.gov >. Ask for their publication concerning the use of a home office for business.

Internet Newsletters (e-mail)

< taxwriter@taxmama.com > put in "Subscribe" to receive free monthly (e-mail) newsletter, *TaxMama*, for information about U.S. tax laws affecting you as a business owner.

• SUCCESS SECRET 68 •

Know how to attract, treat, and keep business customers.

Customer Service

One of the advantages a home business can offer potential customers is personal attention to their needs and wants that larger companies cannot provide. This does not mean you have to work twice as many hours to provide your goods and services; however, it means you can pay attention to details that demonstrate to customers that you care about the quality of work your business provides them. The following sections contain tips and guidelines to help you let customers know they are important to you.

What You Can (and Cannot) Provide for Your Customers

Your business cannot be all things to all people—that's why you do market research—to find the *right* customers or *niche* for your business. Here are decisions you will have to make about what your business can or cannot give your target customers:

Customer "Extras"

Business experts say it's the little "extras" that help you cement customer loyalty. Here are some suggestions for "perks" you might want to provide your customers:

- ❖ Free delivery and pick-up.
- ❖ Custom designs or services tailored to the client's needs or preferences.
- ❖ Extended warranties or guarantees.
- ❖ Special sales for loyal customers.
- ❖ Cash or credit to loyal customers for their referrals of new paying clients.
- ❖ Thank-you "gifts," such as cards, specialty foods, or event tickets.

Am I going to give the best prices, outstanding service, or excellent quality? Business experts say it is impossible for a business to provide all three and stay in business. The goal, then, is to strive to provide two of these three business goals. How then do you decide which two? By analyzing how you work and what your target customers most want. You can find this out by doing customer surveys and encouraging their feedback.

Tactics for Finding (and Keeping) Customers

As mentioned, if you have done the preliminary research into your business idea and completed a business plan, you should already have an idea who your best customers are. The goal now is to find them. Here are suggestions:

- ❖ **Do cold-calling.** Michelle Clevenger personally delivered her business flyers to small businesses in her area then followed up with phone calls to those she knew would be good customers for her desktop publishing business.

❖ **Encourage referrals.** Again, with every project she does, Clevenger asks her customers if she can add a credit line with her
business name and contact information. It helps other potential
customers see samples of her work and recognize who is
responsible for it.

❖ **Spread the word.** Tell everyone you know—friends, business
acquaintances, family, others—about your new business. Carry
cards with you all the time—even to the grocery store. Even if a
person you happen to see there cannot use your business,
chances are she will know of someone who can.

❖ **Speak out.** Many groups are looking for speakers. If you can talk
on a topic of interest to them, you have an excellent way to not
only garner new customers from the audience, but also to attract
people who read the press release the group sends local media
to announce upcoming events and speakers—*like you!*

There are other ways to get new customers—and marketing is
an ongoing process with your business. The goal is to *keep* customers you get because, according to what women business owners say over and over, word-of-mouth referrals from satisfied
customers is a primary means of getting new customers.

Automate Your Customer Service

As your business grows, with the many demands on your time, you
may find it difficult to respond immediately to new and prospective
customers' requests for information. Here are some ways to acknowledge them as well as provide the information they need to
decide whether your business can help them:

❖ Have a Web site set up with the products and services your business offers. Include the URL on all your correspondence, promotional materials, and other advertising avenues. (See chapter
13, Going Online.)

❖ Consider the capabilities of voice mail. It permits you to give a
longer explanation than does an answering machine, plus offers
options from which your customers can choose to get more specific information.

❖ Fax-back and automated e-mail responses to customer requests
may be possibilities if you have a large demand for information.

Fax-back programs vary in their prices and capabilities, so you may want to talk to an office specialist for some suggestions. For automated e-mail, you can talk to your Internet Service Provider (ISP) to plan a service that fits your business.

Handling Customer Complaints

As one author's book title suggests: *A Complaint Is a Gift* (see *For More Information* on page 298). Complaints are your customers' way of letting you know that you're not meeting their expectations. Joann, with her wall-papering and painting business, says: "When I had my first complaint, I was devastated. It really upset me that my customer was not satisfied. Fortunately, after I talked to my customer, I realized I had misunderstood what she really wanted. I changed what she wanted at no cost and my customer was happy again."

How you react and handle these complaints will determine whether you will continue to keep customers and can affect the prospects of new customers coming to you. Here are some suggestions to help you resolve their grievances:

✣ **Do not take the complaint personally.** This is hard to do, especially if you *are* the business. Your customer is not saying they *hate* or *dislike* you—just that they were not satisfied with a certain service or product.

✣ **Listen to the specifics.** Let customers first vent their complaint then review with them what specifically made them unhappy.

Discuss with them how you might rectify their complaint: Refund their money? Redo the job or service? Acknowledge your mistake? If possible, grant them the option they prefer, or offer another solution on which you both can agree.

Many times, however, customers do not complain to you—they simply go to a competitor. Even worse, they may spread the reason they were unhappy, and prejudice other potential customers against you. To prevent this, regularly take customer surveys—both informal or formal—about your service; take note of regular customers from whom you have not heard in some time. Personally call them to ask whether you can do anything for them, and if there is a reason you have not heard from them lately.

Contented Customers: How to Let Them Know You Care

Business experts say it costs less to keep a regular customer satisfied than to get a new one. To keep your customers pleased . . .

* **Follow through on your promises.** If you offer a guarantee, next-day service, free delivery, or another benefit, make sure your provide it.
* **Respond promptly.** No matter how backed-up you are with work, return customer calls as soon as possible after they contact you. If you cannot handle their immediate requests, give them an approximate time when you will be able to devote your full attention to them.
* **Give them a little extra.** If you can give a customer a new lead for more business, a helpful hint, or something else they didn't expect, you demonstrate that you care about them and their success. They will appreciate your thoughtfulness and be more likely to return again or give you referrals.

Dealing with "Challenging Clients"

One fact of running your own business that other home-business owners warn about is that you will not be able to please some customers—no matter what you do. In the worst-case scenario, some even sue for one reason or another. Attempts to please unreasonably demanding customers can cost you valuable time and money—you may never be able to please them anyway. Business owners who learned the hard way offer these tips to avoid that "hellish customer."

* **Establish policies for your business operations.** Write your business policies down in customer handbooks or flyers, and discuss them with your customers for clarification.
* **"Read" potential customers' body language.** If you get a sense from conversations that a customer is never satisfied (perhaps

they put down others in your field, imply they are always right and everyone else is wrong, or blame others for their failures), then follow your instincts and politely refuse them.

❖ **If they have a reputation for being difficult, tell them you will get back to them.** Meanwhile, try to talk to other business owners with whom they have dealt. To be fair, remember that there are two sides to every story, and certain business relationships simply aren't compatible.

❖ **If your business dealings involve a contract, have your lawyer review it.** She'll be able to advise you of its ramifications and what is and is not your legal responsibility.

Impressing Customers

Because *you* are your business, the first thing customers notice is your attitude. Being friendly when you first meet prospective customers can be an incentive for them to contact you for business. Whether you exhibit at a trade show or handle phone inquiries, be pleasant, courteous, and respectful.

People do not necessarily want to be your "pal" (even though many women business owners say their customers become friends as well as patrons). What people *do* want is to be treated *with respect.* You don't necessarily have to *like* every customer, but you must recognize that each customer does deserve your *respect* as a human being. Make eye contact with all customers, thank them for their inquiries or their business, send them personal notes of appreciation, and let them know you care about them in any way you can. This sounds so simple but can be overlooked easily, especially by business owners who are solely profit-driven.

Overcoming Discrimination

Of course, certain discrimination—based on age, race, gender, and such factors—is illegal in the workplace. Still, as a woman and home-business owner, you may face subtle prejudice from customers or other business owners with preconceived and narrow views about who or what business a woman can operate. However, there is no longer a time and place for such prejudice, as is demonstrated by these statistics and examples:

✤ **Gender-based:** "The number of women-owned firms in general has increased by 78% between 1987 and 1996, and the number of people they employ by 183%" (NFWBO). When Joann started her wallpaper and painting business ten years ago, there were few women in her field, and she was usually hired by women. Now, she says, she competes with many men (and other women) in this industry and feels that customers are more concerned about her experience and skill than whether she is or isn't a woman.

✤ **Non-traditional businesses:** "The fastest-growing fields for women in business are in non-traditional business sectors like construction, wholesale trade, transportation, agriculture, and manufacturing." Just look at *Working Woman* magazine's annual profile and listing of America's top women-owned businesses. The May 1998 issue featured women who owned and operated multimillion-dollar businesses in areas such as producing scrap metal, auto distributorship and finance, lumber, banking, television and film production, and many other once-male-dominated enterprises. In one suburban area, a woman-owned lawn-mowing business is one of the busiest in the area (she operates the machinery along with her employees).

✤ **Race-based:** "Businesses owned by women of color are growing three times faster than the overall rate of business growth and faster than the growth rate of women-owned businesses in the U.S. [grew 153% between 1987 and 1996]" (NFWBO). Talented and educated minority women who may have felt they hit a "glass ceiling" or "wall" in their past jobs are starting their own businesses to fulfill their dreams and help others close to them.

✤ **Age-based:** As the "golden years" of baby boomers get closer, many are retiring or planning to start businesses doing something they enjoy. Esther Fox, who started a part-time business called Poetry-on-Demand* calls people such as herself "Empty-Nest Entrepreneurs." She says, "Our children are young adults and planning their own lives now, and I (along with many of my

---

*Esther Fox's Poetry-on-Demand is business #99 in *More 101 Best Home-Based Businesses for Women.*

friends) am looking for ways to bring in extra income and work that would bring fulfillment."

With so many "barriers" falling, many entrepreneurial avenues are now open to all women. Should you encounter any prejudices against yourself or the business you operate, be polite but don't tolerate it. Be confident in your skills and conduct your business with professionalism. Let the quality of your product or service speak for itself.

Treatment That Drives Customers Away

Business owners and experts concur that if you treat your customers well, you can develop their loyalty. However, even your most faithful customers will eventually abandon you if your treat them in the following ways:

* **Not enabling them to contact you.** Customers call when they want something. If they cannot reach you or you do not get back to them promptly, at least to acknowledge their call or letter, they will give up and go to someone who will respond. If you work away from your home office often, consider getting a cell phone or pager, or arrange to have call-forwarding.
* **Not being truthful in your communications or actions.** As the adage says, "Your actions speak louder than your words." Deliver what you promise and advertise; otherwise do not say it.
* **Not being concerned with a customer's dilemma.** It is impossible to meet every customer's needs, but if a person calls you for a product and/or service you cannot provide, he or she will appreciate your giving a lead to someone who can—even if it's a competitor. The person will be likely to remember your helpfulness and perhaps become your customer or give good referrals.
* **Not recognizing customers for their faithfulness.** It never hurts a business to thank customers through cards, thank-you notes, and other expressions of appreciation. Bert Schwarz enjoys entertaining her customers at her annual open house every Christmas.

Treat your customers like you would want (and like) to be treated, and your business will thrive.

_____

For More Information
Books

AMA Handbook for Customer Satisfaction: A Complete Guide to Research, Planning & Implementations by Alan F. Dutka (Lincolnwood, IL: NTC Publishing Group, 1995).

A Complaint Is a Gift: Using Customer Feedback as a Strategic Tool by Janelle Barlow and Claus Moller (San Francisco, CA: Berrett-Koehler Publishing, 1996).

The Arthur Andersen Guide to Talking with Your Customers by Michael J. Wing and Arthur Andersen LLP (Chicago: Upstart Publishing, 1997).

Aftermarketing: How to Keep Customers for Life Through Relationship Marketing by Terry G. Vavra (New York: Irwin Professional Publishing, 1995).

Calming Upset Customers by Rebecca Morgan (Menlo Park, CA: Crisp Publications, 1996).

Customers for Life: How to Turn That One-Time Buyer into a Lifelong Customer by Carl Sewell and Paul B. Brown (New York: Pocket Books, 1998).

How to Conduct Your Own Survey by Priscilla Salant and Don A. Dillman (New York: Wiley, 1994).

How to Win Customers and Keep Them for Life by Michael LeBoeuf (audiocassette ed., 1997).

The Street-Smart Entrepreneur by Jay Golz (Omaha, NE: Addicus Books, 1998).

_____

• SUCCESS SECRET 69 •

Make networking and bartering work to help foster your business.

Networking

Networking, as was discussed in previous chapters, is a low-cost way to announce your business and generate leads to more business, plus it gives you an opportunity to exchange information ideas with other business owners. Networking is about giving as much as getting information from others. Patricia C. Gallagher, author and marketing entrepreneur, says: "Never underestimate any place you go to speak or meet with others in business. At every talk I gave, or event I attended—no matter how small—I gained some information or leads to help my business." Doree Romett, a giftologist and owner of a home-based gift basket business, says: "The benefits of networking with other home and small business owners has been so incredible and invaluable for me, both personally and professionally. Networking allows others to get to know you as a person and a professional, which builds customer confidence and friendships. People like to do business with those they consider friends and those who are confident regarding their product/service."

Here are some guidelines to help you improve your networking skills:

* Do some research before you attend the business or social event. Find out what type of businesses or people will be there, and whether it is a formal event or a business card exchange or function.
* Decide what your purpose is for attending—to help promote your new business? Assess the business group to see whether it is an appropriate association for your business? To meet a specific person or persons?
* Take along cards, brochures, and a small tablet with a pen to make notations to help you remember important details about those you meet.
* Arrive early so you will not be uncomfortable walking into a full room.
* Talk with as many people as you can, and help others by introducing newcomers to people you already know. Give a little "plug" for your friend, for example: "Jane, I want you to meet Doree. Her gift baskets are outstanding!"
* Follow up with a note to the sponsor of the event and anyone to whom you promised more information.

You cannot spend all your free time going to meetings, but if you choose the right ones, your business is bound to benefit from these networking opportunities. As Annette Yost, a home-based customer relations specialist and young mother of two girls, says: "The value of networking for me has been what I have learned from the business experiences of others and the sharing of their knowledge."

Bartering

Bartering, as was discussed in chapter 6, can be a way to get products and services your business needs but you cannot afford, as well as a way to promote your business. By joining and participating in business barter exchanges or groups, you also increase your visibility in your business community, resulting in more contacts and referrals. Be sure not to overdo it, though, because your business still needs cash flow. Do not forget to discuss tax considerations related to bartering with your accountant.

For More Information

Books

Business by Referral: A Sure-Fire Way to Generate New Business by Ivan R. Misner and Robert Davis (Austin, TX: Bard Press, 1998).

The Secrets of Savvy Networking: How to Make the Best Connections for Business and Personal Success by Susan Roane (New York: Warner Books, 1993).

• SUCCESS SECRET 70 •

Be a business professional.

In my book, *More 101 Best Home-Based Businesses for Women*, I discuss some myths about home businesses. "Myth #5" is: "If I work from home, I can be much more casual in how I dress and how I treat my customers."

The reality is yes, you can dress more casually (unless you have a home office that receives customers), but how you treat your customers should be as professional as any business protocol dictates. Here are professional points:

❖ All your business materials and correspondence should be professional-looking and include no spelling errors or write-overs.

❖ Promptly return business calls and be on time for client appointments.

❖ Be sure customers can rely on you for dependable and reliable service or goods.

❖ Be a member of a business association or professional trade group.

❖ Conduct yourself with confidence and as the expert you are.

You are the executive in charge and responsible for your business's procedures. Working from home does not diminish the fact that if you do not take your business seriously, no one else will either.

Your Business Ethics

Besides being honest, you will need to face ethical dilemmas appropriately. Because your business is *you*, your actions influence your business's image to your customers and business associates. Know what you will do and will not do with your business. One home-business owner was contacted by a man who produced infomercials. He suggested she personally promote some of her business ideas. She says: "I sent him a letter that I was not interested because, for my business, I felt self-promotion just was not 'me' and I was afraid I would lose my credibility among my customers." Here is some advice on how to face certain ethical issues.

❖ If you say your product is 100 percent American-made, be sure all of it is—not just some parts of it.

❖ Do not offer or accept any gifts or money in return for specialized business favors.

❖ If you have a mailing list, consider whether you are going to sell your list to others. (Or do you advertise the fact to customers that you *do not?*)

❖ Be wary of where you lend your name in connection with politics or causes.

❖ Do not denigrate your competitors to attract new business. Instead, in your ads emphasize how your business's products and/or services best meet your clients' needs. Let your customers decide which business they want to patronize.

✣ Take responsibility for any of your mistakes or actions that had negative repercussions with your client.

You will not always find a reference of what is ethical and is not, but if you value honesty and truthfulness, generally your business ethics will reflect those, too.

• SUCCESS SECRET 71 •

Know when and how to hire the best help for your business.

Family Help

As a home business grows, so do the demands; and often the time comes when you need some help. The first place you might look is your own family—depending on their ages and capabilities. Paula Kay's business, Ageless Placements, Inc., has been so successful over the past three years that she was able to hire her sister full time. And when her married daughter did not want to put her first baby in child care, Paula hired her, too, and had her daughter bring the baby to the office. "It was a little distracting," Paula says, "but it is satisfying knowing I am helping my family out, and it gives me more time to focus on my business and how to improve it."

When Joann first started her wallpapering, she was a divorced mother, so she would take her children along to help when the customer didn't mind. Her younger children enjoyed helping her paste or cut strips and she hired her older daughter one summer to actually assist her with papering. On the down side, one woman who started a costume business said her daughter resented the time she helped in the business.

Each family situation and business is different and has to be worked out for what is best for the entire family.

Hiring Your Children

Children can be involved in all sorts of ways with your business. LaDonna Vick, whose mail-order company specializes in home-business resources, lets her six-year-old daughter staple booklets together and her three-year-old daughter help pick the colors for her booklet covers. Vick says: "When you get your family involved, even in the smallest way, they have a better understanding of what you do as a work-at-home mom."

If your children are older and you want to hire them, first check with your local and/or state authorities as to the child-labor laws and the number of hours children are permitted to work for your business. Then consult with your accountant as to how your recordkeeping should be set up. Your accountant can also let you know what wages can be deducted, whether Social Security needs to be withheld, and for what tax breaks you might qualify, according to current laws.

Business experts urge you to document the hours your children worked, the jobs they did (tasks should be business-related), and how much you paid them—comparable to the standard rates you would pay an (unrelated) employee to do this job. You will need this documentation if you should be audited by the IRS, as well as for your own records.

Pros and Cons of a Family Business
If you are thinking of hiring family members, here are some considerations:

Pros:
+ Children feel important that they are helping the business support their family.
+ You can work your schedule to take vacations at times of the year when there are smaller crowds or you can take "spur-of-the-moment" day and short family trips.
+ Children learn first-hand the principles of entrepreneurship and often go on to start their own businesses.
+ Children learn good "work ethics" and what it takes to earn money.
+ You may get to know your children better and vice versa.

Cons:
+ Some children will resent being asked to work in the business.
+ Some parent/child or sibling relationships do not work well together (this can apply to adult children as well!).

❖ Parents may not respect their children's opinions about business decisions.
❖ Parents may assume children will want to "take over" the business someday and the children will feel guilty if they do not continue working in the family business when they become adults.
❖ The business can interfere and spill over into family fun time and life.

_____

For More Information
Miscellaneous Sources

Family Business Books, Biz Books, Inc., 120 W. Morehead St., Suite 100, Charlotte, NC 28202, or e-mail: < bizbooks@amcity. com >.

LaDonna Vick, founder and creator of Mommy's@Work, "Your Home Business Resource Place," < www.momsnetwork.com/ suites/ momsatwork >.

Paula Kay, Ageless Placements, Inc., 8130 66th St., N, Suite 4, Pinellas Park, FL 33781. Specializes in recruiting older workers to assist seniors in their homes with daily living. Business opportunity available (manual, training, and "tools" to start your own agency—not a franchise).

_____

Independent Contractors

If you need assistance or expertise, you might want to hire an independent contractor, but you may face potential IRS problems if the worker comes into your home to do the job. Generally, a person is considered an independent contractor if she works at her own pace in her own office or workshop, uses her own tools, and performs similar work for other businesses. If you have questions about IRS designations (there is a whole list besides these three) regarding who is a company employee and who is an independent contractor; about how to contract with someone (or about being hired as an independent contractor yourself); or wish to access a whole list of

Virtual Assistants to the Rescue!

With today's level of technology, you can often hire virtual assistants (VAs) from remote locations to provide office support services. Shane Brodock, a professionally trained virtual assistant operating out of Florida, says, "VAs are more than just remote secretaries. They learn their clients' businesses and work closely with them to help take those businesses to the next level where they become more productive and effective." Brodock continues, "Since the typical VA charges by the hour, the service is more cost-effective than hiring on-site assistants and paying for their time whether there is work to be done or not."

Note: Make sure you check the tax and legal regulations of the state (or country) in which your VA lives. Also follow state and federal regulations regarding your hiring of any virtual assistant, whether as an employee or independent contractor. For a virtual assistant, go to < www.homestead.com/sohosolutions >

topics, call the IRS directly at (800) 829-3676 or download the publication from its Web site: < www.irs.ustreas.gov >.

The reason the IRS is concerned about independent contractor status is that companies and corporations take advantages of so many workers (Read *Income Opportunities'* article, "Under the Corporate Thumb," November 1997, by Diana Hembree, Linda Molnar, and Diana Reiss-Koncar, p. 23). It is best if you hire an independent contractor (or are hired as one) to have a contract drawn up by a lawyer familiar with such business contracts.

When to Subcontract Your Work
If you are hired to do a particular job that includes parts that are not in your area of expertise, you can subcontract those jobs to other specialists. Again, you will want to have a lawyer draw up a

contract with such stipulations as the contractors use their own equipment, set their own hours, are responsible for paying their own taxes, and adhere to any other job expectations or stipulations that need to be followed.

Another option is to work with a temporary agency to do clerical jobs, errands, and other tasks so you can be free to concentrate on your clients' needs. Knowing when to delegate and "let go" of some routine business operations often helps the productivity and growth of a business.

If you decide to hire one or more regular employees, you will first have to check to see if your local zoning will permit employees working in your home. With the hiring of regular employees, you will have to think about other considerations such as interviewing prospective candidates, taxes, benefits, additional liability insurances, hours, and how comfortable you will feel having someone in your home and vice versa. Again, consult with your accountant concerning hiring employees or workers.

Other Home-Based Business Owners
Teaming Up

"Women-owned home-based firms are as likely as men-owned to operate as 'virtual corporations,' collaborating with other firms on a project-by-project basis, bringing complementary skills to the relationships" (NFWBO). Bert Schwarz, owner of a home-based antique business, regularly teams up with the owner of a historical restaurant for advertising purposes.

Jane Mitchell, who creates gourmet cheesecakes from her home kitchen, teams up with Peggi Clauhs and Winnie McClennen, mother and daughter who teach gourmet cooking lessons in their home-based Cooking Cottage (and take students on worldwide culinary tours). Mitchell will be invited to teach dessert-making classes as a guest instructor.

Sally Silagy teamed up with artist Lynn Petersen to come up with "The Garden Lady," a character featured on Sally's greeting cards < www.GardeningGreetings.com >. By teaming with other home-business owners, you, too, can create your own entrepreneurial web in which you can help one another grow your businesses and meet your customers' needs. If you would like to work with other women entrepreneurs, meet them by joining home and small business associations in your area or national organizations that have local chapters (see Resources on page 398).

Another way people are teaming up is through "virtual offices." Using an online service and specialized software, you can "meet" on the Internet with other home-business owners or workers.

———

For More Information
Books
Teaming Up: The Small Business Guide to Collaborating with Others by Paul and Sarah Edwards (New York: Tarcher/Putnam, 1997 < www.paulandsarah.com >.

"Virtual Office" Online Services
HotOffice Virtual Office Service, HotOffice Technologies, Inc., < www.hotoffice.com >.
Netopia Virtual Office, Netopia, Inc. (510) 814-5000, < www. netopia.com >.
Lotus Instant! TEAMROOM. Lotus Development Corp., < www. lotus.com >.

———

Other Help Sources
Hiring a Sales Representative
If your business makes a product that could be produced fast enough to keep up with a big demand and sold wholesale, you might want to consider hiring a sales rep who is familiar with selling items in your industry. Many reps would rather deal with larger producers, but if you ask for referrals, go to trade shows, or look in wholesale directories, you may find several who are willing to represent your product and help you increase sales.

Cheryle had a home-based business producing handmade wool dusters from the sheep she raised. A sales rep approached Cheryle at a craft show and exhibited samples of Cheryle's dusters at wholesale craft shows all over the country. The rep sent Cheryle the orders (for which she paid the rep a percentage) and shipped the dusters directly to the customers through UPS (who came to her house daily and billed her weekly). Unfortunately, Cheryle developed carpal tunnel syndrome in both wrists and stopped making the dusters, but she did continue to sell her naturally dyed wool and yarn, which she spun on her antique spinning wheels.

There can be a considerable expense involved in providing samples for your rep and the commission you must pay on sales in the rep's territory, and you must be able to produce enough to supply the customer demand. Unfortunately, not all sales reps are reputable, so if you are considering hiring a rep, do thorough research into his or her background to make sure the rep is suitable for your product and is someone you can trust.

Employees—Sheltered Workshops

If your business involves a repetitive procedure such as packaging, putting documents on microfilm, or performing other jobs like labeling, you might want to consider contacting a local private or county nonprofit, vocational training agency for adults with developmental disabilities. Under supervision, some of these adults learn skills they can eventually use in a regular job. For others, working like any one of us and earning money of their own provides a sense of self-worth and accomplishment.

At some sheltered workshops, groups of their workers will contract out to do cleaning, landscaping, and other such jobs. They take pride in doing a job well and love the camaraderie with their fellow workers. Contact your local sheltered workshop or the organizations listed below if your business could use such assistance.

For More Information
Sheltered Workshop Information
ARC of the United States (formerly the Association for Retarded Citizens of the United States), 500 E. Border St., Suite 300, Arlington, TX 76010, < www.thearc.org >.

Goodwill Industries International, 92000 Rockville Pike, Bethesda, MD 20814, < www.goodwill.org >.

• SUCCESS SECRET 72 •

Know how to stay fit when you work from home.

Home Fitness Tips

With all the hours you put in with a home business plus all your other family and household duties, the last thing you may think of doing is *more* work. Actually, being healthy and fit will help you cope with stress and the demands of such a hectic life. Working at home can lead to a temptation to snack more and exercise less as you sit in your office chair, or it can offer more opportunities to live a healthier lifestyle than when you worked as an employee.

Women polled on the Internet site "The Women's Network" (< www.ivillage.com/work/index.html >) said they gained more weight than they liked since they started to work at home. However, women business owners have endless ways to keep themselves in shape—jogging, walking, home gyms, gardening, etc. Here are some tips to help you stay fit and trim at home:

❖ Check with your physician before you embark on any new exercise routine.

❖ Hire a professional trainer (a number have home offices).

❖ Find a routine you enjoy. One woman writer has a weight-lifting exercise routine on Tuesdays, Thursdays, and Saturdays; and jogs two miles Mondays, Wednesdays, and Fridays. If the weather is too cold or inclement, she runs on her treadmill to music on the radio.

❖ Stock your refrigerator with yogurt, fresh fruit, and vegetables for healthful meals and snacks.

❖ If your neighborhood is safe or has sidewalks or a park, go for a brisk walk. A number of home-working moms have jogging strollers for their young children.

❖ If you have not exercised before, build up your exercise time slowly and gradually.

❖ Alternate weight-bearing exercises like walking, dancing, or jogging with strength-training to help keep the calcium in your bones.

❖ Put exercise in your daily schedule and it will become part of your everyday routine.
❖ Exercise with another home-based working mom if you need motivation.

You may gain weight when you first start working from home, but if you discipline yourself, do a form of regular exercise you love, and plan your meals, you can be wise, healthy, and—perhaps someday due to your business—wealthy!

• SUCCESS SECRET 73 •

Learn some techniques to reduce stress.

Emergency Coping Tips
If you are "home alone" and feel stressed—by deadlines; interruptions by family, neighbors, and extended family; telephone calls from customers demanding immediate attention or your son's school principal; or some small or major crisis that arises—coping can be difficult. Here are some tips to keep you from going crazy if you feel overwhelmed or are facing an emergency.

❖ **Pray for strength!**
❖ **Breathe!** Many people who are tense breathe shallowly. Take some deep breaths and relax the tense muscles in your chest.
❖ **Take a minute** to gather your senses and decide what has to be done first and to determine whether this problem needs immediate attention or can wait until you can figure out a strategy to resolve it.
❖ **Resume normal activities.** If this problem can hold a while, go back to your regular schedule to get yourself into a working mode again so you're not paralyzed by the problem itself. Often by resuming your normal activities, your brain can start to think of ways to solve this dilemma.
❖ **Keep a sense of humor.** Unless it has to do with life or death, you will get through this!

❖ **Schedule** a block of time to deal with this problem.

Dealing with Burnout

As exciting as it is having your own business, sometimes the long hours, the increasing demands related to business growth (or the stress of non-growth) can take its toll on you. If you begin to resent your work, dread the next day's tasks, or have overall negative thoughts about your business and think the 9 to 5 routine wasn't so bad after all, you may be experiencing burnout. Sometimes a business that was a creative outlet for you has turned into more production and administrative headaches and less fun than it was.

Here are some suggestions from psychologists on how to deal with burnout:

❖ Take some time out to reflect on your values and what is important in your life and how your business can fit into that "picture."
❖ Take classes or workshops in your industry. You may come up with new ideas or spin-offs for your business.
❖ Do not try to be involved in your business seven days a week. Try to set business hours then "close your doors" after those hours. Spend time with family and friends, and helping others. Other people can refresh you, provide some feedback and support with your problems, and give you a new outlook on life.
❖ Downsize your "things" list—such as material goods, debts, and so on—and "upsize" your personal relationships and creative thinking.
❖ Leave some "white space" in your own daily schedule to meditate, pray, reflect. Yoga and other forms of meditation have had a comeback over the years. They can help teach you relaxation and calming techniques.
❖ Realize things could be worse, and be thankful for what you have.

Burnout can happen to anyone who is emotionally and physically drained due to work and other pressures. You can keep your enthusiasm for your business if you do not let it control you and if you keep looking for ways to be creative with it.

For More Information
Books

90 Days to Stress-Free Living: A Step-by-Step Guide by Norman Shealy
(Rockport, MA: Element, 1999).

The Complete Idiot's Guide to Managing Stress by Jeff Davidson (Indianapolis, IN: Alpha Books, 1996).

Preventing Job Burnout: Transforming Work Pressures into Productivity by
Beverly A. Potter and Phil Franks (Menlo Park, CA: Crisp Publications, 1995).

• SUCCESS SECRET 74 •

Know how to make the most of your vacations.

Entrepreneur Travel Tips

One of those ways to prevent burnout is to schedule a vacation.
This can be difficult if you are a sole proprietor; but if you do not take
the time, no one will offer it to you. One advantage of being your
own boss is you can take a vacation when it suits you. With a little
planning, even with a demanding business, you can take time off and
enjoy it. When Pam, who had a busy bookkeeping business, was finished with the tax season, she would "reward" herself by taking her
family to a hotel resort for a couple of days. Pam got the opportunity to spend uninterrupted time with her children and they appreciated the break from their studies and routine as well.

Here are some suggestions to help you plan the vacation you
deserve:

❖ Schedule the time on your calendar or work tasks that will fill
those days.

❖ Plan several short trips, which will be easier to plan and catch
up from.

❖ If there are clients who may need you, team up with other home-
business owners who can fill in for you. For example, four

lawyers who practiced in similar areas of law teamed up to cover one another's vacations—some of which lasted for a month. They sent letters to each of their clients saying when they were leaving and who would be handling calls.

❖ Try to coincide your vacations during "slow times" for your business—after holidays, for example.

❖ Decide whether you want to stay "connected" via fax, telephone, or e-mail—or be totally away from the business.

❖ Go without unrealistic expectations that this will be the "perfect" vacation. Just plan to "go with the flow," and you will be less upset with lost luggage, rude service, or inclement weather. Just be glad you are having a much-needed break.

Vacation Write-Offs
It will be up to you to decide whether to combine your vacation and some business. Some business owners want to get away totally. Some will schedule the vacation first according to the family's wants and then see if they can incorporate business-related side-trips; others have to travel on business and do their relaxation on the side. One home-business owner whose husband was born in Germany was able to deduct some of her travel expenses to that country because she could purchase items for resale in her business and visit one of her major suppliers who is based there.

Deductions for mileage, tolls and parking costs, hotel costs, meals, materials, and business-related courses can apply to your trip. Unless your spouse or family is employed in your business, though, their expenses are usually not deductible. Of course, keep all receipts and consult with your accountant *before* you go on vacation for some tips about keeping expense records, etc.

Staying Connected on Vacation
If you are planning to take an extended vacation, you might want to stay "connected" with your clients and or home office. Here are some suggestions to help you do this:

❖ Do some research into the places where you will be traveling to see if you will be able to plug in your fax or other equipment.

❖ Talk to other home businesspeople who have traveled and kept in touch with their business for some tips.
❖ Research the Internet and your local business technology store for the latest equipment like "smartphones," cellular phones that offer wireless Internet access and e-mail services to non-corporate consumers. Read publications like *HomeOffice Computing* < www.smalloffice.com > and other home-office publications (see Resources on page 398), which regularly review the latest home-office wireless equipment.
❖ Use office centers like Kinkos to help with faxing, photocopying, and other small business services.

Everyday technology improves so that we can reach people (or be reached by people) even from remote places thousands of miles away. It can be a blessing or a curse, depending on your business's needs and personal concerns. Either way, you now have options and choices and more freedom than ever before to run your business away from your home office.

• SUCCESS SECRET 75 •

Be a "green" entrepreneur.

If you read business publications, you will see profiles of entrepreneurs inventing products from recycled materials—from shoes to safe ground cover for playgrounds—and featured businesses that publicize their efforts to be environmentally concerned. Joyce Chambers has a creative part-time business as a "professional pendant designer," using recycled paper to create beautiful jewelry. Her business has helped her earn her way through college. She has even written a how-to booklet about this "green" art.

If you participate in such recycling efforts, let your community know about it. It may bring customers who are similarly concerned to do business with you.

Recycling Tips:
❖ Use paper supply companies that use recycled paper stock and note that fact on your promotional materials to let customers know you are environmentally concerned.

* Use ecological packaging, biodegradable bags, or reusable items that customers can return for a cents-off discount.
* Recycle your cartridges. Have them refilled or buy equipment made by companies such as Canon, with a program that lets you return used cartridges at no cost.
* Use nontoxic and natural cleaning materials and fluids in your business.
* Participate in your community recycling programs.
* Brainstorm for unique ways your business can recycle and reuse, then promote that fact to your customers for good public relations.
* Donate a savings bond for a drawing for youth who participate in a clean-up day.
* "Adopt" a portion of highway if your state has a program like the one in Pennsylvania that will erect a sign with your business's or organization's name on it in return for your keeping that stretch of highway clean.
* Look for ways related to your business that you could invent a unique environmental product or solution.

For More Information
Publications
Ecopreneuring: The Complete Guide to Small Business Opportunities from the Environmental Revolution by Steven J. Bennett (New York: Wiley & Sons, 1991).

"How Anyone Can Create Fashion Jewelry at Home for Fun or Profit," by Joyce Chambers, 1998. Send $5 check or money order to Joyce Chambers, PAPER ART ORIGINALS, 2526 Lamar Ave., Suite 231, Paris, TX 75460.

In Business, 419 State Ave., Emmaus, PA 18049. Business magazine for all sizes of green businesses.

Internet Sites
< www.emagazine.com > *E Magazine,* an environmental magazine.
< www.greenbiz.com/ > "Green Business Letter" Includes links, sample issues, etc.
< www.recycle.net/recycle > "Recycler's World." Lists materials wanted, waste exchanges.

Associations

Co-op America and the National Green Pages, 1612 K St. NW, #600, Washington, DC 20006. An organization for environmentally concerned businesses; publishes a newsletter and the *National Green Pages*, a directory of "green" businesses and resources.

Government Sources

Environmental Protection Agency (EPA). Provides information and publications about matters related to environmental protection. (202) 260-2090 (see Resources on page 398 for address).

Supplies

Earth Care Paper, Inc., P.O. Box 3335, Madison, WI 53704. Sells recycled paper and products.

12

Managing and Maintaining a Profitable Business

A woman is like a tea bag. You never know how strong she is until she's in hot water.

—Eleanor Roosevelt

Once your home business is launched, organized, and maintained, you will face the inevitable up-and-down cycles of operation and the obstacles of surviving costly business mistakes. Learn to recognize common signs of business trouble so you can deal with the problems before they escalate. The best way to do this is to consult your team of business experts when you feel that you are losing control or are unsure of how to handle a business problem. Many business mistakes can be avoided altogether if you regularly seek professional advice.

This chapter will present you with success tips to help you cope with some of the most common problems entrepreneurs face in struggling to keep their businesses going and growing.

317

• SUCCESS SECRET 76 •

Learn to avoid mistakes that can "kill" a new business.

Here are some tips to help you avoid costly mistakes that can lead to the demise of your home business.

Preventing Trouble

You cannot predict bad (or good) business fortune, but you can control some of the mistakes that could put you out of business. As the old saying goes, "Hope for the best and prepare for the worst." Here are some tips to help you be prepared for that "worst":

✤ Make a list of potential business problems as you review your financial and business plans. Sometimes you cannot visualize these problems until your business is up and running, so review your plans often and always be prepared to change them as needed.

✤ Decide which of those problems could surface first and visualize how that problem could affect your business.

✤ Plan your attack and defense. For example, if you anticipate you are not going to have enough in your budget for advertising, plan alternative and low-cost methods to promote your business instead.

✤ Start small and grow instead of going big at first then having to cut back. For example, before you have that expensive state-of-the-art greenhouse built onto your house or in your backyard, build an inexpensive one with framing and plastic. Establish a customer base before you make major expenditures and put yourself into deep debt.

Additional Business Busters to Avoid

✤ **Underpricing your products or services.** As discussed in chapter 10, Pricing and Profits, you must determine the price that will be fair to your customers yet high enough to cover your expenses and your profit margin. Add value to your business by promoting your service, your expertise, or your quality so customers will pay what your service or product is worth to them.

Is Honesty the Best Policy?

When starting a home business, you may be unsure of what exactly you can and cannot promise your customers in delivering products and services. Here are some tips that will help you be honest with your customers and not lose them to your competitors:

❖ Do emphasize the strongest benefits your customer can expect from using your product or service. Do not exaggerate, but stress the positive aspects of the customer doing business with you.

❖ Do let your customers know the value of your products or skills through your promotional materials. Tell them about legitimate testimonials, referrals, awards, and certifications you have received as a result of your business.

❖ Do not promise your customers something you cannot deliver. Rather than take on a project you are not capable of completing, be ready to refer customers to others who can meet their needs.

❖ Do not insult your customers' intelligence. Nowadays, many consumers do their "homework" before they pay someone to do the job. Listen to what they want, welcome their input, and tactfully make suggestions so you can come to an agreement on exactly what is to be done.

You may risk losing some sales, or even customers, with your honesty. If you are fair, however, those who do business with you will develop a trust that can make them customers for life!

❖ **Wasting time on too many little projects with little compensation instead of concentrating on the larger, more lucrative ones.** You don't have to eliminate those smaller jobs, just intersperse a few of them along with the big jobs.

❖ **Failing to set the professional "tone" for your business.** Just as you set limits on children's behavior, you also have to set the "rules" clarifying how you do business when you first meet with clients. If you have an at-home child-care business, for example, set policies to deal with parents who are constantly late in picking up their children or late in making payments. Sit down and make up a "business policies" list and let your customers know what you expect from them, just as they have the right to expect certain things from you.

Shared Home-Business Problems

If you talk to other women business owners, you will often find that they face similar problems, which is one purpose of networking—to hear how others solve common problems. Here are some solutions to problems you may be facing, such as:

Inconsiderate Clients

Clients sometimes think they can call you any time because you work from home. When you work from home, you can choose to work after hours, but that does not mean customers can expect to reach you at all hours or interfere with your personal activities. Unless you give permission to a client, when you are finished for the day, let your voice mail take any after-hour calls. It will help to set limits to those who would take advantage of your home location.

Cash Shortage

You're likely to have little money coming in as your business goes through its start-up phase. My thirteen-year-old son told me when I began writing and publishing full time that I should get a "real" job like all the rest of the moms so I could buy him the expensive sneakers he wanted. Women home-business owners often have problems justifying to their families the need to economize in order to save or raise money for their business start-up and growth.

Women who solved this problem demonstrated to their families that they were as committed to starting their business as to any job they could have on the outside. They often "reward" their families for their support by taking them out to eat or for a fun day trip. Try to stress the benefits of their working from home (without making unrealistic promises!) and emphasize how much their support is important to your success.

Facing Isolation

A recent article said that some of the popular coffeehouses have become a place that home-business owners go to get some "human contact." If you are feeling isolated, team up with another woman business owner periodically for a walk or a coffee break at the local bagel shop. You can share one another's problems and just get out of the house. Joining (or forming) a local business association also helps to provide social contact.

These are just a few of the problems home-business owners face every day. When you experience problems, remind yourself of the reasons you started a home business and of all the benefits you have with a home business.

Tackling Business Problems

Deciding that you have a problem is one of the first steps to overcoming it. Once you have acknowledged this fact, you can begin to solve it in the following steps:

✤ Face the fear of the problem, and stand up to it by realizing that it is not going away.
✤ Analyze it by asking: What is the problem and how did it become a problem? For example, were your energies focused on your marketing and you neglected to keep track of your cash flow?
✤ Plan your strategy to attack it. What steps should you take toward resolution? Do you need to call on an expert? Decrease your expenses? Do more promotions?
✤ Persist until you resolve your business problem. Some business problems are easier and faster to solve, like redoing a job for a customer, but others may take longer to fix. For these bigger problems, use the support of your family and business experts.

LaDonna Vick says: "I signed up for a business opportunity to sell a product I knew little about. I wasted a lot of time and money on this business. I knew within my heart that it would not work for me. Needless to say, I didn't stick with it. I found when I started

Business Danger Signals

How do you tell whether your home business is headed toward danger? Here are some signals to alert you:

❖ Absence of a structured business or financial plan to guide you.

❖ Being very busy, but seldom achieving any of your business goals.

❖ Losing more money than you are making after at least two years in business.

❖ Customer complaints escalating.

If you see these signs or begin to feel your business is "out of control," it is time to pull back and consult with your "entrepreneurial team of experts"—your life partner, accountant, business coach, marketing expert, and others who can give you unbiased assessments of your business problems.

doing what came naturally and what I enjoyed, the pieces began to fall together. Lesson: Work at what you love to do, and I guarantee you'll be more likely to stick with it and succeed."

Learning from Mistakes

To paraphrase a familiar adage, "Sometimes the best lessons learned are the hardest ones." This is repeated here to let you know you will make mistakes as entrepreneur, but a mistake is only harmful if you fail to learn from it. Liz Folger says this about her home-business experiences: "Wow, have I made a mistake or two! I think my biggest one is the marketing department, in thinking I needed to pay big bucks to get my product or service out there. In reality, there are many FREE ways to get your name out there. Sure, they will take time, but they don't cost a dime. As a work-at-home mom on a small marketing budget, this idea works well for me."

For More Information
Books
The Creative Problem Solver's Toolbox by Richard Fobes (Corvallis, OR: Solutions Through Innovations, 1997).
Fail-Proof Your Business: Beat the Odds and Be Successful by Paul E. Adams (Los Angeles: Adams-Hall Publishing, 1999).
How to Reduce Business Losses from Employee Theft and Customer Fraud by Alfred N. Weiner (Vestal, NY: Almar Press, 1998).

Internet Sites
< www.streetfighter.com > Street Fighter Marketing, Inc. Consulting organization that helps small businesses develop innovative answers to problems.

• SUCCESS SECRET 77 •

Learn strategies that ensure business success.

Delegate for Success
There comes a point in your home business when you realize you will have to delegate some responsibilities to others. Here is how to "let go" and still feel "in control."

* Decide what it is that you do best for your business, and what others can handle just as competently.
* Pick the best people for those jobs you do not (or would rather not) handle well—even the household chores. Judy Tamagno, mother of five children, recognized Appaloosa horse watercolor artist, and creator of porcelain-sculpted jewelry and figures, says: "I've been able to do much artwork over the years because I delegated the household chores to the kids! It was good for them because they learned to be self-sufficient in many household tasks. Even my boys know how to keep a neat room, do their own laundry, and whip up a meal."

Pam Adzima, who started her home business remanufacturing toner cartridges seven years ago, advises: "Surround yourself with talented people, and ask for help when you need it—delegate!"

✤ Communicate effectively with those to whom you delegate tasks so they understand the goals and directions of your business. The better they comprehend which way your business is headed, the better they will serve the needs of your customers. If you advertise the friendliness of your business to customers, make sure the person who answers the phones or e-mail reflects that when they deal with your customers.

Learning to let go of some responsibilities to the right people can give you more freedom to be creative and productive.

Questions to Help You Stay in Business

As mentioned before, you will inevitably make wrong decisions in your business. Oftentimes the biggest mistake is not consulting our experts *before* we embark in a new direction with our business. Ask questions, starting with yourself:

✤ **Am I organized?** The better organized you are, the better you will know which steps to take next toward advancing your business.
✤ **Am I being realistic with what I can expect to accomplish?** You may wish for phenomenal growth, but realistically, it is better to grow at a pace within your financial and knowledge "zone."
✤ **Do I know all I need to know to run my business?** Never stop learning! Maryanne Burgess, sewing entrepreneur and publisher of the *Designer Source Listing*, says: "Savvy entrepreneurs never stop learning. Whether you are planning your future enterprise or wondering how to improve the business you own, you have one important thing to do: educate yourself."
✤ **Do I keep track of my business's cash flow?** To ensure that your business survives, predict your monthly cash requirements and cash availability. This requires you to keep careful records so you will know if the money coming into your business (fees, sales) will be sufficient enough to pay the money going out (bills).

Entrepreneurs need to be wise enough to know when to ask questions that can help prevent potential problems from occurring. Asking is no reflection on one's ability to run a business—in fact, it is a smart person who realizes she cannot know everything herself and knows which experts do have the answers she needs!

For More Information
Books
201 Great Ideas for Your Small Business by Jane Applegate (Princeton, NJ: Bloomberg Press, 1998).
Street-Smart Entrepreneur: 133 Tough Lessons I Learned the Hard Way by Jay Goltz (Omaha, NE: Addicus Books, 1998).
Tips & Traps for Entrepreneurs: Real-Life Ideas and Solutions for the Toughest Problems Facing Entrepreneurs by Courtney Price and Kathleen Allen (New York: McGraw-Hill, 1998).

• SUCCESS SECRET 78 •

Take advantage of licensing, or getting a trademark or patent for your business.*

Trademarks, Copyrights, Patents
To protect your business and its products, name, or invention, you will want to know how to get a trademark, copyright, or patent for your product. Here are some tips:

Copyright
Copyright protects literary, dramatic, musical, or artistic works, motion pictures, software, and other intellectual property. You can protect this by putting your copyright symbol and notice © like Sally Silagy has with her "Garden Lady" character (see figure 12.1). If you wish, you can write for copyright forms to formally register your work (or groups of works) for around $20; however, this is

---

*Consult with an attorney familiar with trademark, patent, and copyright laws and protections to prevent your infringement of others' rights or yours being violated.

not necessary because you receive the copyright the moment you create something that is uniquely yours. Registration of your copyright, though, enables you to sue for infringement of your work. You cannot, however, copyright ideas—only works that have been created.

You also must not use another's work (such as Disney characters) in your crafts without permission or a licensing agreement. If you are using a design in your publications and promotional materials, you can, of course, create your own, hire an artist, or use copyright-free designs offered for sale like those by Dover Publications. Contact the Copyright Office for more information.

Licensing

If you wish to sell products related or associated with established businesses, you will need to contact these companies or institutions regarding the possibility of arranging a licensing agreement. You would then pay a percentage of your gross sales of the products using the name or likeness of these protected products.

Figure 12.1 Copyright example of Sally Silagy's "The Garden Lady"

Patent

If you invent something like Karen Alvarez's Baby Comfort Strap, you will have to apply for a patent to protect it. Your type of invention will determine the type of patent you receive: design, utility (how it is used), or a new plant (flower, variety of fruit, etc.). This can be a lengthy (and costly) process, with no guarantee that your invention will bring you monetary rewards. Talk to other women inventors and patent attorneys who can give you an idea of the entire process involved in protecting your creation.

Trademark

If you are considering getting a trademark (name) for your business name, product, or anything else that's intended to set it uniquely apart, you will want to contact the proper state and federal offices (see *For More Information* below). A trademark search will have to be conducted to make sure no one else is using a similar trademark. You can do that through companies that specialize in trademark searches, go to U.S. Patent and Trademark Depository Libraries (PTDLs) located throughout the country, use CD-ROMs, or conduct online searches. Request publications on the trademark procedures and what can and cannot be trademarked from the Patent and Trademark Office.

For More Information
Books
Bringing Your Product to Market by Don Debelak (New York: Wiley, 1998).

The Copyright Permission and Libel Handbook: A Step-by-Step Guide for Writers, Editors and Publishers by Lloyd Jassin and Steven Schecter (New York: Wiley, 1998).

Patent, Copyright, & Trademark: A Desk Reference to Intellectual Property Law by Stephen Elias (Berkeley, CA: Nolo Press, 1996).

Trademark: Legal Care for Your Business & Product Name by Stephen Elias and Kate McGrath (Berkeley, CA: Nolo Press, 1998). Copyright-free designs.

Internet Sites

< www.copyright.com > Copyright Clearance Center.

< www.fplc.edu > Patent, copyright, trademark information by Franklin Pierce Law Center.

Government Sources

Federal

United States Copyright Office, The Library of Congress, 101 Independence Ave., SE, Washington, DC 20559-6000, (202) 707-9100, < www.loc.gov/ >. For copyright application.

U.S. Patent and Trademark Office, Washington, DC 20231, (800) PTO-9199 (786-9199), < www.uspto.gov >. Write or visit the office's Web site for more information on patents, trademarks, and copyrights and their listing of publications like *Basic Facts about Patents, Basic Facts about Trademarks*, etc.

State

Contact your state's Department of Commerce or other office to inquire about registering your trademark with them.

• SUCCESS SECRET 79 •

Know how to prevent your business from being sued.

Preventing Lawsuits

Preventing lawsuits against your business is both smart and economical, which is why you want to have a business lawyer *before* any trouble could possibly ensue. It is wise to have liability insurance to help protect your business and possibly your personal assets (see also "Insurance for You and Your Business" in chapter 4). Hopefully, your business will never need a lawyer. If, however, you are formally notified about an impending legal action, you will have an attorney with whom you can confer immediately instead of trying to find one in a stressful situation. Here are some suggestions to avoid lawsuits:

Legal Documents for Your Home Business

Using appropriate legal documents for your home business transactions can help keep you out of court! Here are some commonly used document types.*

❖ Contracts regarding the delivery and performance of your services or products.

❖ Subcontracting agreements.

❖ Liability and waiver documents.

❖ Ownership arrangements.

❖ Corporation structures.

❖ Continuance of your business in the event of your illness, injury, or death.

*Budget into your start-up costs the price of having a lawyer who specializes in business or your industry advise you which documents you should have for your business and how you should use them.

❖ Promptly deal with small problems associated with customer complaints, product guarantees, and so on before they escalate to something larger.

❖ Keep inside and outside areas where customers or delivery persons walk free of snow, ice, and obstacles.

❖ Refer clients elsewhere if you have heard (or did research) that they have been involved in a number of lawsuits.

❖ Follow local, state, and federal licensing and regulations that apply to your specific business or its location. Read industry and business publications to be aware of any law or regulation changes. Ask for often free or low-cost publications about these restrictions so you will be informed.

❖ Get in the habit of putting agreements on paper for both parties to sign. For example, many publishers assign an article without a contract. A wise writer will draw up her own based on the conversation with the editor and send it to them for their approval and signature. This way both parties are in agreement as to due date, rights sold, payment, expenses reimbursed, and so on. Consult with your lawyer if you have any doubt about how to write it up.

✤ Do not get behind on your work—especially work that involves deadlines. Missing your deadline could cost your clients money—and could cost you, too, if they decide to sue for lost profits.

What to Do If You Get Sued

If the worst should happen and you receive notice about legal actions, immediately contact your lawyer—not the person or company who is initiating the lawsuit. Then write down all the circumstances involved to help you recall the incidents and their chronological order, including dates, people involved, etc. This will help your lawyer better understand what transpired and save money on time and research. Discuss all your resolution options, including arbitration and mediation (alternative dispute resolution or "ADR"). Fortunately, many lawsuits are settled out of court, but it still is an experience no businessperson wants to experience in terms of their time, money, and image to their business.

Taking Bad Accounts to Small-Claims Court

Some business suits can be filed in small-claims court, depending on the amount and circumstances involved. Generally, litigation that takes place through this legal avenue is cheaper and faster, and the decisions are just as binding as any court judgment. If you choose this avenue or are summoned as a defendant, do some legal research in a local law library; organize and prepare with documents supporting your claims or defense; and follow proper court protocol regarding dress, speech, and behavior. Talk to your attorney or a paralegal for some additional tips and advice.

———

For More Information
Books
The Legal Guide for Starting and Running a Small Business by Fred S. Steingold (Berkeley, CA: Nolo Press, 1998). Contains information on small-claims court.

What to Expect in a Lawsuit and How to Make Sure Your Attorney Gets Results by Ken Menendez (Santa Monica, CA: Merritt Publishing, 1998).

Internet Sites

< www.courttv.com/legalhelp/business/ > Court TV Legal Help's Small Business Law Center, with information on finding a business lawyer and helpful links.

< www.nolopress.com > The Web site of Nolo Press, publisher of many books on law and your business.

• SUCCESS SECRET 80 •

Learn how to manage your business inventory.

If your business produces more than one product or even type of service, you will want to have an efficient production system and keep accurate records of your products or you could lose both customers and money. Here are some tips for you.

Production

Nikki, who sells a variety of personal craft items—from purses and jewelry bags to ornaments and tote bags—spends about twenty hours a week in production and one day selling her items at the thirty craft shows she attends per year. Sharon, who sells her wood products to over 300 shops in the country, says: "My bookkeeping was so disorganized in the beginning that I was not even sure which customers had paid for their orders! Now I have a computer (and software) to print my order forms and have a record-keeping system that works for me."

If you sell your product wholesale or retail, you have to have a production schedule that can meet the demand for your product. For wholesale or selling through catalogs, generally you may have to produce hundreds or more of your product. If you have more of a one-of-kind product, you will have to be able to command prices that will compensate for the time involved in producing so few pieces.

Forecasting how much you need to have on hand can depend on various factors such as:

❖ Previous year's sales
❖ The seasonality of the product (is it targeted to specific holidays?)
❖ The overall economy and trends
❖ Your promotions regarding certain pieces

Women home-business owners recommend you test-market your new pieces by giving away or selling samples at small shops or shows. If the response is good, then set up a production line that is efficient and works for you. To fill her $5,000 worth of orders in her small home, Sharon has an assembly line set up. She cuts out all her pieces at once in her basement; sands them in an old outdoor chicken coop; stains and paints the pieces in her garage; and packs her items in boxes in her living room. (Sharon, her husband, and their three children are hoping to move to a larger place where she can have a regular workshop!)

Setting Up an Inventory System
Talk to other businesspeople in your industry or go by the trade publications and/or software manual recommendations to keep accurate books and inventory. If you fear learning your software, take classes, hire a college student majoring in computer programming or business; ask (or pay) a friend who understands how to operate the software you purchased to teach you; or get instruction books, videos, or CD-ROMs and teach yourself.

For More Information
Inventory Software
SOHOMaster 2.1 by One-On-One Software. Look for this at your favorite software retailer.

• SUCCESS SECRET 81 •

Know how to repair bad business credit.

If for any reason your past credit history is less than perfect, here are some steps you can take to help restore it.

❖ Stay away from credit repair organizations unless they are highly recommended by other professionals. Many are scams, so consult with your lawyer before you sign any contracts with them.

❖ Contact your creditors if you are unable to make payments to see whether you can work out an acceptable payment agreement.

❖ Talk to a financial advisor who may be able to give you some steps to take to solve your financial dilemma.

❖ "Downsize" your living expenses; sell off some seldom-used business equipment or work part time to pay off the bills you owe as quickly as possible.

❖ To rebuild your credit, offer to prepay your orders until you are able to convince your customer of your stability.

❖ Prevent it from happening again by building your business at a pace at which you can pay for the items you need and as the demand of your customers justifies your expenditures.

For More Information
Books
The Insider's Guide to Managing Your Credit by Deborah McNaughton (Chicago: Dearborn Financial Publishing, 1998).
Solving Credit Problems and Your Credit: A Complete Guide. Order booklets from the Consumer Information Catalog, P.O. Box 100, Pueblo, CO 81002, < www.pueblo.gsa.gov/ > .

• SUCCESS SECRET 82 •

Know what to include when signing business contracts.

Business deals are still sealed today with a handshake, but written contracts ensure that each party knows what to expect of the other.

Just because a consultant or business offers you a contract does not mean you have to sign as is—in fact, you should never do that unless you understand all your rights and obligations. An agent once told me, "Everything is negotiable."

A good contract is one that is fair to both parties; sometimes each has to concede a little in order to come to terms.

Go over any contract with your lawyer to clarify any language that confuses you. Write up the specifics you would like and give them to him or her to write into the contract. Also get legal advice when contracts involve the following:

* Hiring subcontractors or being hired as an independent contractor.
* Being liable for any damages that your services could cause in the process of your operations.
* Being requested to sign a non-competing clause for a period of time.
* Deciding payment and reimbursement terms.
* Business confidentiality terms—how restricting are they? and for how long do they apply to you?

Research this company's practices and treatment of other businesses. If you do not get good feedback, and your lawyer concurs, just say "No" to a questionable contract and go elsewhere. After all, as the owner of your own home business, it's your decision.

For More Information
Books

The Most Valuable Business Legal Forms You'll Ever Need by James C. Ray (Naperville, IL: Sourcebooks, Inc., 1997).

Wage Slave No More!: Law and Taxes for the Self-Employed by Stephen Fishman (Berkeley, CA: Nolo Press, 1996).

Internet Sites

< www.nolo.com > Nolo Press's "Self-Help Law Center," with books and articles about contracts, Independent Contractors, and home and small business legal concerns, and other legal topics.

13

Going Online

Though having a Web site for your home business will not guarantee you more customers, it will provide opportunities for your business to reach markets unobtainable through typical forms of advertising and promotion. Since you do not need a storefront on the Internet, potential customers cannot "see" your size—only your advertised products or services and related information. This allows small businesses to compete with larger businesses just by being present on the Internet.

As Internet use increases daily, all businesses will continue to see the impact it has and will continue to have on society into the next century. If you are considering getting a Web site for your business, take time to thoroughly understand how it can best serve your business. I hope the tips and resources presented in this chapter will provoke you to do more research about how this technological revolution can better serve you and your home venture.

• SUCCESS SECRET 83 •

Know how the Internet can
help your home business.

Internet Statistics

Every day more people are getting connected to the Internet. The U.S. Department of Commerce announced last year that the Internet is doubling every 100 days. In one of his online articles, Dr. Robert Sullivan, business expert and Web designer, says: "Forty percent of ALL small businesses now use the Internet; and Internet commerce, which was $10 billion dollars in 1998, is estimated to grow to $50 billion by 2002."

How Home Businesses Can Use the Internet

The National Foundation of Women Business Owners (NFWBO) said that the share of women business owners with home pages tripled from 1997 to 1998. Here are popular ways to use the Internet to help your home business.

Web Site

Hiring a Web designer to lay out a basic, business Web site can start at around $2,000 and range up to $8,000 (some large companies may pay as much as $100,000!). Additional charges will include fees for hosting, domain registering, and site updating, as well as costs to promote and publish your Web site. Low-cost

Women Business Owners and the Internet

The National Foundation for Women Business Owners (NFWBO— < www.nfwbo >) says, "Women business owners are taking a more proactive approach than men business owners in adopting new technology and using the Internet to grow their businesses."

alternatives include designing your own (free) home page in conjunction with your local ISP (Internet Service Provider), with commercial servers (such as AOL), or with sites like "The Women's
Network" (iVillage) that have easy steps to help you create a one-
page, business home page.*

Research
Even without a Web site, the Internet offers endless research opportunities to access business information at many sites like these:

✤ *Business Ideas:* Liz Folger's site < www.bizymoms.com >
   Mother's Home Business Network < www.homeworkingmom.
   com > .
✤ *Financing Info:* Insider Reports < www.insiderreports.com/index.
   html#3 > (Search Outback Library).
✤ *How-to & Start-up:* The (SBA's) Online Women's Business Center
   < www.onlinewbc.org > ; The Business Owner's Toolkit < www.
   toolkit.cch.com > .

Networking
You can share information and find solutions to business problems
by connecting with other home-business owners through Web
rings, chats, message boards (like those here at iVillage), and
home-business newsgroups, at sites such as these:

✤ Field of Dreams < www.fodreams.com > .
✤ Mom's Network Exchange < www.momsnetwork.com > .

Advertising and Marketing
✤ **Business Web Site:** Small business expert Kimberly Stanséll
   advises, if you are going to have a business Web site, to: "Take
   your time and determine the objective of your Web site. Otherwise your site may be just another puff piece about you or your
   company and be an ineffective marketing tool."
   Dr. Sullivan advises: "You should have ongoing information on
   your site—a reason for potential customers to come back."

---

*To start building an *i*Village site, go to < auth.ivillage.com/cgi-bin/home-
pages/display_homepages_login.cgi > .

Use services like "Submit It! Online" to announce your Web presence to search engines so you can be listed on their sites. <www.submit-it.com> ($59) or <www.siteowner.com> (free).

❖ **E-mail:** Provide information to potential customers through invited e-mail (not unsolicited e-mail, called "spamming"), by using avenues such as e-zine advertising, publishing, and discussion group participation. Do not forget to also add your business signature (a tagline at the end of your e-mail message) to all your customer e-mails. BizWeb contains excellent articles (see Resources on page 398).

Without a Web site you can market your business by offering to host a newsgroup, online forum, message board, or chat session, which will help position you as an industry leader. You could also ask managers at other sites your potential customers visit whether they would like to post your articles or edited chat transcripts (for free).

For More Information
Books
HyperWars: 11 Strategies for Survival and Profit in the Era of Online Business by Brian Judson (New York: Scribner, 1999).
The Internet Glossary and Quick Reference Guide by Alan Freedman, Alfred and Emily Glossbrenner (New York: Amacon, 1998).
The Online Business Atlas by Douglas E. Goldstein with Joyce Flory, Ph.D. (New York: McGraw-Hill, 1996).

Internet Sites
<www.bizweb2000.com> BizWeb. Excellent online marketing techniques/articles and free e-zine.
<www.isquare.com> Small and home-business information (and free online newsletters); articles on small business topics, including "Why Your Business MUST Make Use of the Internet" by Dr. Robert Sullivan, e-commerce expert and author of *The Small Business Start-Up Guide; United States Government—New Customer.*

Universal E-Mail Account Benefits

Whether you have a commercial or a local Internet service provider (ISP), you should consider getting a universal e-mail account for your business for several reasons, including these:

❖ You can access your e-mail wherever you can "hook" into a computer and Web browser, even while you are traveling.

❖ You can separate your business-related e-mail from personal messages.

❖ You present a more professional image, depending on which universal account you use.

< www.kimberlystansell.com > This is the Web site of Kimberly Stanséll, entrepreneurial trainer and author of *Bootstrapper's Success Secrets: 151 Tactics for Building Your Business on a Shoestring Budget.*

Software for Creating Your Own Web Site
(Check also at office supply and software retail stores.)

Adobe PageMill 3.0 < www.adobe.com > enables you to build a Web presence.

Microsoft Front Page < www.microsoft.com/frontpage > provides easy Web site construction.

My Internet Business Page < www.mysoftware.com > (800) 325-3508.

Internet Malls and Your Home Business
Just like the craft malls over the past decade opened to provide a storefront for many skilled artists and craftspeople, so, too, have "storefronts" opened all over the Internet. Even big flea markets are posting their regular vendors' ads on the Internet. Here are

some points you will want to consider before linking your site with an Internet mall.

✤ Successful malls are those that market heavily to bring potential customers to the site.
✤ The mall's operators are knowledgeable about online marketing.
✤ Contacting other businesses to see what kind of response they have had since joining this mall will help you determine potential effectiveness.
✤ The mall should use a variety of marketing and linking techniques so your site receives more traffic.

The Internet may or may not be worth the expense for advertising your home business. Do your research into any malls you are considering. Look over other mall sites like < www.malls.com/ awesome > , The Awesome Mall of the Internet. Do not overlook, though, doing your own registering of your site in the many existing search engines. Also register your business with the many women's sites such as Field of Dreams < www.fodreams.com > and home-business sites like Mom's Network Exchange < www.momsnetwork. com > and Web rings where you can list your business for free.

Internet Realities
Before you decide to get a site for your business, consider some realities of having an Internet site:

✤ You can spend big money for a site and still have no one come. Web designing can be free (your own one-page site), or can cost many thousands of dollars for an extravagant site.
✤ Internet viewing is unique from other media. People easily become impatient looking for information so it should be arranged in an understandable order or visitors will click somewhere else.
✤ Like a newsletter, designs, photos, and simple graphics make a site more interesting and more attractive, but if they take too long to download, visitors will not return.
✤ Marketing your site is ongoing and constant. It takes work. Once you have a site built, you have to constantly "work" it to help your share of the millions of visitors to the Internet find their way (hopefully) to your site.

Two Examples of Women Business Owners Using the Internet

"Women business owners are exploring the Internet with greater zeal than men business owners." —NFWBO

Here are two examples:

Louise Spindler of the Ann Hemyng Candy, Inc.'s Chocolate Factory, Trumbauersville, Pennsylvania < www.chocolateshop.com > says, "We have been contacted by many corporations and have done corporate logo molds (in chocolate) for them or special packs for events they are having, all through our Internet site. This (corporate) business would not have developed without our Web site."

Rochelle B. Balch, of RB Balch & Associates, Inc., Glendale, Arizona, started her home-based, computer consulting business in 1993 when she was downsized out of a job. Balch's business offers contract/custom programming, small office support services and all types of related PC support. In 1997 it grossed more than $2.4 million. Rochelle's Web site, < www.rbbalch.com >, contains helpful and timely computer-related articles, and describes the services her business offers to potential customers. She is also the author of the book, *C-E-O & M-O-M, Same Time, Same Place* (Glendale, AZ: RB Associates, 1997), which she describes on her site as a book that, ". . . will inspire you to 'go for it' and learn to understand that prioritizing is the key for keeping your sanity."

These are just two of the many women today who are using the Internet for their businesses. You can find others listed on many women's business Web sites (see Resources on page 398).

Tips for Finding an Internet Service Provider

❖ For normal Internet use, you should only need a dial-up service such as Point to Point Protocol (PPP).

❖ As opposed to the commercial online services, ISP costs average $20 per month for a "flat fee" account.

❖ Make sure your ISP has either an 800-number or a listing of local numbers through which you can access the Internet at a good speed with no toll or connection charges.

❖ Your ISP should have plenty of technical support and good response.

• SUCCESS SECRET 84 •

Know what should (and should not) be included on your Web site.

Legalities and the Internet
Here are some legal recommendations you should consider in having an online site:

❖ Thoroughly research the domain name you choose for your Universal Resource Locator (URL) to make sure you are not infringing on some other company's trademarked name. Experts also advise you to get a federal trademark for your domain name and display your trademark.

❖ If you have written material on your Web site, you should also copyright it.

❖ Some businesses selling online goods and services may come under state, federal, or international laws. You must obey truth in advertising. If you are unsure your advertising is following FTC rules, call its Public Reference Branch (202) 326-2222 or visit its site: < www.ftc.gov > .

❖ Get permission to place any other link on your Web site.

❖ Do not infringe on any other site's copyright. You cannot use graphics, articles, original designs, etc. from another site without permission.

You are responsible for everything on your Web site. If you are unsure about any legal questions, check with an attorney knowledgeable with Internet usage.

For More Information
Books
Cyberlaw: What You Need to Know About Doing Business Online by David Johnston, Sunny Handa, and Charles Morgan (North York, Ontario: Stoddart Publishing, 1997).

Internet Sites
< www.cyberlaw.com > Jonathan Rosenor's CyberLaw™.
< www.findlaw.com > FindLaw™ Internet Legal Resources.

What to Include on Your Site

When visitors do find your site, what will they see? Here are some tips for making a good "first Internet impression."

❖ Ask your Web designer to make sure your site is viewable by both Macintosh and PC users, and for both major browsers, Microsoft Internet Explorer and Netscape Navigator. Your site can look quite different in another browser—and not always better.
❖ Make your site interesting and full of information that will be helpful to the visitor. If you cannot spend time updating the information every day, consider a much more manageable "weekly tip."
❖ Register your site with search engines, using several key words that will help people find your site when they enter a category in a search engine.
❖ Study other successful business sites to get some ideas of how to improve yours.

One woman spent over half a year researching information about effective Web sites before she had hers designed. Learn all you can, and keep learning by reading Internet-related publications. Then start simply and let your Web site "evolve" to fit the needs of your visitors (and potential customers).

For More Information
Books
121 Internet Businesses You Can Start from Home: Plus a Beginner's Guide to Starting a Business Online by Ron E. Gielgun (Santa Rosa, CA: Actium Publishing, 1997).
Making Money in Cyberspace by Paul and Sarah Edwards (New York: Putnam, 1999).

Internet Sites

< www.actium1.com > Actium Publishing with "Internet Start-Ups," and helpful information.

< www.poorrichard.com > Helps people set up Web sites by Peter Kent, author of *Poor Richard's Web Site: Geek-Free, Commonsense Advice on Building a Low-Cost Web Site* (Lakewood, CO: Top Floor Publishing, 1998).

• SUCCESS SECRET 85 •

Understand how to market and maintain your Web site.

According to data from International Data Corporation (< www.idc. com >), the number of small businesses with sites on the Web will be 4.3 million by the year 2001; and the average overall revenues of small businesses using the Internet is $3.79 million.

Attracting Customers to Your Web Site

Here are some suggestions to make your site stand out from your competitors':

Offer Customers a "Secure" Site

If you take credit card orders over your Web site, make sure your site is a "secure server." Secure sites are indicated by an "s" added to http, right before the URL (regular URL: http://; secure server URL: https//). Whether you arrange security for your Web site after getting a merchant account or contract with another business for the secure site, it will be a definite advantage. Customers are likely to order products from you rather than your competitors who don't advertise such security.

❖ Personalize your site with your photo and some interesting information about you and your business, and make it easy for people to contact you.

❖ If customers have been pleased with your business's service and/or product, get permission to post these endorsements on your home page.

❖ Put the value of your business on your home page—for example: "specializing in special orders, guarantees, speedy service."

❖ If you also publish a newsletter (snail mail) or e-mail, have the latest issue online; or if you wrote a book, have some excerpts from it—especially some helpful tips for your visitors.

❖ Write articles in industry publications and in your tagline, put your Web site and e-mail address.

For More Information

Books

Advertising on the Internet by Robin Zeff and Brad Aronson (New York: Wiley, 1997).

Internet Security Handbook by Williams Stallings (Foster City, CA: IDG Books, 1995).

Online Marketing Handbook by Daniel S. Janal (New York: Van Nostrand Reinhold, 1996).

Internet Sites

< www.charge.com/ > Charge.Com specializes in firms that specialize in small and home-based operations that do business online.

< www.e-digest.com > site of *E-Digest,* a weekly free marketing newsletter for Internet Entrepreneurs. To subscribe, visit the site.

< www.wilsonweb.com/webmarket > Web Marketing Today Info Center.

Software

Raptor Firewall < www.axent.com > Computer security software for taking online credit card orders, etc.

• SUCCESS SECRET 86 •

Apply basic tips for your Web site's survival.

Here are some tips for surviving on the Internet:

❖ **Be patient.** Just because you have an Internet site does not mean you will get thousands of instant orders. Despite the phenomenal increase in the number of people connected to the Internet, the majority are not yet accustomed to purchasing items on the Internet. Business experts say the most popular items currently are appliances, stocks, computers, and electronics.

❖ **Remember its benefits.** It's open 24 hours a day, offers global market potential, and is easy to update.

Make Sure Customers Know How to Access Your Web site

Be sure to include your Web site address (URL) on or in all the following:

❖ Your business cards, brochures, and other promotional and print materials.

❖ Your e-mail "signature" (the tagline on all your electronic mail messages).

❖ Your business stationery.

❖ All your classified and display ads, including telephone directory ads.

❖ All your product labels or hang tags.

❖ Taglines of any articles you write for publications or Internet sites.

❖ Handout sheets for any courses or workshops you teach.

❖ Any magnetic car signs or signs you are permitted to post outside your residence for your home business.

❖ The foreword or end of any booklets or books you write.

✤ **Put your "signature" on all e-mail correspondence** and your site address on all your promotional materials, which include your Web site's URL.

✤ **Participate in message boards** and chats, write guest articles, and so forth. In your credit line, always include your URL. The Chocolate Factory, a handmade chocolate company run by a mother and daughter team, includes its site address (< www. chocolateshop.com >) on all their candy labels. They ship their candies all over the world.

✤ **Do not give up.** As with all marketing, it takes time until you find the right "key" to unlock those millions of Internet customers' doors.

For More Information
Books
HyperWars: 11 Strategies for Survival and Profit in the Era of Online Business by Bruce Judson (New York: Scribner, 1998).

• **SUCCESS SECRET 87** •

Promote your business's Web site using e-zines.

Women business owners are exploring the Internet with greater zeal than men business owners, with over 47% of women business owners currently subscribing to an online service compared to 41% of men business owners (NFWBO).

An "e-zine" is an electronic magazine. Ads in e-zines are generally low-cost and are sent out to thousands of people—but not as spamming. The purpose of your ads is describe your business and encourage potential customers to click on a hyperlink placed at the end of your ad, leading them to your Web site. From there, you can have an online order form or other instructions for either getting more information about your business and/or products.

E-zines are like print publications in that they target certain customers, so before you place any ads in them, make sure you study their content and audience so you can choose the best ones that will reach your target market. Once you have narrowed your selection, code your ads so you can evaluate the results each ad brings.

With a little bit of research, your best advertising avenue may be no more than an e-mail away.

For More Information
Internet Sites
< www.DrNunley.com > Web site of Dr. Kevin Nunley, Internet marketing expert (also has the site, < www.BizGuru.com > with low-cost advertising strategies, etc., for "home biz workers").
< www.everythingemail.com > Mary Houten-Kemp's EVERYTHING E-MAIL™ (has e-mail tips, glossary, and other relevant information).

E-Zine Samples
The A.I.M. Ezine—Includes regular Internet marketing tips and articles to over 308,000 of its subscribers. To subscribe, send a blank e-mail to: < subscribe-Inet-mailer@send.memail.com >.

Software
Eudora Pro Email 4.0 < www.eudora.com > e-mail management.

14

Planning for Your Business's Future

Change is the law of life, and those who only look to the past or present are certain to miss the future.

—John F. Kennedy

• **SUCCESS SECRET 88** •

Know how to safely grow your business.

Once your business has reached its break-even point (see Glossary on page 376), you'll want to start thinking about business growth and in what direction to take your business. Of course, this will have to be a decision based on your personal and business goals, as well as your financial resources. Some women are satisfied with their customer base and want to keep their business at a certain level, while others want to expand it as much as possible.

If you decide to work toward future growth of your business, you should consider all the ramifications entailed with business growth. You may have to delegate many routine business activities to focus only on this goal. Another problem is your competitors may become more aggressive in their marketing efforts as they see you

349

as a potential threat to their business's profits. Lastly, you may have to seriously pursue venture capital to fund your business's expansion plans.

As your business becomes more established, there are other considerations you should consider such as your future retirement, passing your business to your heirs, and even the possibility of franchising your business if it is successful. Besides wanting your business to be successful, you may also want it to play a role in "giving back" to your community. These topics and others are presented in this chapter.

Expansion Dilemma

Many home businesses have literally started from kitchen tables and have gone on to be multimillion-dollar enterprises. Others with modest start-ups have stayed modest—or worse, expanded into failure. As was discussed previously, once you begin to expand, you will have to delegate more duties, hire others, and quite likely find yourself going from being main product or service generator to being administrator. This is the case for Paula Kay with Ageless Placements, who has hired her sister and daughter to handle the operations while she now oversees the business, plus develops ways to expand it into a business opportunity for others.

If you find yourself unable to handle the demand for your products or services, you will have to consider these options: turn down business and refer overflow to other home businesses, raise your prices, or explore hiring options (see chapter 11, Open for Business).

Expansion Tips

Here are some expansion considerations you may want to ponder:

❖ Analyze all your options before you rush headlong into expansion. Decide what you can or cannot do or if this is one of your business goals.

❖ Do not be in a hurry to expand. Concentrate on cementing customer loyalty before you rush off to start something new. Ask yourself whether the quality and service your present customers have come to expect could suffer if you expand.

❖ Realize that expansion will most likely change your role as sole proprietor to "boss," entailing more management duties.

❖ Consider all the uncertainties. Ask yourself whether an expansion is going to eventually bring in more money. Will you be taking too large a financial risk? Is it going to jeopardize your present business or take more time from your family or other pursuits you care about?

Take in these considerations, talk to your family about an expansion's risks, consult with your financial experts, contact women business owners whose businesses have expanded, and then—and only then—make a decision about the expansion of your business.

Bigger Is Not Always Better
One mother with a home-cooking business says that right now, with her children still small, she really does not want to expand further. She says she has enough business supplying to caterers and working with another home business that uses her products; she likes her current business pace so she can volunteer at her children's school and other activities.

Liz Folger, author of the *Stay-at-Home Mom's Guide to Making Money* (Prima Publishing), advises: "Don't forget why you chose to work from home in the first place. For me, it's to raise my daughters myself. Raising does not mean, 'I'll play with you in a few minutes' every time they come to me for my attention. It does mean taking time for your kids. They grow up so quickly, and you can never have yesterday back. Live today to the fullest."

Consider, too, ways you can expand without moving your business from home—such as outsourcing extra work, investing in new technology, teaming up, or bartering with other home-business owners.

———

For More Information
Internet Sites
< www.bizymoms.com > Liz Folger's Web site. Contains resources, business ideas, articles, and other information for work-at-home moms.

———

Moving Out and Relocation

As discussed in chapter 9, Resources for All Entrepreneurs, one way a number of home businesses expand is to be accepted into small business incubators. One rural family business selling family hot-sauce recipes has taken this route to successfully expand their food-related business using the incubator's resources and experts. If you are considering moving your business out of your home, ask yourself the following: Do I want to purchase, lease, or rent facilities? How will this move affect my cash flow? Is there a location suitable for my business, convenient to my customers, and at a good location to attract new customers? Is moving out necessary for expansion?

For More Information

Publications

The Entrepreneur's Relocation Guide by Kimberly Stanséll, 1997. FREE while supplies last. Send your request for a copy along with $3.00 to cover shipping and handling to Kimberly Stanséll, 6308 W. 89th St., Suite 306, Los Angeles, CA 90045 (only requests with shipping and handling fee will be processed); or visit < www.kimberlystansell.com > .

Money to Expand Your Business

If you are thinking of expanding your business, one of the best reasons for doing so is that your sales indicate the potential market is there to support your growth. Banks, investors, state agencies, the SBA, and other lenders are more likely to lend you the money you need, because they have more of a guarantee that their money will be repaid. You should, however, go through the formal process of drawing up or revising a formal business plan.

From your business plan, draw realistic projections to present to potential lenders. If your business offers potential for employment of other workers, do not forget other funding options. Your state's economic development department, for example, may have funding for which your business may qualify. Again, do thorough research into all the possible options that may be available to you.

• SUCCESS SECRET 89 •

Consider how to explore additional business avenues.

Franchising or Turning Your Business into a Business Opportunity

If your business could be operated successfully in other parts of the country (or world), you may want to think about franchising it, selling it as a business opportunity, or licensing it. This involves studying what franchises and business opportunities like yours exist. Your first step is to research what is involved in these types of expansion. Talk to lawyers specializing in franchising and other methods of expansion; talk to other women franchisors (see chapter 2, Starting-Out Steps) or sellers of business opportunities; consult with other experts at SCORE or Women's Business Development Centers; and visit franchise shows to see what is involved.

Tanya Wallace, founder and franchisor of Toddlin' Time parent/toddler play programs, says she franchised her business in 1992 "as a way of offering the Toddlin' Time system to other communities, as it proved to be very successful with mine. Franchising seemed to me a way of keeping my system intact, ensuring that franchisees would follow specific guidelines for operating their centers, which I felt was necessary in a business dealing with children." Wallace is also the co-author with Caroline Hull of *Money-Making Moms: How Work at Home Can Work for You*, which can be ordered through her Web site at < www.moneymakingmoms.com > or through bookstores.

Business Spin-Offs

Both Paula Kay with Ageless Placements, Inc., and Deborah Cohen, president of Home Remedies of NY™, took their successful businesses and packaged them into affordable business opportunities consisting of start-up manuals and various training or consultation and support. Both women want to give others the head-start opportunities to start a home-business venture.

Deborah Cohen says: "Once my business was successfully up and running, I was approached by other individuals interested in starting a home-based business like mine. After consulting with business advisors, several attorneys, family members, and friends, I decided to document the HRN* business in a comprehensive business manual so that others could benefit from my experience."

She continues: "We opted to market the business to stay-at-home moms specifically because, as a stay-at-home mom myself, I had created the business to be adaptable to the lifestyle of today's busy mom. . . . To date, of the 25 HRN's operating across the country, 19 are operated by stay-at-home moms."

Diversifying may be the most cost-effective and logical method of expanding your business—and often yields lucrative results. Bert added her mail-order business selling country curtains when people saw her ad in a country-decorating magazine.

For More Information
Books
A Woman's Guide to Her Own Franchise Business by Anne Small. (Greenport, NY: Pilot Books,† 1986).
Franchise Bible: How to Buy a Franchise or Franchise Your Own Business, 3rd ed., by Erin J. Keup (Grants Pass, OR: Oasis Press, 1995).

Internet Sites
<www.pilotbooks.com> Pilot books.

---

*HRN is a service that refers qualified home maintenance and repair contractors to local homeowners who need these home repair services.
†Pilot Books has been a leading publisher of franchising information since 1959. For a listing of additional publications, visit their site (listed on page 406) or call (800) 79-PILOT for a catalog.

Business Opportunities

Ageless Placements, Inc., Paula Kay, P.O. Box 48513, St. Petersburg, FL 33743; (727) 547-4337.

Home Remedies of NY, Inc.™, 1539 Hewlett Ave., Hewlett, NY 11557-1511; (516) 374-8504; e-mail < homremdies@aol.com > or visit < www.homeownersreferral.com > .

Magazines

Entrepreneur Magazine hosts franchise expos around the country, as well as featuring franchise and business opportunities in their publications. Also visit the Web sites it sponsors: < www. entrepreneurmag.com > and < www.bizstartups.com > .

(Also see chapter 2, Starting-Out Steps, for more information on franchises and business opportunities.)

• SUCCESS SECRET 90 •

Have a succession plan for your heirs.

Business experts say that a majority of family businesses never survive the succeeding family generations because their businesses lack a succession plan. If you would like to see your home business stay in the family, here are some suggestions to help form a plan:

Women Business Owners Pass Their Businesses Down

In a 1995 study for their "Trendsetter Barometer" in which they interviewed CEOs of 435 companies identified in the media as the fastest-growing U.S. businesses over the previous five years, Coopers & Lybrand, L.L.P., discovered that "The majority of women CEOs (59 percent) said they plan to pass their businesses along to a close family member, such as a child, a spouse, or other close relative. But less than one-third of women business owners (30 percent) have a formal written succession plan in place."

❖ Realize that you will not live forever, and if you hope your children or family will take over your business someday, start discussing this possibility with them now.
❖ Involve the children in your business, but do not force or expect them to want to continue in your place.
❖ Talk to a lawyer and a financial advisor to work out the legal arrangements and documents while everyone can have input.

• SUCCESS SECRET 91 •

Know how to sell your business profitably.

Considerations Before You Sell Your Business

As stated previously, if you are a sole proprietor of a service business, you are the business. Without you, the business offers its customers no guarantees that it will be operated with the same attention to quality and service. Chris Carroll sold her home-cleaning business to become her comedian husband's agent. She says the man and woman who bought it went out of business in three months. They did not know how to operate it for growth, and Carroll's customers did not like the way the new owners operated.

For just this reason, the selling value of a one-person service or small product business is typically lower than the value of bigger businesses. This does not mean all one-person, home-service businesses have little value. It all depends on the specific type of business, how long it has been operating, and the customer base and growth it has to sustain it—no matter who owns it.

Business experts suggest you work on establishing a business that can stand on its own before you think of selling it for any profit. Consult with a lawyer familiar with selling and buying businesses before you sell. If you have a partner or other owners, then they may offer to buy your share out. Plan ahead if you are entertaining the thought of selling your business to reap the best benefits from a sale.

For More Information
Books
How to Sell Your Business—And Get What You Want! By Colin Gabriel
(Westport, CT: Gwent Press, 1998).

• **Success Secret 92** •

Know what to consider in buying a business.

Buying a business can give the owner the following advantages: existing sales records, existing assets that can make getting a loan easier, more opportunities to purchase it (monthly payments with options to buy, etc.), and an existing customer base. If you would like to buy a business to run from your home, here are some suggestions:

❖ Research to see whether it is "do-able" from home and permitted by zoning laws.

❖ Look at the competition to get an idea of potential growth.

❖ Have a lawyer and your financial advisor go over the business debts, financial records, etc.

❖ Assess your own skills in running this business. Do you know anything about it? Is the present owner willing to stay on as an advisor to help guide you?

Pam Adzima had started re-manufacturing toner cartridges from home seven years ago, and slowly built her business. She says that, with her growth, "I decided to buy out a local company with 5,500 square feet of office space and a trained employee. On the day of the closing, the former owner stole all the assets and left the company bankrupt. It took three months of no salary for me and working two jobs (with four kids) to get back in the black."

Fortunately, Adzima's story had a happy ending: "Today I have eight employees, my husband and parents have joined me in business, and we are approaching one million in sales." Adzima has also expanded to selling computers.

Buying a business may seem like an ideal way to go, but proceed with caution before you invest any money.

For More Information
Internet Sites

< www.entrepreneurmag.com >   "Business Resale Network," located on *Entrepreneur Magazine's* Web site. Contains a comprehensive listing of existing businesses for sale.

• SUCCESS SECRET 93 •

Know how to survive a business bankruptcy.

Unfortunately, sometimes due to overextending one's business spending, not paying attention to cash flow, or to unforeseen circumstances such as illness or family crises, you may not be able to see your way out of your financial troubles other than to file for bankruptcy. Among the options you might try are arranging a payment plan with your creditors or borrowing from family, friends, or business associates. You can also go to a nonprofit consumer association in your area that provides debt counseling. Perhaps they can help you set up an installment plan, if you can afford it along with your living expenses. If your business cannot generate enough income for you to recover, consult with an attorney about what filing for bankruptcy entails and how it can affect your future credit rating.

You can build your credit back slowly using secured credit cards or sometimes by providing proof of steady earnings. Of course, the best action is to prevent business and personal bankruptcy by spending wisely and slowly as your business grows.

For More Information
Books

How to Hold or Fold: What to Do with a Business in Trouble and How to Deal with the Aftermath by Lisa Rogak (Grafton, NH: Williams Hill Publishing, 1999).

• SUCCESS SECRET 94 •

Know how to plan for your retirement.

An important factor new entrepreneurs often overlook is planning for retirement. New business owners may not realize that most retirement planning experts estimate that each of us will need around 60 percent to 80 percent of our present annual income to support *every one* of our retirement years! Add to this that the Social Security Administration says the present Social Security system only contributes about 23 percent for the average retiree's income, and the constant speculation by politicians that the Social Security or Medicare Trust Fund may go broke in future years. You can see why it is crucial to start early to ensure financial security for your later years.

A recent study by The National Foundation of Women Business Owners reported that even though women business owners discuss retirement issues more frequently and offer their employees a larger number of retirement investment options than do men who own businesses, *some 51 percent of these women-owned businesses have no retirement plans.* Fortunately, movements like the recent legislation, the Taxpayer Relief Act of 1997, and a 1998 joint campaign by the NAWBO and the Department of Labor to educate women entrepreneurs about retirement savings plans are encouraging more women business owners to establish retirement plans.

Why else should a small business owner or self-employed woman set aside money for retirement?

❖ Each retirement dollar saved is worth eight to ten times the original amount over a 30- to 40-year span due to compounded interest. Thus, the earlier you start, the more you will have for retirement.
❖ A retirement account offers one of the best tax shelters you can have.
❖ It helps you develop self-discipline and set a regular pattern for saving.
❖ Having a retirement plan for any workers you may hire will attract and retain employees and help foster loyalty among them.

Once you have committed to starting a savings retirement plan, where do you go from here?

First, consult with a financial advisor before you select any plan. Ask your accountant, another woman business owner, your banker, or members of a business association to which you may belong for names of advisers they recommend.

In choosing the best plan for you, first set down a realistic and affordable budget—not just for the present, but for your predictable future. Next, take time to read, research, and talk to other self-employed individuals and small business owners about why they chose their particular retirement plans.

Any of a number of retirement plans may suit your needs. You will need to consult with your financial advisor for a more extensive explanation of each plan and to periodically adjust your retirement plan to any changing financial circumstances concerning your business's operations or your status as a self-employed individual. Hopefully, your hard work over the years as an entrepreneur will bring you success, and you will be rewarded with a financially independent retirement.

___

For More Information
Books
10 Minute Guide to Retirement for Women by Kerry Hannon (New York: Macmillan General Reference, 1996).

___

• SUCCESS SECRET 95 •

Take the opportunity to use your business to help others.

It is very gratifying to use your business to help other women entrepreneurs, schools, or organizations in your community. The NFWBO states: "Many women business owners have relied upon mentors when getting their businesses started."

LaDonna Vick of Mommy's@Work says: "I lend my expertise to the local schools whenever possible. The teachers really enjoy having me there, and it gives me a chance to show my daughters that because I work at home, I'm able to come to their schools."

You may be able to help in youth entrepreneurship programs, or have high school students or college interns assist you in running your business while learning valuable entrepreneurial skills.

You could teach entrepreneurship courses at adult evening schools or participate in nonprofit organizations' fund-raising events that help serve the less fortunate in your community. (See also Entrepreneurship Education under Resources on page 398.)

You can also be a mentor to other women entrepreneurs through the SBA Mentor program, or by networking with other women who own home businesses. Jeanie Swisher, who has been an entrepreneur, says that her personal motto is "If I have only one life to live—if I can help others get what they want in life, then I will get what I want, too." Swisher attributes her success in life "to a genuine love for others, a deep sense of fair play and the innate determination to succeed." And many women who have been helped by mentors become mentors to others in business ventures—the shared knowledge is passed along to help other women achieve their dreams!

For More Information
Books
Making the Rules by Jeanie Swisher, (West Chester, PA: Spectrum, 1998). Focuses on the many aspects of running your own business, including start-up, direct mail, multi-level marketing, Internet and Web development tips. To order, send your name and address and $16.95 to SPECTRUM PUBLISHERS DIRECT, making the rules, 35 South High Street #4001, West Chester, PA 19382.

Newsletters
Swisher's online newsletter, *UP-TO-SPEED Business News* about marketing, direct mail, and networking. Type "subscribe" in the subject and e-mail to <uptospeedbiznews9@usa.net>. Print edition available.

15

Miscellaneous Business Ventures & Preparing for the 21st Century

We've got to have a legacy of leadership. We've got to bring along a generation of women who are going to confront twenty-first century realities.

—Jewell Jackson McCabe, business woman, activist, and president of the National Coalition of 100 Black Women

• SUCCESS SECRET 96 •

Know how to use mail order to increase business sales or how to start your own mail-order venture.

Millions of products are bought and sent daily in the mail. With the growing number of businesses selling items from the Internet every day, mail-order sales are going to continually increase. The advantage of the Internet is that a home business does not need to put together and mail a catalog when full-color items can be displayed on a Web page for millions to view. Most mail-order busi-

Two Biggest Mistakes in Mail Order

Terry Thomas, publisher of *Mail Order Marketing News*, says the two most common mail-order business mistakes are:

1. "Unrealistic expectations—if you think you are going to become rich in one or two months, you are most likely not being very realistic. You must be willing to stick to a plan and slowly build your business," says Thomas.
2. "Thinking that one product will make you rich is short-term thinking," says Thomas. "You must build and maintain a catalog of related products to sell to your customers over and over again. Think in terms of markets! Identify a market with an unfulfilled need, and find products to fulfill that need," continues Thomas.

For a sample of Thomas's mail-order newsletter, send $1 to TJT Publications, P.O. Box 55685, Valencia, CA 91385.

nesses use a combination of advertising, by mailing their catalogs and maintaining their Internet sites to feature special items.

What the Internet has done is provide a storefront for small businesses that target narrow markets for products such as fishing flies or collectibles. One person sells an average of 700 collectible candy dispensers a week from her townhouse; a young man has a multimillion-dollar business selling ATV parts from his garage via the mail. One woman's daughter paid for her college junior year spent in Scotland when she noticed out-of-date, collector bean toys being sold in Scottish shops. She purchased them for a few pounds and shipped them home to her mother, who offered them for sale on the Internet site set up specifically for collectors of this toy.

If you have knowledge of a collectible or have a product or products that could sell well to a nationwide market, then you may want to consider selling these items using mail order. Georgeanne Fiumara, founder of Mothers' Home Business Network < www. homeworkingmom.com >, says: "Choosing the right product to sell is the first and most important first step for anyone who wants to start a mail-order business. The ideal product will be easy to describe, desired by a well-designed target market, affordable to ship, and can be sold for at least four times your cost to produce or purchase."

Fiumara continues: "Do you have an expertise in any field? If so, you can transform your knowledge into an information product. Selling information in the form of newsletters, books, booklets, audiotapes, or videotapes will also allow you to have exclusive rights and full control of your offering."

Creating Your Own Catalog

With thousands of mail catalogs being sent to consumers as well as groups and organizations, you might consider putting together your own catalog of products and mailing it to your customers. Full-color catalogs are expensive and beyond the price range of many home businesses, even though a number of very big catalog houses were started from the founders' homes.

With no previous experience, Bert put together her own mail-order catalog featuring the lace curtains she carries in her home-based antiques and country items store. She did most of the layout herself and hired a professional photographer to take the color photos she included. Bert sent the catalog to the mailing list she garnered from previous customers who had ordered through a display ad she placed in Country Sampler and her 800-ordering number.

The catalog was not a total failure (Bert did receive a number of orders from her catalog mailing), but generally it was not worth the expense and time involved. "My best advertising venue for mail order has been the responses I have received from my curtain display ad in Country Sampler magazine, followed up with direct mailings of the curtain brochures," says Bert. "I do not think I would do another one (catalog). I did not realize how well the brochures that I get from the lace company have worked for me. All I had to do was develop a better marketing strategy. That's the key to the whole thing. The catalog doesn't really matter if you have the right product and find the right market for it."

If you would like to put together your own catalog, learn all you can about doing it—take courses, start small, and build slowly (see *For More Information* below). Make sure you have a mailing list of potential buyers like Bert did, or you will be wasting money you could use elsewhere in your business operations.

Selling to Catalog Houses

You may want to sell just a few items of yours to a catalog house. Most products submitted for acceptance in catalogs are rejected because of size, production problems, and lack of sales appeal. However, if you wish to try, contact the catalog company in which you are interested and inquire about their product-submissions procedure. Catalog buyers say to choose your best-selling item, one that is unique and one that you can mass-produce should your product become popular.

For More Information

Books/Directories

Home-Based Catalog Marketing by William J. Bond (New York: McGraw-Hill, 1994).

How to Create Successful Catalogs by Maxwell Sroge (Lincolnwood, IL: NTC Business Books, 1995).

How to Start a Home-Based Mail Order Business by Georgeanne Fiumara (Old Saybrook, CT: Globe Pequot Press, 1996).

Mail-Order Success Secrets, 2nd ed., by Tyler Hicks (Rocklin, CA: Prima Publishing, 1998).

National Directory of Mailing Lists, edited by Ken Barry (New York: Oxbridge Communications, 1998).

Associations

Direct Marketing Association, 1120 Avenue of the Americas, New York, NY 10036, < www.the-dma.org > . Offers professional development, training seminars, workshops, library and information services. Annual conference and exhibition and carries a direct marketing publications catalog.

Federal Trade Commission, Public Reference Branch, Washington, DC 20580, (202) 326-2222, < www.ftc.gov >. Oversees truth in advertising and the mail-order industry. Order their Mail-Order Rule booklet.

National Mail Order Association (NMOA), 2807 Polk St., NE, Minneapolis, MN 55418. Excellent for small mail-order businesses; monthly newsletter: "Mail Order Digest." Web site, < www. nmoa.org > includes "Mail Order Marketing Tips," "Six Mail Order Pointers," and "How to Pick the Right Product."

Mailing List Brokers

Compiler's Plus, Inc., 100 Paragon Dr., Montvale, NJ 07645-1745. Sales leads and mailing lists.

Mail Management Software

Mailer's Software, 970 Calle Negocio, San Clemente, CA 92673-6201, < www.800mail.com >. Bulk mail software.

Mail Order Wizard, Haven Corp, 802 Madison St., Evanston, IL 60202-2207.

MySoftware Company, 1259 El Camino Real, Suite 167, Menlo Park, CA 94025-4227, (800) 325-3508, < www.mysoftware.com >. Has easy-to-run software for mailing and database needs. Write, call, or visit their Web site.

Online Catalog Tool

If you want to create an online catalog, try *Catalog-on-a-Disk* by EmmaSoft, which is a cost-effective toolkit for creating and distributing your electronic product catalog. You can install your catalog on your Web site or issue it on disk, using unlimited pictures and words. For information, write EmmaSoft Software Company, Inc., P.O. Box 238, Lansing, NY 14882-0238, or visit < www.catalog-on-a-disk.com/ >.

Shipping Packages from Home
Airborne Express (800) 247-2676.
FedEx (800) 463-3339. Free FedEx Ship software for regular shipments <www.FedEx.com>.
UPS (800) 742-5877.
Contact each company for occasional and regular pickup expenses from your home.

Video
"Money From Home—How to Succeed in Your Own Mail Order Business" by Gary Reed, produced by Quality Plus, P.O. Box 2455, Payson, Arizona 85547, (520) 474-8140, <www. qualityplusco.com>. Write, call, or visit Web site for current video price.

———

• SUCCESS SECRET 97 •

Know how to turn your ideas into inventions.

Karen Alvarez, president of The Baby Comfort Company, LLC, devised a better strap to keep children safe after her young son fell out of a grocery shopping cart. If you have a good idea for a new product, Alvarez says: "My advice to anyone who wants to take a product concept to market is make sure there *is* a market. Make some disclosure agreements and ask some people you respect for their opinion on what you are thinking. If you can make a prototype of the concept/product, that would be very helpful for them to see."

Alvarez continues: "Be very careful you don't feed the 'sharks.' There are a lot of business people who will not steal your idea, but others who don't have the imagination will take the credit, so be careful. Ask other moms, too, for their opinions. If you get encouraging feedback, then the next question to ask is how much would you pay in the marketplace for this? Make sure the product can be made for or below that." Karen Alvarez, <www.babycomfort. com>, information/orders (925) 833-8287.

Thomas Register

If you are seeking sources of parts for your invention idea or prototype, or possibly searching for a manufacturer to make it for you, then look in the *Thomas Register of American Manufacturers*, a nationwide listing of manufacturers (available in a 33-volume set or on CD-ROMs). You can also find it in larger public libraries, by visiting the Internet site <www.thomasregister.com>, or by writing for prices and ordering information to Thomas Publishing Company, 5 Penn Plaza, New York, NY 10001.

From Idea to Product

Here are some other tips for taking your idea to market:

❖ As Alvarez advises, make sure there is a market for your product.
❖ Network with and learn all you can from other inventors and do your own thorough research.
❖ Realize the entire process from idea to patented product can be expensive and time-consuming. Inventing a new product and marketing it is like starting an entirely new business that needs a business and marketing plan of its own.
❖ Do a patent search (see chapter 12, Managing and Maintaining a Profitable Business), and if no one has a patent on your idea, see a patent attorney.
❖ Do not fall victim to invention scams. Avoid late-night TV programs and magazine ads!

For More Information

Books/Directories

The Catalog of Catalogs V: The Complete Mail-Order Directory (Bethesda, MD: Woodbine House, 1998).

Inventor's Desktop Companion by Richard C. Levy (Detroit, MI: Gale Research, 1995).

Organizations

Inventor's Awareness Group, Inc., 1533 E. Mountain Rd., Suite B, Westfield, MA 01085-1458.

A volunteer group formed to protect and assist independent inventors. Send a SASE for information about membership and their price of their booklet, *Invention . . . Truth or Consequences*.

Internet Sites

< www.TENonline.org > The Entrepreneur Network hosted by the Zimmer Foundation.

< www.thomasregister.com > Thomas Register (listing of manufacturers).

< www.uspto.gov > U.S. Patent and Trademark Office.

Magazines

The Inventor's Digest, 310 Franklin St., #24, Boston, MA 02110. Bimonthly.

Video

"How to Get Rich with Your Invention," produced by Quality Plus, P.O. Box 2455, Payson, AZ 85547 < www.qualityplusco.com > .

• SUCCESS SECRET 98 •

Know how to find distributors for your products.

Even if you have the product, with patent and a manufacturer ready to produce it, the most difficult challenge may be in finding retailers to carry it or establishing a distribution network to sell it (distributors include sales agents, wholesalers, sales reps, and so on). Here are some tips:

❖ Get some record of customer response and sales.
❖ Attend trade shows related to the product.
❖ Read trade and industry publications to get more leads and potential distributors.

❖ Talk to other inventors to see if they can give you referrals to reputable distributors.
❖ Consult with a marketing firm that specializes in new products. Ask for references.

(Consult with a lawyer before signing any contracts regarding your invention or its distribution!)

For More Information
Associations
❖ Manufacturer's Agents National Association, P.O. Box 3467, Laguna Hills, CA 92654. Publishes a *Directory of Manufacturer's Sales Agencies* (that may also be available in your library) and their monthly *Agency Sales,* in which you may find distributors willing to add to their product lines.

Books
Marketing Your Invention by Thomas E. Mosley (Chicago: Upstart Publishing, 1997).

• SUCCESS SECRET 99 •

Know the best home-business trends for the new century to keep your business progressive.

Taking Your Business into the 21st Century
Here are recommendations for keeping up with new trends:

❖ Stay informed of the ongoing movements in your field and business by reading trade and general business publications, your newspapers' business pages, watching television business and investment shows, as well as studying books and reports by trend specialists (also see *For More Information* on page 372).
❖ Listen to your customers, families, friends, and business associates as they talk about their lives and needs and problems. Any

Using Personal Growth to Help Your Business Succeed

With a home business you usually are the business. Your attitude about yourself and your approach to life is also reflected in how you do business. The following tips can help give you the confidence to succeed—in life and in your home business:

❖ Know your strengths and be honest about your weaknesses; know what personal assets to cultivate and which to improve.

❖ Develop your goals and make a plan to achieve them, one by one.

❖ If your action or performance is criticized, take a step back and see what you might have done better. Ask an expert for help if you are overwhelmed or are simply unsure what to do.

❖ If you get discouraged, read positive customer letters or comments about you or your business or make a list of your accomplishments.

❖ Face your fears, then develop your strategy to overcome them.

❖ Learn to trust yourself and your instincts and develop the confidence you need to go forward. If you act confident (whether or not you feel it), others will perceive you as confident and capable.

❖ Do not be afraid to laugh at yourself and realize that all people—no matter how successful—have self-doubts and make mistakes along the way. The difference is that successful people keep going—and so you can you!

business that will solve a problem or save people time or money will be successful!

❖ Stay current with your business and technology skills for your home office and business by reading, taking courses, and visiting trade shows featuring new products.

❖ Stay alert for new "niches" and customer markets that may open up. Get customer feedback with surveys or samplings.
❖ Think globally with your business as it enters the new century as the Internet and trade programs open markets around the world.

_____

For More Information
Books
Clicking: 16 Trends to Future Fit Your Life, Your Work, Your Business by Faith Popcorn and Lys Marigold (New York: HaperCollins, 1996).
Trends 2000: How to Prepare for and Profit from the Changes of the 21st Century by Gerald Celente (New York: Warner, 1997).

Organizations
The Trends Research Institute, Gerald Celente, Director Salisbury Turnpike, Rhinebeck, NY 12572, < www.trendsresearch.com >. Tracking over 300 trend categories: Consumer, business, family, education, international, etc.

_____

• SUCCESS SECRET 100 •

Prepare your business to better serve the needs of the 21st century customer.

Familiarizing yourself with business trends forecasted by futurist experts will help you better meet the needs of your customers in the coming years. Kimberly Stanséll, entrepreneur and small business expert says: "Small-business owners would be wise to start preparing themselves for a twenty-first century customer, who will be far more difficult to serve. Customers will be more knowledgeable, affluent, demanding, and vocal, and will expect to be catered to regardless of their age, gender, or race."

Forecasts
Here are some other forecasts for the new century by trend experts:

✤ Women's business ownership will continue to grow at a rapid rate, but there will be more joint ventures and teamwork efforts on projects.

✤ Women entrepreneurs are going to strive to have more balance between their business lives and families. They are demanding society recognize that their families are a priority over work and business.

✤ Technology and new home wiring will make it possible for more families to work and learn from home instead of going to traditional jobs or schools. Families will be able to arrange their work and education schedules around the needs of the family as a unit.

Barbara Brabec, home-business author/expert and one of the first to write about the home-business phenomenon in the '80s, says: "We are going to see enormous changes in the kinds of businesses we do from home. I see more computer-related businesses, and that it will be as common for businesses to have a Web site as it is to have business stationery today." Brabec, who has written several books on the crafts movement over the last decades, also says, "Crafts' products will be in demand as a nostalgic 'connection to the past.' " And she concludes, "*Flexibility* and *change* are the key words for a home business's survival in the next century—the challenges of adapting to the changes caused by technological advances and our population trends that will see us going back to small communities, again, filled with home businesses. There will be less demands for products and more demands for service-type businesses at the local level—doing the everyday chores that people do not have time to do anymore because of our hectic lifestyles."

✤ Business trends will grow in the following areas:

Hot Home-Business Trends for the Next Century

✤ **Creative businesses:** Educational products and materials, arts and handcrafts industries, and music programs.

✤ **Personal and home services:** At-home elder and child care, referral services.

✤ **Computer-based business:** Internet industries, desktop publishing, growth in small publishers.

❖ **Health-related businesses:** Alternative medicines, herbalists, homeopathic medicine, personal fitness consultants, massage and stress-free therapies.

❖ **Green and environmental businesses:** Water purification, organic foods, recycling businesses, garden-related products.

❖ **Mature adult services:** Errand assistance, retirement and financial planning, group homes instead of large nursing homes, home-health and living-assistance programs.

❖ **Other:** New world markets, mail order, adventure travel, and new sports.

Businesspeople who are aware of the changing lives and needs of their customers will be better able to meet their demands and will continue to have profitable businesses well into the next century.

For More Information
Books
100 Best Businesses for the 21st Century by Lisa Rogak (Grafton, NH: Williams Hill Publishing, 1999).

• SUCCESS SECRET 101 •

Know how to help continue the growth of women-owned businesses for future generations.

Ways you can encourage the success of women in business include the following:

❖ Urge and support legislation for entrepreneurship for girls and young women in schools and colleges.

❖ Urge banking and lending institutions to be aware of the needs of women business owners.

❖ Join a national and/or women's business group that supports programs for women's entrepreneurship.

❖ Be a mentor to another woman or girl in your family, or your community.

Advocating for Women's Business Development Centers

Just as women once fought for the right to vote, women today must work to help promote women's entrepreneurship. Over the past few years, the U.S. Small Business Administration's Office of Women's Business Ownership has been setting up over seventy Women's Business Development Centers dedicated to economic empowerment of women throughout the states and Puerto Rico. In addition to funding from the SBA and donations, more money will be needed, as women continue to start businesses at twice the rate of men. The additional monies will open more centers, sustain services and programs that support and accelerate women's business ownership, and strengthen the impact of women on our country's economy.

Contact your U.S. senators and representatives and urge them to expand funding to these centers. Successful women entrepreneurs can also contribute financial support and time—by being mentors or conducting workshops at centers or at any of the many women's business conferences held annually around our country. For more information about the Women Business Development Centers or to learn the location of the center nearest you, either call 1-800-8-ASK-SBA or visit the Internet site: < http://www.onlinewbc.org >.

❖ Become a speaker in your industry or career so you can be a role model for other girls and women.
❖ Enjoy the entrepreneurial quest!

Do not give up in the persistence of your own dreams and, along the way, stop and give a hand to other "sisters and daughters in entrepreneurship" who are striving for success in their ventures.

"101 Best Wishes for Success in Your Entrepreneurial Ventures!"

Glossary of Commonly Used Business Terms

Accounting period is a regular period of time, such as a quarter or year, for which a financial statement is produced for a business.

Accounts payable is the money you owe to suppliers.

Accounts receivable is the sum customers owe you for services or goods you have furnished (see also asset).

Arbitration is a method of handling a dispute between two parties in which a mutually agreed upon person or group is chosen to help mediate an acceptable settlement between them.

Asset is any single item of value to its owner, tangible or intangible, that can generate cash; includes accounts receivable, inventory, equipment, etc.

Audit is a formal review and confirmation of financial accounts and records.

Balance sheet is a fiscal statement giving the financial position of a business on a certain date.

Bandwidth is the speed at which information is transferred over networks of the Internet.

Barter is exchanging of goods or business services without the use of money.

Baud is the speed at which computer modems can transmit data. Baud speed is registered in BPS or bits per second.

Bid pricing means estimating all the expenses in finishing a project, then adding your profit margin to arrive at the total price.

Boilerplate is legal language, often labeled the "fine print," that states the details in a business contract or agreement.

Break-even point is the dollar amount your business must make so that sales income equals your total costs. From this point you can determine the prices you must charge for your product or services so that your business will be profitable.

Browser is a software program such as *Netscape* or *Microsoft Internet Explorer* that enables you to read and navigate the HTML Internet documents so you can "search" or "browse" for information.

Business opportunity is a business venture sold by a company or entrepreneur who wishes to expand the company or sell the idea to others who want to start a business. A business opportunity usually is a "package" complete with manual, business forms, and sometimes the equipment. Customer support may or may not be included. Be sure to research any opportunity before you invest any money to make sure it is legitimate and not a scam. Ask for references.

Business plan is a written description ("blueprint") of your proposed business's operations that includes short- and long-term goals, start-up financing needed, financial and marketing plans, the owner's qualifications, and details of the products and/or services it is offering.

C & F (costs and freight) is a commercial designation that means the stated value of a shipment of goods including all costs and freight involved in shipping the goods to their destination.

Capacity is the ability to pay back a debt.

Capital is the net worth of a business or money that can be used for investment purposes.

Certified lender is a bank that is certified by the SBA to participate in the SBA's guaranteed loan program. These banks agree to the SBA's conditions and, in return, the SBA agrees to process any guaranteed loan application within three business days. SBA district offices can provide you with lists of certified banks in your area.

Cold-calling is a form of contacting potential customers by calling (or visiting), unannounced, to inform them of your business products and services.

Collateral is property, stocks, bonds, life insurance policies, savings accounts, and business assets, any or all of which can be held to insure the repayment of a loan.

Contingency fee refers to when a person is paid only if she successfully completes the assigned job.

Corporation is a legal entity that functions somewhat like an individual, legally and for tax purposes. Liabilities are held by the corporation, minimizing the personal liability for owners. Two other unique types of corporation are S corporations and limited liability corporations (consult a knowledgeable attorney for more information).

Current liabilities is the sum of a business's debts that are due and payable within the next 12 months.

Debt financing is borrowing money that is to be repaid over a period of time, usually with interest (short- or long-term).

Deficit is a business's net loss due to expenditures exceeding income, or the excess of liabilities over assets.

Demographics are the statistics of a region's population such as sex, age, income, education, buying habits, and so on that an entrepreneur can use to research the market potential of their business idea.

Depreciation is usually used for tax deduction purposes, in which equipment decreases in value from use over a span of time.

Direct costs are costs that can be traced and designated directly to a specific product, such as the cost of wax in decorative candles.

Direct loans are financial assistance provided through the lending of federal monies for a specified period of time, with a reasonable expectation of repayment. These loans may or may not require interest payments.

Direct marketing includes mailing of promotional materials, face-to-face selling, and other sales methods a business uses to let potential customers know about the goods and/or services it has for sale.

Distribution is the method of getting your product or service to your customers (preferably the fastest and least expensive way).

Distributor is a wholesaler who has purchased the rights to market one company's goods (usually not numerous companies' products as an independent sales representative would do) to customers within a given (though not always exclusive) territory. You are in business for yourself and set your own hours.

Download refers to transferring files to your computer from another computer.

Employer Identification Number (EIN) is a number assigned to a business from the IRS that is to be shown on all business tax returns, documents, and statements. Many sole proprietors and independent contractors use their social security numbers. Contact your local IRS office and consult with your accountant for more information.

Equity is the net value of an asset or business less the liabilities.

Equity financing is a method of getting money in exchange for a share of business ownership.

FAQ stands for "Frequently Asked Questions," which are often listed on Internet sites to help supply answers to common questions on a certain topic or subject.

Fax-on-demand is a communications system that permits callers to dial in requests and information via fax, through selection from a voice-response list or entering touch-tone numbers.

Firewall is a type of computer programming that is used for security so that the network user can see through the "firewall" into the Internet, but other Internet users cannot see through the firewall into your network. Businesses who sell products or services over the Internet use firewalls to protect customers' private information, such as credit card numbers used for ordering.

Fiscal year is any 12-month calendar year used by a business or a government agency as an accounting period.

Fixed assets are assets of a permanent nature such as property, equipment, or buildings that are not usually changed into cash in the course of doing business.

Fixed expenses are those that generally do not change from month-to-month (rent, taxes, etc.).

Flaming refers to hate e-mails, often the result of unwanted e-mail solicitations, as opposed to spamming, which refers to unwanted (or "junk") mail that comes from a business owner over the Web.

Franchise is a business opportunity in which an owner of a business grants, in a written agreement, the right to the purchaser of the franchise to sell and distribute the goods and services under the business's name and/or trademark.

Franchisee is the person who purchases from the franchisor the right to sell and distribute the franchise's products and use its trademark and/or trade name. She pays an initial franchise fee; and may or may not pay ongoing royalty fees and advertising costs; and may or may not be required to purchase the company's supplies needed to operate the franchise.

Franchisor is the owner of a franchise company.

Fulfillment is the operation of receiving orders and shipping and tracking goods sold through direct marketing.

Gross income usually pertains to a business's income before deductions. With your home office, gross income is your business's income minus the expenses that do not relate to your home use. Contact your accountant or local IRS office for "business use of your home" deductions.

Home page is the page your Internet browser loads at start-up; often refers to the first Web site document shown when you visit a new Web site or follow a link.

HTML stands for Hypertext Mark-Up Language, which is the standard format for creating documents and pages on the Internet, the World Wide Web.

Hyperlink, which is often shortened to "Link," is a listing of one Web site's URL on another site's page, usually to provide related information that a user can click on to move immediately, possibly to another entirely different Web site.

Income is money received for goods and/or services as well as from other sources such as rents, investment, and so forth.

Income statement is a detailed statement showing revenue minus all expenses resulting in a net profit or loss for a specific duration.

The Internet is a cooperatively run and globally distributed collection of computer networks. It was started about 20 years ago as a government-funded project to set up communications in the event of a nationwide nuclear attack. It has since been adopted by businesses, organizations, and individuals worldwide to promote commerce and exchange information. The Internet exchanges information via a common set of rules for exchanging data, and is often referred to as the "Information Super-Highway."

Internet Service Provider (ISP) is the company that provides access to the Internet.

JPEG (developed by the Joint Photographic Experts Group) is a Web graphics format used to display photographs and artwork on the Web.

Lead time is the amount of preparation time a business owner estimates it will take to implement a new product or service (research, market testing, etc.). Home-business owners must remember to factor in time for "family crises," both minor and major, which usually happen right before a deadline!

Liabilities includes accounts payable plus all the costs of running a business.

Lien is the legal right to hold or sell property of another for purposes of getting payment for money owned.

Liquid assets refers to assets that can be readily changed into cash.

Liquidation is the selling of a business's assets to pay off debts.

Liquidity is the level to which a company can produce cash within a short time period.

ISDN (Integrated Services Digital Network) is technology that enables multiple digital signals to move through a single, conventional phone wire.

Markup is the difference you add onto the cost of a product that you have either made or purchased wholesale in order to make a profit.

MLM stands for multi-level marketing, a form of network marketing in which distributors not only sell companies' products to consumers but also enlist others to sell these products/ services under their supervision. Also called "downline."

Modem is the device that connects your computer to a phone line, enabling you to send data from one computer to another.

Net profit or loss is the result of subtracting additional expenses and adding additional income to the gross profit or loss.

Netiquette refers to rules of procedure for networking e-mail solicitations and information over the Internet; discourages spamming, passing along others' e-mail addresses, and other discourteous behavior.

Network marketing is part of direct marketing in that you sell products directly to consumers, through home parties or one-to-one.

You are among a number of representatives who are also selling for the company you represent. You may or may not have other representatives under you (downline).

Networking is the exchange of information and leads between business owners and associates with the purpose of encouraging and helping one another's businesses.

Net worth is the business owner's equity in a company as represented by the difference between total assets and total liabilities.

Outsourcing means to obtain goods or services from sources outside a business.

Overhead consists of business expenses not related directly to the production of your services or products; examples include insurance, heat, electricity, etc.

Partnership (general) is an alliance of two or more persons as co-owners of a business-for-profit.

Percentage fee is when payment is made to you based on your ability to make a sale, such as with real estate agents or literary agents.

Personal financial history is a record of your borrowing and repayments, plus a listing of your personal assets and liabilities (extremely important to a lender when you are applying for a business loan).

Plug-in is a feature that basically can be added to a browser, enabling you to receive multimedia features of certain Web pages.

Profit-and-loss statement is a full year's statement of a business's earnings.

Promotion includes everything you do to sell your service or product.

Pyramid is an illegal business scam in which a few people at the top make money at the expense of the many people at the bottom of the list who generally lose their initial (and often substantial!) investment. Many pyramids are disguised and tout themselves as legitimate MLMs.

Retainer is payment made to a business expert or consultant in either a single or regular payments to insure their availability if their expertise is needed.

Sandwich Generation refers to that age group of the population responsible for both their older parents and relatives and for their children and even grandchildren.

Scam is an illegal business opportunity that promises quick profits. Many today offer lucrative work-from-home schemes. Check their references with the Federal Trade Commission and The National Fraud Information Center (see Chapter 2).

Seasonality refers to business buying patterns affected by weather, seasons and/or holidays (such as Christmas or Mother's Day).

Segmentation refers to targeting specific people or businesses that are most likely to buy its products or services through one or more marketing efforts.

SASE is an abbreviation for "self-addressed, stamped (first-class) envelope. An *LSASE* means a long (business-size) self-addressed, stamped envelope. This is often used for a return reply in request of information or a query (often used by professional freelance writers).

Small business incubator is an association of small businesses usually housed in one building to share building facilities, staff, and other business services that a small business could not afford on its own. A number of home businesses join incubators if their business needs to expand out of its home location.

Sole proprietor is a legal form of business ownership, in which the business is owned and controlled by one person. One's name can be used in the business or under a fictitious name (DBA or "doing business as"). The owner is fully liable and personal assets are not protected from lawsuits.

Spamming means promoting or sending unwanted solicitations or materials to unknown users or to user groups on the Internet.

Spreadsheet is a numerical data table consisting of columns and rows related by formulae used by businesses for tracking customer profiles and recording other business data. Software for spreadsheets is often found in office suites.

Tax number (also called sales tax number) is the number given to a business by its state revenue department to enable the purchasing of goods and products wholesale without paying sales tax. You also need this number to go to wholesale shows and to exhibit your goods there. Contact your local state legislator's office for the address of your state government's office.

Time study is an analysis of how much money you need to make
     per hour in order to cover your overhead and operating costs,
     your time involved, and your desired profit margin.

Upload refers to transmitting a file from your computer to another.

URL (Uniform Resource Locator) is the address notation that points
     to a particular document or site on the World Wide Web.

Usenet is the system that disburses a multitude of news groups all
     over the Internet.

Venture capital is financing invested in new or existing firms which
     exhibit the potential for extensive growth.

Way bill is the document sent along with shipped products that ex-
     plains the shipment's costs and route.

Wireless is a telephone system that operates without wires between
     the person's handset and the home station that makes possible
     the call connection to the handset.

World Wide Web is a collection of millions of computers on the Inter-
     net that contain information and multimedia (sound, graphics,
     animation, etc.) that has been put in a single format—called
     HTML (hypertext mark-up language).

For More Information
Books

The SOHO Desk Reference (Small Office/Home Office) edited by Peter H.
     Engle (New York: Harper Collins, 1997) is a comprehensive
     handbook of over 400 subjects containing answers to the many
     questions that arise when running a business.

See also the "Glossary" in *More 101 Best Home-Based Businesses for
     Women* by Priscilla Y. Huff (Rocklin, CA: Prima Publishing,
     1998).

Frequently Asked Questions (FAQs) About Home Businesses

A successful entrepreneur must be persistent in finding answers to important business questions. Here are some of the most frequently asked questions about home businesses:

Q: How do I overcome my fear of starting a home business?
A: Attend a women's entrepreneur conference and/or classes, such as those held by many Small Business Development Centers (< www.smallbiz.suny.edu >) and Women Business Centers (< www.onlinewbc.org >). They offer business-related workshops and networking opportunities with other women entrepreneurs to help give you the confidence, support, and knowledge to start.

Q: What makes a business idea a good one?
A: Any business that can save people time or money, and/or solve a problem of some sort has a good chance of succeeding. Books like Faith Popcorn's *Clicking* and Gerald Celente's *Trends 2000* give insight on our nation's future trends.

Q: What can I do if my home office is not suitable for client meetings?
A: Offer to meet clients at their offices, or contact local business organizations for the availability of meeting rooms or the Executive Suite Association, 438 E. Wilson Bridge Rd., Suite 200, Columbus, OH 43085 (< www.esuites.org >). Executive Suite Association members rent offices by the hour or day.

Q: Should I tell my customers that my business is home based?
A: Unless it gives your business an advantage over your competitors, most customers are more concerned with the quality of your product and/or customer service and your professionalism than where you work.

Q: My business has grown so much that I am thinking of moving it from its home base. How can I make this a smooth transition?
A: Business incubators foster small businesses and help them become independent. Contact the National Business Incubation Association at < www.nbia.org > for an incubator near you.

Q: Is it a myth or fact that grants exist for business start-ups?
A: Most grants target nonprofit organizations and government agencies rather than home or small business start-ups; but your business may qualify for a local, state, or federal grant if it can contribute to your community's development, job potential, or education. Check Gale Research's *Grants on Disc* for a grants' listing (available at larger libraries).

Q: Do I really need a business plan?
A: Starting a venture without a business plan is like building a house without blueprints—you may get it built, but the foundation may not be solid enough to sustain it.

Q: How can I determine what products/services my customers want?
A: Get customer feedback through surveys, questionnaires, or forthright, personal conversations.

Q: What are some things I should do before I ever start my business to help insure its success?
A: Assess your strengths; know your industry; use classes, seminars, and tapes to learn basic business management; and have a well-developed marketing plan.

Resources
The Home Office and Small Business Answer Book: Solutions to the Most Frequently Asked Questions About Starting and Running Home Offices and Small Businesses by Janet Attard (New York: Henry Holt, 1993) < www.businessknowhow.com > .

Readers' Questions
The following are just a sample of the many questions I receive about home and small businesses.

Q: I am trying to find information about opening a consignment store. Do you have any references I may try?
A: Here are two excellent resources for you: *The Consignment Workbook,* by Sue Harris, can be ordered from Scandia International, 133 Olney Rd., Petersburgh, NY 12138; and if you have access to the Internet, the site < www.consignment.org > will be extremely helpful to you.

Q: I thought I could last in my present job for one more year until my retirement, but a new supervisor made my life impossible, so I walked out one day and never went back. In looking for possible ideas for home business, I find most of the profiles of successful women-owned home businesses seem to be geared for younger women with families. Are there home-business ideas for us older people who want to (and incidentally need to) earn our retirement incomes?
A: It is unfortunate you had a bad experience at your former job, but the good news is that many mature adults are starting up very successful part- and full-time businesses. With our increasing life spans, entrepreneurship will become an option for more mature adults in the next century. An excellent book for you to read to give

you some business ideas is *100 Best Retirement Businesses* by Lisa Angowski Rogak with David Bangs, Jr., (Chicago: Upstart Publishing Co., 1994).

You could also start a business helping seniors. Paula Kay started an agency, Ageless Placements, Inc., which recruits older workers to assist elderly people in their homes. She has been so successful that she is now offering to share this business opportunity with others. For more information, write her at 8130 66th St. North, Suite 4, Pinellas Park, FL 33781.

Q: I am trying to start an errand service, but am unsure on the basics of getting started. Can you help?
A: Errand services are also often called "Personal Service Providers," or "Concierge Services." They help people organize their lives and homes by carrying out tasks that their customers do not have the time do. Specializations of this business include errands, shopping, party-planning, bill-paying, moving coordination, bookkeeping, and others. To read more about this service, you can order *How to Start & Operate an Errand Service* by Rob Spina, Legacy Marketing, 403 Hobart Dr., Laurel Springs, NJ 08021.

Q: I have been interested in teaching stress management and self-esteem to women's groups for years. Several of my friends have asked me to speak to the groups to which they belong on a periodic basis. I have a great passion for what I teach and live the principles myself. I know I have the education and the skills, as well as life experiences, to make a huge difference in many lives. What I do not know is how to make this into a business or how to make money at it. I have no idea where to go with the ideas in my head! Please help!
A: Congratulations on your wonderful business idea! Here are some resources that should help you.

Books
How To Make It Big in the Seminar Business by Paul Karasik (New York: McGraw-Hill, 1992).
Speak and Grow Rich, 2nd ed., by Dottie Walters (Englewood Cliffs, NJ: Prentice-Hall, 1996). < www.walters-intl.com >.

Start-Up Guide

Entrepreneur's Start-Up Guide, Seminar Promotion, $59 + shipping and handling. Call (800) 421-2300 to order.

Q: I am interested in growing specialty plants for gardens. Do you have some resources to help me get started?
A: Congratulations on your interest in selling your specialty plants. Here are some suggestions I believe you'll find helpful:

❖ Write to Homestead Growers for their booklet *Profitable Plants: Your Guide to the Best Backyard Cash Crops*. Send $1 for shipping to Homestead Design, P.O. Box 2010, Port Townsend, WA 98368-0080.

❖ Write to Storey's How-To Books for a Country Living, Schoolhouse Rd., Pownal, VT 05261, for a current catalog of books, including several on making a living selling plants and on how to raise certain crops. Also see their Internet site: < www. StoreyBooks.com > .

❖ Sell your plants via mail order with classified ads in gardening magazines. Check your library and magazine stand for samples and write for their ad rates.

❖ Sell your plants wholesale to local nurseries. Contact your county's Cooperative Extension Office (there is one run by the U.S. Department of Agriculture in every U.S. county) for guidance on growing your plants and to get up to date on any regulations that may be required of you regarding raising and shipping your plants.

❖ Expand your line of plants. For example, in some cities, there is a movement to start gardens on vacant city lots (after being cleaned up) to provide specialty crops for local restaurants. Organic foods are going to be in demand in the next century. Also in demand are old-time varieties of tomatoes, peppers (one farmer in my area does very well growing 50 different varieties of peppers for restaurants), lettuces, herbs, etc.

❖ If you live in a rural area, a good book to read is *The Complete Country Business Guide: Everything You Need to Know to Become a Rural Entrepreneur* by Lisa Rogak; $24.95 plus shipping & handling; Williams Hill Publishing, RR 1, Box 1234, Grafton, NH 03240.

Q: I am interested in a candle business. Do you know of any helpful resources?

A: If you are already involved in a certain type of art and/or craft, you will need to decide whether you will be selling your candles wholesale, retail, or as a one-of-a-kind item (to museum or gift shops, for example). If you are to make a profit with your candles, you must approach it like any other business venture in researching your market, writing a business plan, testing your market, and so on.

Here are some helpful resources to help you get started in a candlemaking business:

Books

The Candlemaker's Companion: A Comprehensive Guide to Rolling, Pouring, Dipping & Decorating Your Own Candles by Betty Oppenheimer (Pownal, VT 05261: Storey Communications, 1997); < www.StoreyBooks.com > .

The Complete Candlemaker: Techniques, Projects, & Inspirations by Norma J. Coney. (Asheville, NC: Lark Books, 1997).

Candles That Earn: Creating & Operating Your Own Successful Business by D. Olsen (Seattle, WA: Peanut Butter Publishing, 1991). Order from Barker Enterprises, listed below.

Candle Supplies and Books

Barker Enterprises, Inc., 15106 10th Ave., SW, Seattle, WA 98166; (206) 244-1870; $3 for catalog. Features supplies and books for a candlemaker hobbyist or entrepreneur; < www.barkerco. com > .

The Wax House, P.O. Box 103, Mequon, WI 53092, has the book *Starting a Candle Business* for $12. Call (888) WAX-9711; $3 for catalog.

Q: I am interested in home employment such as stuffing envelopes from home and assembling crafts at home. Are there legitimate opportunities like this?

A: Frankly, it is very difficult to find legitimate work-from-home opportunities. The best way is to contact companies or members of local business organizations to see if they have "overflow" work they hire out. If you do this type of work, however, be aware that:

❖ Certain types of home work may be illegal by local, state, or federal regulations.

❖ You may need to obtain a homeworker's certificate (check at your local state legislator's office for information).

❖ You should contact an accountant to make sure you know the taxes and record-keeping procedures you must follow.

Most (if not all) the home-working ads you see in magazines and newspapers are simply scams. A legitimate employer will offer to pay you for work and not ask you to pay them for information or start-up packages! A good reference is the latest edition of Lynie Arden's book, *Work-at-Home Sourcebook*, in which she lists home work opportunities around the country (many of which require that you live in the vicinity of the company or have certain qualifications). Phrases such as "Guaranteed Profits," "Free Money," "Free Business Kit," "Insider Secrets Revealed!," "Mail-Order System—Continuous Cash Money," and "$100 an Hour to Fill Out Worksheets" are just a few of the phrases and headlines characteristic of scam artists. Do not send any money to them; invest in your own venture or save your money!

Q: I need help pricing my work. I manage databases for non-profit organizations and small businesses and also do mailers and marketing for them. Should I charge them by the document or by the hour? What about postage (I believe they have their own postage meter)?
A: Pricing is difficult in a new business start-up. The goal in pricing a service and/or product is to mark up the labor and material costs sufficiently to cover overhead expenses and generate sufficient profit. You will also have to add on percentages of your taxes, insurance costs, retirement benefits, and your time per hour. Here are some additional tips:

❖ Call other mailing list services in your area (or outside your vicinity).

❖ The mailing services with whom I spoke charged 20 to 50 cents per name and address and their clients paid the postage.

❖ They also recommended that you charge a minimum every time you are hired to do a mailing, no matter how small.

Here are some other resources that may be helpful to you:

❖ Direct Marketing Association, 1120 Avenue of the Americas, New York, NY 10036-6700; < www.the-dma.org >.

Books

Mailing List Services on Your Home-Based PC by Linda Rohrbough (New York: Tab/McGraw-Hill, 1994). Look in your local public library, as it may be out of print.

Priced to Sell by Herman Holtz (Dover, NH: Upstart Publishing Co., 1996).

Q: I am a new entrepreneur and want to know some common mistakes that new business owners often make and what is the key to writing good promotional materials.

A: Here are some mistakes to avoid:

❖ *Mistake #1: Not defining one's target market.* A new entrepreneur should always write a business plan to discover who her potential customers will be and whether there are sufficient numbers of them who will purchase the products and/or services to support the new venture.

❖ *Mistake # 2: Inadequate marketing.* A new entrepreneur has to spend almost 75 percent of her time promoting her new venture and 20 percent of her time marketing even when her business is established. The trick, too, in marketing is to do it as effectively and cost-effectively as possible.

❖ *Mistake # 3: Inadequate research into one's business idea.* A new entrepreneur should constantly learn about her industry—the latest technology and trends, the projected growth in future years, etc.—by reading trade publications, books, attending conferences, and networking with others to keep her business current and competitive to keep and attract customers.

The *key* to writing good promotional materials is to emphasize what is *unique* about your business; what sets it apart from your competitors'. For example, free services that are included, saving money, better customer service, and other benefits all help your customers realize the *value* they will gain when they purchase your goods and/or services.

Q: I have friends and neighbors who hate to pay bills. I thought if I started a monthly service for them and charged a flat fee, it could turn out to be a little business for me. Any ideas about how to get started?

A: There is definitely a need for this service—especially among older adults. Many widows and widowers whose spouses handled all the personal bookkeeping are completely lost when it comes to knowing how to pay their bills, balance their checkbooks, and so on. Your service would be a "Personal Bookkeeping Service." First, check to see if your state requires you to have a certification or license to perform a service like this. Next, consult with your lawyer about liability and confidentiality issues with this type of service. Then take some accounting, bookkeeping, and computer courses (and maybe some geriatric psychology courses) to learn the latest technology and issues.

If you believe there is a market in your area, contact local banks, senior centers, financial advisors and planners, churches, and aging agencies for referrals. If such businesses already exist in your area, also call a local Women's Business Center, Small Business Development Center, or SCORE office, which may offer ongoing consultations and programs for business start-ups. With the first of the baby boomers reaching 65 and over (retirement age) in 2013, this type of service is sure to be in demand into the next century.

Q: Do you know of any jobs that I can do at home without a big start-up fee and without a college degree?

A: There are any number of businesses you can do from home that do not require a college education. What business experts do advise, however, is some background or experience that is helpful in a business you choose to start. To do this, work or volunteer in a position related to your business idea(s). From this you will gain contacts and a "working knowledge" that you can use in your venture.

Many women start a business as an outgrowth of a hobby they have been doing for years. Generally, these are service-type businesses—landscaping or cleaning, for example—and are less expensive to start than product-oriented businesses. Go to your library to look up other books on home-business ideas, as well as to find publications such as *Entrepreneur's Business Start-Ups, Entrepreneur's*

HomeOffice, Income Opportunities, Small Business Opportunities, Working at Home, and other magazines. These regularly feature profiles on entrepreneurs who have started successful home businesses on shoestring budgets. A good book to also read is *77 No Talent, No Experience, and (almost) No Cost Businesses You Can Start Today!* by Kelly Reno (Rocklin, CA: Prima Publishing, 1997).

Q: I am interested in starting a mail-order business. Do you have some sources that would be helpful?
A: With thousands of catalogs and millions of buyers out there, mail order continues to be popular for busy customers to shop from the convenience of their homes. Now, the Internet has also increased its sales of unique products. One person I know sells over 700 popular candy dispensers a week to collectors from his Internet site. If you have a background or knowledge in a certain area, you may be able to sell those items to worldwide customers with your own catalog or Web site. For an Internet business, read *101 Businesses You Can Start on the Internet* by Daniel S. Janal (New York: Van Nostrand Reinhold, 1996) and *121 Internet Businesses You Can Start from Home* by Ron E. Gielgun. Another book to help you get started is *How to Start a Home-Based Mail Order Business* by Georganne Fiumara (Old Saybrook, CT: Globe Pequot Press, 1997) (< www.homeworkingmom.com >). You might also wish to join this excellent association for small business mail-order companies: The National Mail Order Association, 2807 Polk St. NE, Minneapolis, MN 55418-2924.

Q: I am interested in making money with my crafts. Do you know of some helpful resources?
A: If you are already involved in producing a certain type of art and/or craft, you will need to decide whether you will be selling your items wholesale, retail, or as exclusive one-of-a-kind items (to art galleries or museum shops, for example). If you are to make a profit with your crafts, you must approach it like any other business venture in researching your market, setting up a business plan, and so on. Here are some other resources to help you become a "professional crafter."

Local County Extension Offices

These offices, which exist in every county in the U.S. and are listed in your local telephone directory, often sponsor craft and business-related workshops. Part of the U.S. Department of Agriculture, they were established to help farmers (which they still do), but many offices have expanded into other areas such as crafts marketing.

Associations

Write for membership, not information, on a craft business start-up.

The American Craft Council (ACC), 72 Spring St., New York, NY 10012.

The Association of Craft & Creative Industries, P.O. Box 2188, Zanesville, OH 4370-2188.

Books

Creative Cash, 6th ed., by Barbara Brabec (Rocklin, CA: Prima Publishing, 1998).

Handmade for Profit by Barbara Brabec (New York: M. Evans & Co., Inc., 1996).

The Crafts Business Answer Book by Barbara Brabec (New York: M. Evans & Co., Inc., 1998).

How to Start a Home-Based Craft Business, 2nd ed., by Kenn Oberrecht (Old Saybrook, CT: Globe Pequot Press, 1997).

Internet Sites

Barbara Brabec's site: < www.crafter.com/brabec > .

Craft Mark—Advertise your crafts on their site: < www.craft-mark.com > .

Magazines

The Crafts Report (for the professional crafter), P.O. Box 1992, Wilmington, DE 19899-9776; < www.craftsreport.com > .

Q: I am a representative for a home party business selling products for women. How do you rebuild the company's reputation

when another representative and a hostesses ran off with the customer's order money?

A: One woman president of a successful home party business says that, unfortunately, she, too, has had experience with the occasional person taking customers' money and running. She says: "When this happens, it not only hurts us financially, but the reputation stays on forever. If this should occur to you, the representative, you should act with 'high professional behavior.' Follow up quickly with any phone calls, questions, problems, and so on. Make sure that your customers get the products QUICKLY. Own up to the reputation, even though it's not yours, then—without being too defensive—assure your customers that this is not the way you operate. Give out your phone number and address whenever asked, perhaps even volunteering it."

The owner continues: "From a company point of view, we never let the customers go without the product. Even when a rep took off with the money, we reassembled the orders and shipped the products. Our procedure now is for our reps to collect little cash; all checks are made out to our company and we process all credit card orders . . . that way, in case the inevitable happens, we are out only a small amount of money. I would advise any representative to work with a company that has the reputation of backing customers, no matter what!"

Q: I am interested in starting a writing business, doing editorial-related projects that I can do at home. Currently, I am doing research. Can you provide any advice for me?

A: Writing is like any other business in that you should put together a business plan so you know who your markets (and their readers) will be and to help you determine your specialization (what kind of writer you will be). There are a number of markets for non-fiction writers: special-interest publications (such as health, gardening, specific sports, and recreation); trade magazines that target specific industries (such as crafts, computers, writing, food, small and home businesses), publications produced *by* associations (such as journals, newsletters, newspapers); and consumer magazines you see on the newsstands and in grocery stores. If you have any expertise or experience or interest in certain areas, you can target writing articles for these publications. Or you can inquire whether they would be interested in freelance copyediting or other work. You will want to study their publications for their style and format, then get a copy of their writer's guidelines.

If you also want to do work on a local basis, contact industries and companies that need newsletters produced, press releases written, reports developed, and other writing done. Access these businesses by joining a local business association. Also, investigate Internet sites that target visitors in your area of expertise that may invite guest article submissions or columns. Here are some helpful resources:

Professional Information Broker: The Information Broker's Handbook, edited by Sue Rugge and Alfred Glossbrenner (New York: McGraw-Hill, Inc., 1997).

Writing and Editing

How to Make Money Publishing from Home by Lisa Shaw (Rocklin, CA: Prima Publishing, 1997).

How to Start & Run a Writing and Editing Business by Herman Holtz (New York: John Wiley & Sons, Inc., 1992).

Making $$$ at Home: Over 1,000 Editors Who Want Your Ideas, Know-How & Experience by Darla Sims (Fairfield, IA: Sunstar Publishing, 1996).

Self-Publishing: The Complete Guide to Self-Publishing by Tom and Marilyn Ross, Association: Small Publishers Association of North American (SPAN), P.O. Box 1306, 425 Cedar St., Buena Vista, CO 81211-1306; < www.SPANnet.org >.

Writer's Digest Magazine—Published by F & W Publications (same address as Writer's Digest Books). Pick up at local bookstores or visit < www.writersdigest.com >.

Writer's Market—Annual directory of publishers and magazines, published by Writer's Digest Books, 1507 Dana Ave., Cincinnati, OH 45207; (800) 289-0963.

If you would like me to answer a question you might have on a specific home-business idea or topic, I would be happy to help give you some helpful resources. Please see page 408 for my contact information.

Resources

Unless otherwise noted, please send a long (business-size) self-addressed, stamped envelope (LSASE) if you contact any of these listings through the mail.

Associations—Women's and Mothers' Home Business

❖ At-Home Mothers' Resource Center, 406 E. Buchanan Ave., Fairfield, IA 52556, < www.athomemothers.com >. Information and resources for at-home mothers. Publishes the *At-Home Mother Resource Catalog* and *At-Home Mothering Magazine*.

❖ Home-Based Working Moms (HBWM), P.O. Box 500164, Austin, TX 78750, < www.hbwm.com >. National organization for moms (and dads) working from home. Newsletter, networking information, and more.

❖ Mothers' Access to Careers at Home (MATCH), P.O. Box 123, Annandale, VA 22003, < www.freestate.net/match/ >.

❖ Mothers' Home Business Network, P.O. Box 423, East Meadow, NY 11554, < www.homeworkingmom.com >. Home-business guidance; newsletter and resource guide.

Business Ownership (Women's) Associations

❖ American Women's Economic Development Corporation (AWED), 71 Vanderbilt Ave., Suite 320, New York, NY 10169; (212) 692-9100, < www.womenconnect. com/AWED >. The premier national, not-for-profit organization committed to helping entrepreneurial women start and grow their own businesses. It offers courses, one-to-one business counseling, seminars, networking events and peer group support. Its goal is ". . . to increase the start-up, survival and expansion rates of small business." It is based in New York City, but also works with organizations, both in the U.S. and internationally, that want to develop programs for women entrepreneurs based on the AWED models. It also offers telephone counseling with one of its small business experts. Call for hourly fees or more information about its programs.

❖ Business Women's Network, 1146 19th St., NW, 3rd Floor, Washington, DC 20036.

❖ The National Association of Women Business Owners (NAWBO), 110 Wayne Ave., Suite 830, Silver Spring, MD 20910-5603, < www. nawbo.org >. "The premier source of information on women-owned businesses . . . worldwide." Its research branch is the National Foundation for Women Business Owners. < www.nfwb.org >

❖ Women Incorporated, Inc., 333 S. Grand Ave., Suite 2450, Los Angeles, CA 90071, <www.womeninc.com>. A national network of women business owners and women in business. Offers member benefits and sells several helpful publications for women entrepreneurs.

Home-Business (and Related) Associations

❖ American Association of Home Based Businesses, P.O. Box 10023, Rockville, MD 20849 (800) 447-9710; fax: (301) 963-7042, <www.aahbb.org>. "A national, nonprofit association dedicated to the support and advocacy of home-based businesses." Does not sell or endorse any business opportunities.

❖ Home Office Association of America, 10 Gracie Station, P.O. Box 806, New York, NY 10028-0082, <www.hoaa.com>. Send an LSASE for information on membership information and benefits.

❖ Small Office Home Office Association International (SOHOA™), 1765 Business Center Drive, Suite 100, Reston, VA 20190-5326, <www.SOHOA.com>. "Specialize in providing products and services to our members—the small office and home-office professionals—that will help them run a more effective and successful business."

Business Associations

❖ National Association for the Self-Employed, 2121 Precinct Line Rd., Hurst, TX 76054 (800) 232-6273, <www.nase.org>. Offers health insurance and other benefits to members.

❖ National Small-Business United, 1156 15th St., NW, Suite 1100, Washington, DC 20005. Offers health insurance and other benefits to members.

❖ Small Business Service Bureau, 554 Main St., Worcester, MA 01608. Membership is open to any business; offers health insurance to its members.

❖ Working Today, P.O. Box 1261, Old Chelsea Box Station, New York, NY 10113, <www.workingtoday.org/>. "A national nonprofit membership organization that promotes the interests of people who work independently, providing them with the tools they need to prosper."

Associations—Trade*
Check the reference sections of public and college libraries for the current editions of these directories.

❖ *Encyclopedia of Associations,* (current edition) Gale Research, Detroit, MI.

❖ *National Trade and Professional Associations of the United States,* published annually by Columbia Books, Inc., 1212 New York Ave., NW, Suite 303, Washington, DC 20005.

---

*Note: Trade associations in your industry may or may not have start-up business information, but they do provide members with networking opportunities (trade shows, conventions); current publications (newsletters, journals, guides, etc.); marketing information; assorted benefits, legislative advocacy in behalf of the industry; future outlooks and trends for your industry, and more. Research to see which associations best suit your home business.

Associations—Special Interest

❖ American Craft Council (ACC), 72 Spring St., 6th floor, New York, NY 10012. Membership is open to those with interest in skilled American craft; is a national educational organization dedicated to the advancement of the American craft movement.

❖ Small Publishers Association of North America (SPAN), P.O. Box 1306, 425 Cedar St., Buena Vista, CO 81211-1306, <www.SPANnet.org>. Nonprofit organization that is the "national voice of the independent publishing association"; founded by Tom and Marilyn Ross, authors of self-publishing and business books.

❖ Volunteer Lawyers for the Arts, 1 E. 53rd St., Sixth Floor, New York, NY 10022, (212) 319-ARTS (2787). Association that assists artists, writers, and arts organizations in answering arts-related legal questions. Write or call for the location of an office near you or visit their Web site.

Books

201 Great Ideas for Small Businesses by Jane Applegate (Chicago: Dearborn Financial, 1998).

C-E-O & M-O-M, Same Time, Same Place by Rochelle Balch (Glendale, AZ: R. B. Balch & Associates, Inc., 1997) <www.rbbalch. com>.

Dive Right In—The Sharks Won't Bite: The Entrepreneurial Woman's Guide to Success by Jane Wesman (Upper Saddle River, NJ: Prentice Hall Trade, 1997).

The Enterprising Woman by Mari Florence (New York, NY: Warner Books, 1997).

Launching Your Home-Based Business: How to Successfully Plan, Finance and Grow Your New Ventures by David H. Bangs, Jr., and Andi Axman (Chicago, IL: Dearborn Trade, 1997).

The Perfect Business: How to Make a Million from Home with No Payroll, No Employee Headaches, No Debts, and No Sleepless Nights! by Michael Leboeuf (Columbus, OH: Fireside, 1997).

Starting a Home-Based Business by Entrepreneur Magazine Group (New York: John Wiley & Sons, Inc., 1996).

Books and Publications (Business-Related) Through the Mail

Contact for a current listing of their publications.

❖ Business Books—Women's (a division of EastHill Press), 6114 LaSalle Ave. #599, Oakland, CA 94611, <BusBks@aol.com> (e-mail).

❖ Jeffrey Lant Associates, P.O. Box 38-2767, Cambridge, MA 02238, <www.worldprofit.com>. Many money-making publications.

❖ Lewis & Renn Associates, 10315 Harmony Dr., Interlochen, MI 49643. Start-up business books.

❖ The New Careers Center, *Whole Work Catalog*, 1515-23rd St., P.O. Box 339-CT, Boulder, CO 80306. Books on specific businesses and careers.

❖ Pilot Books, 127 Sterling Ave., P.O. Box 2102, Greenport, NY 11944-2102, (800) 79-PILOT <www.pilotbooks.com>. Small business guides and franchise publications.

Bookstores—Online

Amazon.com <www.amazon.com>.

Barnes & Noble <www.barnesandnoble.com>.

Borders Books <www.borders.com>.

CD-ROMS
Information on business start-up, usually carried in office supply stores.

Adams Streetwise Small Business Start-Up (Adams Corp.), (781) 767-8100, < www.
adamsmedia.com >.
How to Really Start Your Own Business (Inc. Business Resources); (800) 468-0800,
< www.inc.com/ >.

Internet Sites
(with home and small business information/sections)
< www.bizoffice.com/library/library.html > —Vast amount of home-based business
information and related links.
< www.bizproweb.com > —Productive site for small and home-based businesses
and professionals.
< www.digital-women.com > —"Digital-Women was founded to create a place for
women from all over the world to come and gather resources, business advice
and tips, marketing tips, sales techniques and any other business tools they
needed to aid them in their success."
< www.ibm.com > IBM's Web site includes helpful "Small Business Center."
< www.ipl.org > —Internet Public Library by University of Michigan's School of
Information. Contains useful Web sites on business and other topics.
< www.ivillage.com/work/index.html > —The Women's Network, *iVillage,* a com-
prehensive informational site for women, including profiles of successful women
business owners, weekly chats with Mompreneurs™ Patricia Kobe and Ellen H.
Parlapiano, plus articles and a message board *(The Self-Employed Woman),* and
a weekly chat hosted by Priscilla Y. Huff (e-mail: < CLBestHBB@ivillage.com >
for home-business questions).
< www.microsoft.com/smallbiz/ > —Microsoft Small Business Kit CD along with
offers and resources for conducting business on the Internet.
< www.momsnetwork.com/suites/momsatwork > —Site of LaDonna Vick, founder
and creator of Mommy's@Work, "Your Home Business Resource Place," a mail-
order company specializing in home-business resources. For free monthly
newsletter, e-mail < mommywork@smartbot.net >.
< www.myria.com > —"The Magazine for Mothers" offers 80 discussion boards
and features, including home-business articles to "enlighten, inform, and encourage moms everywhere."
< www.paulandsarah.com > —The information-packed Web site of home-business
experts Paul and Sarah Edwards.
< www.ProfitableWomen.com > —Great Minds Think Alike (GMTA).
< www.isquare.com > —"The Small Business Advisor," with business success in-
formation by Dr. Robert Sullivan and other business experts.
< www.smartbiz.com > —Smart Business Supersite.
< www.tsbj.com > —The Small Business Journal.
< www.tjobs.com > —The Telecommuting Jobs Page, which lists positions at com-
panies looking for home-based workers. Check for references before signing any
contracts, and read *The Virtual Office Survival Handbook: What Telecommuters and
Entrepreneurs Need to Succeed in Today's Traditional Workplace* by Alice Bredin
(New York: John Wiley & Sons, Inc., 1996). See also < www.fodreams.com/
tele.html > —for home/telecommuting opportunities.
< www.toolkit.cch.com > —The Business Owner's Toolkit —Has thousands of pages
of information on starting, planning, financing your business, including articles on home-based businesses.
< www.visa.com/smallbiz/ > —Small business site for Visa business cardholders
(good links for business funding and women's business ownership).
< www.womenconnect.com > —Women's Connection Online. Wide variety of infor-
mation for women, including home and small business information.

< www.workingsolo.com > —Web site of Terri Lonier, author of *Working Solo* and other helpful small business books.

Canadian Business Resources

❖ The Association of Independent Consultants Toronto, 2175 Sheppard Avenue East, Suite 110, Willowdale Province, Ontario, Canada M2J 1W8.
❖ Barternet Trade Exchange, 2-456 Notre Dame Ave., Winnipeg, Manitoba, Canada R38 1R5.
❖ Biz Resource Group, #6-2316 McCallum Rd., Abbotsford, BC, Canada V2S 3P4 *USA Address:* #6-2316 McCallum Rd., Sumas, WA 98295, < www.bizresource. com >. Offers workshops and a newsletter for small businesses.
❖ The Canadian Business Women's Network™, (250) 518-0567, < www.cdnbiz-women.com >. Resources and support for women's enterprises in Canada. Home Based Education Centre, 6432 188 St., Surrey, BC, Canada V3S-8V1. Write for information (price, ordering information, current edition, etc.) about spiral-bound book: *Things to Look for When Starting a Computer Business.*
❖ National Home Business Institute, 366 Adelaide, Toronto, Ontario, Canada M5V 1R9.
❖ *PROFIT: The Magazine for Canadian Entrepreneurs,* 777 Bay St., Fifth Floor, Toronto, Ontario, Canada M5W 1A7. Six issues per year; write for subscription information.
❖ Women Business Owners of Canada (WBOC), 1243 Islington Ave., Suite 911, Toronto, Ontario, Canada M8X 1Y9, (416) 236-2000, < www.wboc.ca >. A national, nonprofit organization launched in 1998, whose purpose is to "be a primary source of information to all [female] business owners, from (Canada's) coast to coast."

Internet Site
❖ Canadian Small Business, < www.about.com >. Small-business links, events, and a free newsletter.

Government
(See also Chapter 9, "Resources to Help You.")

Federal
The U.S. Small Business Administration (SBA) offers an extensive selection of information on most business management topics, from how to start a business to exporting your products. This information is listed in "Resource Directory for Small Business Management," which can be obtained *free* from your nearest SBA office. The SBA has offices throughout the country. Consult the U.S. Government section in your telephone directory for the office nearest you. For more information about SBA business development programs and services, call the SBA Answer Desk at (800) U-ASK-SBA (827-5722) or visit the Web site: < www.sba.gov/ >.

For information on the location of the following SBA-related business support offices nearest to you, write the following address, call the SBA Answer Desk, or visit the related Web site.

❖ Business Information Centers (BICs)—Operated by the SBA offices located in some U.S. cities, which offer state-of-the-art technology, informational resources, and on-site counseling; (800) 827-5722.
❖ Commerce Business Daily— < cbd.savvy.com >. This site has the full text of announcements issued by the Department of Commerce on procurements, contracts, requests for product and service needs of U.S. government agencies.

❖ Consumer Product Safety Commission (CPSC), Publications Request, Washington, DC 20207. The CPSC offers guidelines for product safety requirements.

❖ Government Publications of Interest to Small Business. These are available from the Government Printing Office (GPO), which sells them through GPO bookstores located in over 24 major cities and listed in the Yellow Pages under the "bookstore" heading. You can request a "Subject Bibliography" by writing to the GPO, Superintendent of Documents, Washington, DC 20402-9328. Or GPO, P.O. Box 3719754, Pittsburgh, PA 15250-7954.

❖ Office of Women's Business Ownership, < www.sba.gov/womeninbusiness. com > .

❖ Service Corps of Retired Executives (SCORE)— < www.score. org > , (800) 634-0245. A national organization sponsored by the SBA of volunteer business executives who provide free business counseling and seminars.

❖ Small Business Development Centers (SBDCs)— < www.smallbiz.suny.edu/roster.htm > Sponsored by the SBA in partnership with state and local governments, universities, and the private sector, these centers are available in over forty-six states, the District of Columbia, Puerto Rico, and the Virgin Islands. Write or call the SBA or look in your telephone directory's white pages under "Small Business Development Centers" for an office nearest you.

❖ *The Consumer Information Catalog,* P.O. Box 100, Pueblo, CO 81002, < www.pueblo.gsa.gov > . This is a catalog of free and low-cost federal publication, including the *Resource Directory for Small Business Management,* which lists home and small business publications. Write for a catalog or visit the Web site.

❖ U.S. Business Advisor— < www.business.gov > .

❖ U.S. Census Bureau— < www.census.gov > ; (301) 457-4100. The U.S. Census Bureau has *CenStats,* a fee-based subscription service on the Internet that can help you find the demographics of certain populations and areas, which will help you in market research. For more information, call or visit their Web site.

❖ The U.S. Department of Agriculture (USDA), 12th St. and Independence Ave., SW, Washington, DC 20250. The USDA offers publications on selling to the USDA. Its county extension offices (one in every county in the U.S.) also offer publications and programs on entrepreneurship. Contact the office in your county for more information.

❖ The U.S. Department of Commerce (DOC), Office of Business Liaison, 14th St., and Constitution Ave., NW, Room 5898C, Washington, DC 20230, < www.doc.gov > . Provides listings of business opportunities available in the federal government and refers businesses to different programs and services in the DOC and other federal agencies.

❖ U.S. Department of Labor (DOL), Employment Standards Administration, 200 Constitution Ave., NW, Washington, DC 20210, < www.dol.gov > . Offers publications on compliance with labor laws (some home businesses are prohibited by DOL regulations).

❖ U.S. Department of Treasury, Internal Revenue Service (IRS), P.O. Box 25866 Richmond, VA 23260, (800) 424-3676, < www. irs.ustreas.gov > . The IRS offers information on tax requirements for home and small businesses.

❖ U.S. Environmental Protection Agency (EPA), Small Business Ombudsman, Crystal Mall—No. 2, Room 1102, 1921 Jefferson Davis Highway, Arlington, VA 22202, < www.epa.gov > . The EPA offers more than 100 publications designed to help small businesses understand how they can comply with EPA regulations.

❖ U.S. Food and Drug Administration (FDA), FDA Center for Food Safety and Applied Nutrition, 200 C Street, SW, Washington, DC 20204, < www.epa.gov > . The FDA offers information on packaging and labeling requirements for food and food-related products.

❖ U.S. Postal Service— < www.usps.com > .

❖ U.S. SBA, 409 Third St., SW, Sixth Floor, Washington, DC 20416.

❖ Women Business Centers— < www.onlinewbc.org > . Over sixty centers existing around the U.S. offer business start-up programs, workshops, and counseling for women entrepreneurs. Write or go to the Web site for a center near you (also see a listing of them in *More 101 Best Home-Based Businesses for Women*).

Entrepreneurship Education

❖ American Woman's Economic Development Corporation (AWED). Entrepreneurial training and counseling for women; courses for those in the New York City region; and telephone business counseling for a fee. (See "Business Associations.")

❖ Edward Lowe Foundation, 51990 Decatur Rd., Cassopolis, MI 49031, <www.lowe.org/smallbiznet>. Free monthly business e-mail newsletter, *smallbizNotes*. Provides information services, research, and educational experiences that support small businesses. Linked to *Edge Magazine* online: <www.edgeonline.com>.

❖ Kauffman Foundation, <www.entreworld.org>. The Kauffman Foundation's "World of Resources for Entrepreneurs" features their listing of best resources for small-business owners.

❖ Muhlenberg College Institute of Entrepreneurship, 24 and Chew Sts., Allentown, PA 18105. Offers entrepreneurship program.

Virtual Entrepreneurship Education

Ohio University College of Business— <www.cob.ohiou.edu> "MBA Without Boundaries."
University of Phoenix— <www.uophx.edu.com>.
Women's University— <www.womensu.com>.

Expos, Trade Shows, Conferences*
(See also "Trade Shows" in Chapter 8, "Advertising.")

Conference
Junior League of Oakland-East Bay, Inc., 3685 Mt. Diablo Blvd., Suite 251, Lafayette, CA 94549, <www.jloeb.org>. Annual Women's Business Conference.

Expo
Entrepreneur Magazine's Small Business Expos are held annually in selected cities around the country. Call (800) 421-2300 for dates and locations.

Internet Sites—Trade Shows
<www.expoguide.com/shows/shows.htm>—Find trade shows, conference, or exhibits that parallel your home business.
<www.tscentral.com>—Trade show site by TSCentral, 149 Cedar St., Wellesley, MA 02474.

---

*Many home, trade, and women's business associations have yearly conferences that have specific home and small business themes and/or workshops, as do SBDCs and other women's organizations. Contact them for the dates of any upcoming events they may sponsor.

Home Study

❖ Distance Education and Training Council (DETC), 1601 18th St., NW, Washington, DC 20009-2529, < www.detc.org >. Write for a brochure of schools offering home study courses.

❖ Graduate School USDA (U.S. Department of Agriculture), Ag Box 9911, Room 1112, South Agriculture Bldg., 14th St. & Independence Ave., SW, Washington, DC 20250-9911. Correspondence courses on accounting, auditing, editing, library technology, and others. Write for a copy of their current course offerings.

Correspondence Schools

Write for a more extensive listing from the Distance Education and Training Council (DETC) listed previously.

❖ Foley-Belsaw Company, 6301 Equitable Rd., Kansas City, MO 64120-9957. Computer programming, upholstery, etc.

❖ International Correspondence Schools, 925 Oak St., Scranton, PA 18540-9902, < www.icslearn.com >. Catering/gourmet cooking, child day care management, interior decorating, etc.

❖ NRI Schools, 4401 Connecticut Ave., NW, Washington, DC 20078-3543, Accounting, computer-based bookkeeping, desktop publishing, etc.

❖ Professional Career Development Institute, 430 Technology Parkway, Norcross, GA 30092-3406. Medical billing, tax preparation, travel agent, etc.

❖ Stratford Career Institute Inc., 233 Swanton Rd., Ste. 121, St. Albans, VT 05478-9911. Accounting, business management, Internet specialist, etc.

Virtual Courses

Women's U., Elyse Killoran, 176 Woodbury Rd., Hauppauge, NY 11788, < www. womensu.com >. Business coaches and other resources.

Publications

Magazines

Look for these magazines and others on home-business topics at your local newsstand or bookstore (such as Barnes & Noble, Borders Books, Waldens).

❖ *(Entrepreneur's) Business Start-Ups*, Subscription Dept., P.O. Box 50347, Boulder, CO 80323-0347, < www.BizStartUps. com >.

❖ *(Entrepreneur's) HomeOffice;* Now published online: < www.HomeOfficeMag. com >.

❖ *Home Business Connection*, Cutting Edge Media, 29 S. Market St., Elizabethtown, PA 17022. Twelve issues.

❖ *HOMEBusiness Journal*, Steffen Bldg., 9584 Main St., Holland Patent, NY 13354-0403, < www.homebizjour.com >.

❖ *Home Business Magazine*— < www.homebusinessmag.com >

❖ *HomeOffice/Small Business Computing*, P.O. Box 53543, Boulder, CO 89323-3543, < www.smalloffice.com >.

❖ *Income Opportunities*, P.O. Box 5300, Jenks, OK 74037, < www.incomeops.com >.

❖ *Opportunity Magazine*, 18 E. 41st St., New York, NY 10017, < opptnty@aol.com > (e-mail).

❖ *Opportunity World*, 28 Vesey St., #257, New York, NY 10007-2701, < oppworld @aol.com >.

❖ *Spare-Time Magazine*, Kipen Publishing. Corp., 5810 W. Oklahoma Ave., Milwaukee, WI 53219-4300, < www.spare-time.com >.
❖ *Wealth Building*, 6827 W. 171st St., Tinley Park, IL 60477, < www.wealthbuilding. com >.
❖ *Working At Home*, Subscriptions Dept., P.O. Box 5484, Harlan, IA 51593-2984.
❖ *Working Woman*, P.O. Box 3276, Harlan, IA 51593-2456, < www. workingwoman-mag.com >.

Newsletters (Specialty)
❖ *The Comic Bible*, monthly publication for comedy writers and comics. For more info, send e-mail to < ComicBible@aol.com > or write May Ann Pierro, The Comic Bible, P.O. Box 995, Kings Park, NY 11754-095.
❖ *Creative Expressions*, "Newsletter for Greeting Card Entrepreneurs," 6 issues, $15.95/yr. to Sally Silagy, *Creative Expressions*, 189a Paradise Circle, Woodland Park, CO 80863; < www.GardeningGreetings.com >. Tips and resources.
❖ *NewsletterNameplate*, Ruddle Creative, 111 N. Market St., Ste. 715, San Jose, CA 95113; < www.ruddle.com >. Newsletter with information and tips for newsletter publishers.
❖ *ShowcaseNews*, Select Entertainment, Inc., 853 Broadway #1516 NYC 10003; coverage of Off-Off Broadway Shows and independent films, distributed monthly to casting directors and talent agents in New York City < www.buzznyc.com/showcsenews >.
❖ *Spilled Candy*, Lorna Tedder, editor, P.O. Box 5202, Niceville, FL 32578-5202. Bimonthly newsletter with self-promotion tips for authors and writers— < www.spilledcandy.com >

Other
Small Business Success, Pacific Bell Directory, Communication Dept.-CWS11, 2375 Northside Dr., San Diego, CA 92108, (800) 848-8000. Annual publication with excellent small business articles and resources. Write or call for a current copy.

Radio
"Marketing Minute" by Marcia Yudkin, marketing expert; seen every week on The Job Show, Saturday mornings, WABU-TV 68 Boston; WNBU-TV 21 N. Hampshire; WZBU-TV 58 Providence/Cape Cod and simulcast at < www.jobshow.com > and occasional commentaries on WBUR radio's Morning Edition.
"Small Business Minute" by *Home Office Computing*, on a CBS radio station in your area— < www.cbsradio.com >.
"Smart Tip of the Day" by Rieva Lesonsky, Entrepreneur Media's editorial director. For a listing of nationwide stations, visit < www.entrepreneurmag.com >.
"Success Weekend"—Home-based, syndicated talk radio show, focusing on home-based businesses by Michael Lamp and Jane Beterbing; heard in Reno, NV, and Colorado Springs, CO, (AM 1460). For a newsletter, send to Success Weekend, Box 1385, Wichita, KS 67201; or go to Web site: < www.moneyroom. com >.
"The Today's Black Woman Radio Show & Newsletter," with Jennifer Keitt. For information, send a LSASE to P.O. Box 9462, Coral Springs, FL 33075.

Resources for People with Disabilities
(See also Chapters 9 and 10.)

❖ National Organization on Disability, 910 16th St., NW, Suite 600, Washington, DC 20006; < www.nod.org >.

❖ National Rehabilitation Information Center, 1010 Wayne Ave., Suite 800, Silver Spring, MD 20910; < www.naric.com/naric >.
❖ The President's Committee on Employment of People with Disabilities, 1331 F St., NW, Third Fl, Washington, DC 20004; < www.pcepd.gov/pubs/fact/supportd.htm >.

Start-Up Business Guides and Small Business Catalogs
(Write or call for catalogs.)

Entrepreneur's Start-Up Guides, 2392 Morse Ave., P.O. Box 57050. (800) 421-2300. Specific businesses.
National Business Library's Start-Up Guides, P.O. Box 21957, Santa Barbara, CA 93121. (800) 947-7724. Specific businesses.
Price Waterhouse Small Business Guides, Small Business Services, 6500 Rock Springs Dr., Bethesda, MD 20817. Covers small business management issues.
U.S. Chamber of Commerce, Small Business Institute, 1615 H St., NW, Washington, DC 20062; (800) 429-7724; < www.usccsbi. com > Offers software, audio, videos, books, and other resources.

Supplies and Equipment
(Contact for a current catalog.)

Business Forms, Checks, Labels, Tags
❖ NEBS®, Inc., 500 Main St., Groton, MA 01471; (800) 225-6380; < www.nebs.com >.
❖ RapidForms, 301 Grove Rd., Thorofare, NJ 08086-9499; (800) 257-8354; < www.rapidforms.com >.

Containers, Boxes, Bags, Packing Tissue
❖ Robbins Container Corp., 222 Conover St., Brooklyn, NY 11231; (718) 875-3204.

Office Supplies
❖ PENNY-WISE Office Products, 6911 Laurel Bowie Rd., Suite 209, Bowie, MD 20715 < www.penny-wise.com >.
❖ Quill Office Products, Quill Corp., 100 Schelter Rd., Lincolnshire, IL 60069-3621; < www.quillcorp.com >.
❖ VIKING® Office Products, 950 W. 190th St., Torrance, CA 90502; (800) 421-1222; < www.vikingop.com >.

Papers
(Desktop publishing, certificates, business stationery, etc.)

❖ Paper Showcase, P.O. Box 8465, Mankato, MN 56002-8465.
❖ Premier Papers, Inc., P.O. Box 64785, St. Paul, MN 55164.

Television
❖ *Small Business 2000*, PBS TV show on small business issues < www.sb2000.com >
❖ *Working from Home* with Paul and Sarah Edwards. A weekly, half-hour series on the Home & Garden Television network— < www.paulandsarah.com >.

❖ Home Shopping Network, One HSN Dr., St. Petersburg, FL 33729, <www. homeshopping.com>.
❖ QVC/Vendor Relations, 1385 Enterprise Dr., West Chester, PA 19380, <www. qvc.com>.

Videos

❖ *Home-Based Business: A Winning Blueprint.* SBA Publications, P.O. Box 46521, Denver, CO 80201-46521.
❖ *Setting Up a Home-Based Business.* American Institute of Small Business, 7515 Wayzata Blvd., Suite 201, Minneapolis, MN 55426, (800) 328-2906.

Miscellaneous Sources
Company Information—Contracting Number

❖ Design and Web Hosting Services, Contact: Dr. Robert Sullivan, Information International, Box 579, Great Falls, VA 22066, bobs@isquare.com (e-mail).

❖ Dun & Bradstreet, 899 Eaton Ave., Bethlehem, PA 18025, (800) 333-0505, <www.dnb.com>. Can provide background reports on businesses (contact for fees) and a free D-U-N-S® number, which is part of D & B's Data Universal Numbering System that allows you, among other things, to gain a federal contract by registering with the government's Central Contractor Register (CCR). Also sells "Resource Toolkit" for business owners, which includes merchant status to accept credit cards, business forms and agreements, business publications, Web site trial offer, and more.
❖ Gebbie Press, Inc., P.O. Box 1000, New Paltz, New York 12561-9984, <www.gebbieinc.com>. Publishes the *All-in-One Media Directory,* listing all U.S. radio, TV, magazines, and newspapers; available in print, on disks, or on mailing labels. Web site visitors may download Gebbie's entire weekly newspaper and TV station databases.

How to Contact the Author
If you have any comments, questions, or business ideas you want to share, or would like a free copy of my newsletter *101 BEST & MORE HOME-BASED & SMALL BUSINESSES FOR WOMEN UPDATES: The Latest Facts, News, & Tips for Self-Employed Women,* please send a LSASE to Priscilla Y. Huff, Box 286, Sellersville, PA 18960. Send e-mail to <pyhuff@cynet.net> or visit my Web site at <www.selfemployed-woman.com>.

Business Ideas

The following are the best home-based businesses for women presented in *101 Best Home-Based Businesses for Women, Revised 2nd Edition*, and *More 101 Best Home-Based Business Ideas for Women*. (Each business idea profile also lists related business ideas to give you additional possible money-making ventures to consider!):

101 Best Home-Based Businesses for Women, Revised 2nd Edition

Special Event Services

1. Balloon Decorating
2. Gift Baskets
3. Gift Reminder Service
4. Party and Event Planner
5. Party Rentals
6. Reunion Planning
7. Videotaping Service
8. Wedding Planner and Consultant

Home Services

9. Cleaning: Blinds
10. Cleaning: Carpets and Rugs
11. Cleaning: Homes and Apartments
12. Estate Sales
13. Garage Sales
14. Housesitting
15. Interior Design
16. Lampshades
17. Referral Service
18. Wallpapering and Painting
19. Welcoming Service

Personal Services

20. Child Care
21. Credit Consulting
22. Special Dating Service
23. Elder Care Services
24. Errand Service
25. Financial Consultant
26. Image Consulting Service
27. Inventory Service
28. Personal Salon Services
29. Professional Organizer
30. Résumé Writing Service
31. Shopping Service
32. Tutoring Service

Health Services

33. Home Health Care
34. Medical Claims Processing

35. Personal Fitness Trainer
36. Personal Weight Management Consultant
37. Reflexologist

Sewing Services
38. Alterations
39. Costumes
40. Curtains, Draperies, and Shades
41. Custom Apparel
42. Custom Cushions and Pillows
43. Patterns
44. Upholstery

Pet Services
45. Pet Grooming
46. Pet Sitting
47. Pet Transportation

Business-to-Business Services
48. Answering Service
49. Billing Service
50. Bookkeeping
51. Business Consultant/Coach
52. Business and Office Support Services
53. Business Plan Consultant
54. Business Writing
55. Consultant for Home-Based Businesses
56. Information Broker
57. Janitorial Service

58. Medical Billing Services
59. Medical Transcribing
60. Process Server
61. Professional Practice Consultant
62. Temporary Help Service
63. Video Production Services/Multimedia Production Services

Entertainment Businesses
64. Children's Parties
65. Clowning
66. Novelty Message Service
67. School Programs, Assemblies, and Presentations
68. Tour Services
69. Toy and Game Inventor

Green Businesses
70. Environmentally Concerned Businesses
71. Flowerscaping Service
72. Garden Consulting
73. Growing Herbs
74. Plant Maintenance Service
75. Wreaths

Craft Businesses
76. Airbrush Art
77. Calligraphy

78. Candles
79. Chair Caning, Rushwork, and Weaving
80. Dollhouses
81. Framing
82. Furniture Art
83. Greeting Cards
84. Jewelry
85. Photography
86. Silk and Fabric Flower and Plant Arranging

Computer Businesses
87. Computer Consulting
88. Graphic Artist/Designer
89. Newsletter Publisher (Desktop)
90. Newspaper Publisher (Desktop)

Food-Related Businesses
91. Catering
92. Food Delivery Service
93. Just Desserts
94. Selling a Family Recipe

Other Business Ideas
95. Engraving
96. Finding Service
97. Freelance Writing
98. Home Art or Music School
99. Mail Order
100. Sign-Painting Business
101. Tax Preparation Service

More 101 Best Home-Based Businesses for Women

Pet and Animal Businesses
1. Specialty Animal Breeding: Bison
2. Pet Day Care
3. Pet ID and Registration Services
4. Pet Detective
5. Animal Behavioral Consultant
6. Pet Specialty Items

Business-to-Business Services
7. Administration Business (Overflow) Service
8. Advertising Agency
9. Business Organizer
10. Client Prospecting Specialist
11. Customer Relations Database
12. Coupon Advertising and Mailing Service
13. Executive Director Services
14. Human Resources Consultant
15. Time Management Specialist

Children's Businesses
16. Educational Consultant
17. Doula Services
18. Making Children's Furniture
19. Nursery Decorating Service
20. Parenting Specialist
21. Parties-in-a-Bag
22. Special Child (and Elder) Day Care
23. Special Subjects Independent Contractor

Computer and Internet Businesses
24. Classified Ads (Internet Business)
25. Collectors' Site (Internet Business)
26. Computer Cleaning (Computer Business)
27. Desktop Video Production Company (Computer Business)
28. Internet Marketing Specialist (Internet Business)
29. Information Technology Consultant (Computer Business)

Creative Businesses
30. Baskets
31. Ceramic Crafts
32. Crafts and Sewing Supplies (Mail Order)
33. Decorative Screens
34. Home-Based Art Gallery
35. Inventor's Consultant
36. Leather Craft
37. Laces and Lace Crafts
38. Metal Craft
39. Shoes (Custom-Made)
40. T-shirts
41. Wall Pieces

Entertainment Businesses
42. Comedy Writing
43. Storytelling
44. Fan Club Management
45. Local Radio or TV Show
46. Pony Rides and Petting Zoo
47. Science Shows

Environmental and Green Businesses
48. Compost and Soil Production
49. Edible Landscaping
50. (Home) Fruit and Vegetable Stand
51. Hedge Trimming and Landscape Lighting
52. Interior Landscaping
53. Topiary Business
54. Water Garden Design

Food-Related Businesses
55. Barbeque Set-ups
56. Cake Decoration
57. Cooking School
58. Flavored Honeys
59. Jams and Jellies
60. Personal Chef and Suppers-to-Go
61. Vegetarian Consultant

Health-Related Businesses
62. First Aid and CPR Instructor
63. Health Insurance Consultant
64. Homeopathic Counselor
65. Medical Health and Records Management
66. Postsurgery and Recuperative Care-Giving Agent
67. Massage Therapist
68. Rolfer
69. Speech Pathologist

Home Services
70. Window Cleaning
71. Closet/Storage/Pantry Organization
72. Handy Women
73. Laptop Inventory for Home Owners
74. Records and Information Searcher
75. Relocation Consultant
76. "Smart" Homes Designer

Baby Boomer and Senior Services
77. Financial Services
78. Gerontology Consultant
79. Nostalgia-Related Products
80. Retirement Life Planner
81. Specific Product Development: Assistance Products

Personal Businesses
82. Announcement Services
83. Budget Expert
84. Consumer Complaint Letters

85. Customized Calendars
86. Laundry Service
87. Makeup Artist or Facialist
88. Nail Salon/Manicurist
89. Spirituality Counselor

Specialty Travel Services
90. Emergency Travelers' Service
91. Homestay
92. Independent Travel Sales Rep
93. Women's Self-Defense Instructor

Word Businesses
94. Abstracting Service
95. Book Packager
96. Children's Writer
97. Freelance Magazine Writer
98. Legal Digesting Service
99. Poetry-on-Demand—Custom Rhymes for Every Time
100. Public Relations Specialist
101. Technical Writer

Index

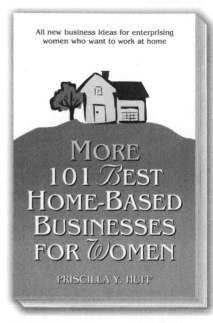